Far Afield

Far
Afield

A Sportswriting Odyssey

S. L. Price

THE LYONS PRESS
Guilford, Connecticut

An imprint of The Globe Pequot Press

10 9 8 7 6 5 4 3 2 1

Printed in the United States of America

Library of Congress Cataloging-in-Publication Data

Price, S. L. (Scott L.), 1962-
 Far afield : a sportswriting odyssey / S. L. Price.
  p. cm.
 ISBN-13: 978-1-59921-144-2
1. Price, S. L. (Scott L.), 1962– 2. Sportswriters—United States—Biography.
3. France—Social life and customs. I. Title.
GV742.42.P75A3 2007
070.4'4079609–dc22
[B]   2007010594

For Fran

There was the one morning in December when I glanced left and saw Mont Sainte-Victoire, its base swathed in fog, its upper flanks washed by a buttery radiance, and though cars hurtled at me and the twisty, narrow road demanded full attention, I couldn't stop staring. Optical illusion, I know, but still: The mountain was floating on air. There were nights when I stepped into a cool wind coursing the hills with a sound like breathing, and stared at a moon so snow white that it stung the eyes. There was the sunburn in winter, the smooth, steamy coffee at The Bastide in the heart of Aix, the wide, wet Cours Mirabeau just steps away. There were the streams of students unimpressed by the statue-still mime, the plane trees beheaded and stripped for winter; the unhurried couples moving along buoyed by a sense of rich congratulation, for everyone, the foreigners most of all, knew how lucky they were. We were fortunate, yes: For the $3.00 bottles of quality red, for the $4.00 prescriptions, for being there. Wasn't this the South of France? Wasn't this Provence?

To say those four words, to tell people this was home then, always elicited a slight pause, as if they didn't know whether to say, "What's that?" or "Shut up." In the popular mind, "South of France" means one of life's good keys got turned. No one goes to Provence to suffer. You saw them everywhere: Americans with very cool eyeglasses, very white teeth, and time to burn. The foolish ones rolled their eyes and complained about French driving or bureaucracy, as if by complaining they could somehow neutralize their own embarrassment, short-circuit the inevitable envy. To say you live in "the South of France" isn't subtle; it isn't like saying you live in Greenwich or Short Hills. It's a new boob job, a stretch limo: Sooner or later, the fact of it demands explaining.

We lived outside a village between Aix and Marseille in a small mountain range known as Le Chaine de L'Etoile, "Star Chain," surrounded by stands of pine, a panorama of exposed limestone, and hamlets of unforced charm. Our *children were healthy and blond. They took to the language with endearing rapidity, and in the late fall of 2003 helped harvest the olives from the gnarled trees in our yard. The olives were driven to a nearby press, where they produced the tangy olive oil in which, whenever I felt like it, I mixed a little salt and dipped shreds of torn baguette. I would bring the roof of my mouth down on the bread, forcing the oil to the back of my throat before chasing it with a swallow of wine.*

At those moments, of course, I was sure I was living a tale of escape. But that's not what this is, after all.

One

Giants lived here once. . . . In Vachel Lindsay's day, in
Carl Sandburg's day, in the silver-colored yesterday, in
Darrow's and Masters' and Edna Millay's day, writers and
working stiffs alike told policemen where to go, the
White Sox won the pennant with a team batting average
of .228 and the town was full of light.

Nelson Algren, *Chicago: City on the Make*

The mystery box opened, and there they sat—Algren, David Mamet,
Saul Bellow, Studs Terkel, Upton Sinclair, Mike Royko, Ring Lardner—
the whole loud, unwieldy school of Chicago writers, one dozen books
packed together and then tossed by the 1,500-mile ride into a jumble
of accusation, a nifty dare: So what are *you* going to do? On top lay a
note from the editor of the *Chicago Tribune*. "Chicago has always been a
city of great stories," she wrote. "I'd like to read some of yours."

Well. It was the winter of 2002, and I had been chewing over a job
offer from the *Trib* for weeks, a great one: Write a column in America's
best sports town, for one of the few ambitious newspapers left, with an
old friend as boss. The courtship had followed the usual steps—a phone
call, a flight, a we-love-you interview, a letter with salary and perks and
an ironclad signature. Most important, I had been handed that rarest of
career gifts: leverage. Writing for newspapers or magazines isn't like other
jobs; nothing you do translates easily to the bottom line. The talent traffic in air—opinions, critiques, quotes, ideas, information. Judgments are

subjective; no one really knows who's any good, and when another pub-lication comes sniffing, your bosses regard it as much a validation as a threat. Coveted from the outside, you become more coveted inside. It's rare. It's nice.

But the leverage works only when wielded with conviction; you must be willing to quit. I'd had a good decade at *Sports Illustrated*, with a promise of more to come. The managing editor, Terry McDonell, said he'd match any salary offer: Leaving, on the most obvious level, made lit-tle sense. But my friend at the *Tribune*, an assistant managing editor now, had been a wily boss long ago in California, smart enough, week-in and week-out, to manipulate my grim and overbearing ambition. "I just want to be great," I would say back when we worked together, as if I really had a choice in the matter. He knew: Nothing would lure me better than arrogance. So the box of books opened, and Bellow and Mamet and Lardner glanced up from their typewriters and said, *Greatness? You've got to go through us first.* For weeks, I left it squatting in the middle of my office floor like a provocation, and after a time I swear I almost could hear the city—Jews and blacks, salesmen and hacks, couples juiced by passionate loathing, the cold and the corruption, the wind, idiocy, regret, baseball, riding the El, the Dan Ryan—rising out of it in a constant murmur of punch-in-the-face prose. I'd trip over the box on my way to my desk, see it when I spoke on the phone, and the voices in the box kept chattering away. I finally shoved them on a shelf so they'd shut up already.

I loved newspapers. For a decade, I had lived for the thrill and tor-ture of daily deadline, the buzz of breaking news—so much that it had taken me more than a month to decide to go from the *Miami Herald* to *Sports Illustrated* in 1994. So here was my chance to go back. Here, too, was leverage, and a chance to . . . what exactly? Two nights before I was set to fly to New York to meet with McDonell, it hit: He's going to ask what it will take to keep me. Someone positioned to grant the answer was about to ask life's central question: *What do you want?*

I was forty. There was another baby due in a month. There was a house in Washington, D.C. that, after three years and an interminable round of construction, had started to feel like home. What did I want? I wanted to tear it all up. I wanted to tear it all down. I was forty, sinking slowly into the American routine, and I knew: Thick-waisted, midwestern, Cubbies-loving Chicago would only take me deeper. I wanted what I'd always wanted, but now had the power to get. Away. I wanted to go where no one talked like me, where nothing was easy again, where *SI* was just another way of saying yes. I wanted to see beer ordered at breakfast, cigarette smoke at every meal, uncomprehending glances, cheating customs officials, three-hour lunch breaks, bricks hurled in a soccer riot. I wanted bad teeth, tunnel-scraping trains scaling Swiss alps, funny blue currency, men who dress like adults, tortured efforts at conjugation. I wanted to be a walking argument, the American loosed in a hostile world.

"Give me Europe," I said. "Let me take a year to cover sports there."

And McDonell didn't laugh. Once in a lifetime, maybe, it's that easy. The Summer Olympics were returning to Athens in 2004, the U.S. was at war in Iraq and widely despised, and now the magazine could range about, taking the temperature country to country before the biggest, most controversial sporting event of the new century. "You're the artist," McDonell said, officially uttering the first foreign word I would hear in my new assignment. In my ten years writing for newspapers in Chapel Hill, Memphis, Sacramento, and Miami, in my years writing for *SI*, I had been called many things—but never that. Yet he kept going, and I resisted the urge to giggle, to look over my shoulder to see if he was speaking to someone who had walked in behind me. "The gig is what you make it," he said. "Don't let the editors here grind you up."

We had our choice: anywhere on the continent. We picked the South of France because my wife, Fran, speaks the language, but there was also the thrill of saying, "Yes, we're moving to the hills of Provence," so casually, so coolly, as if this was just another link in our charmed chain of adventures, as if we were just like people who had money. And the fact was, we had been tapped in some way for so long; we had lived in San Francisco, Miami, and, now, Washington, D.C.—each a city with undeniable mystique, each beautiful and odd. Not only that, but as a sportswriter I had stumbled into these places with eerily impeccable timing—to San Francisco in the late '80s with Bill Walsh's 49ers dynasty and the World Series Giants and Oakland A's, to Miami in the '90s with its premier college football team and new pro baseball and hockey franchises, to Washington in 2000 just before superstars Michael Jordan, Steve Spurrier, and Jaromir Jagr ran aground there and Maryland basketball won its first national championship. I'm capable of delusion. I would be sure that some greater power was at work, that I'd been chosen somehow, if not for the disasters.

I didn't think it strange the first time, when I was in L.A. with the Giants in 1987 and the earthquake threw me out of bed, nor even when I sat in the upper deck of Candlestick Park in 1989 and felt the stadium jump when the worst quake to hit the Bay Area in eighty-three years shook the World Series. But after Hurricane Andrew—the worst storm to hit Miami in six decades—rolled over Dade County in 1992, I began to wonder. In the summer of 2001, two weeks before September 11, I actually congratulated myself for moving my family to D.C., where, at the time, 2 inches of snow was considered calamitous. Then the plane shot into the Pentagon. Then our post office closed and neighbors wore rubber gloves for fear of letters laced with anthrax. Then a pair of snipers roamed the area gunning down women and children. I'm no fool; I know none of these events were about me. Still, each spasm of fear felt like payment, some kind of cosmic counter to a lifetime of good fortune. When, in the summer of 2003, I went to Manhattan for two days to work on a story and the city suffered its worst blackout in over thirty years, it seemed only right. "It really does happen wherever you go, doesn't it?" said a friend.

He still doesn't realize: I wouldn't want it any different. I grew up in a rich neighborhood with no money, in a smart family seeded with a strange pride and a contrary bent. I've waited a lifetime for whoever's in charge to tap my shoulder and say, "You don't belong here." Like most neurotics, I get nervous when things are too easy or pleasant; the longer I stay in a pitch-perfect place like Boulder, Santa Barbara, or Martha's

Vineyard, the more I want to see something smash. I didn't really live in San Francisco or D.C., not in my head, and I certainly don't live in "the South of France" now; I still come from the town where no one young wants to be, where the restaurants shut down early and the nights are owned by bar drunks railing at the TV. I've never read a book about expats immersed in Provence, or the repairing of some soul and villa in Tuscany; it all smelled a bit too pat, too quaint for words, and I've never been much good at quaint. So France—France now—was perfect. France had disowned Bush's Iraq adventure; France, by all accounts, had no use for Americans anymore. Still, I couldn't resist stacking the deck. Looking for a house, I had the choice of seven Provençal beauties. I picked the one closest to the region's strangest sight: two massive cooling towers at the power plant in Gardanne that, every fresh and glorious morning, spew a hellish brew of smoke and steam in seamless imitation of the nuclear facility at Three Mile Island.

Ten months of preparation, worry, wondering—all of it led to this: On the fourth day of September of 2003, after twenty-four hours and rushed changes in New York, Frankfurt, and Paris, our plane approaches Marseille. Fran sits upcabin with the baby, Charlie. Our seven-year-old son Jack, my three-year-old daughter Addie and I sprawl across the last row in the back of the plane, the two kids stoned on red-eye exhaustion until, just twenty minutes before landing, passing out for the first time. We land. I shake Jack. Addie—in a clear show of superior female strength—scampers over her brother's prone body without a second look. I shake him again. He moans, clenches his eyes shut. The other passengers are moving out; the French flight attendants pretend to ignore us. I lift Jack by his arms and, while yanking out what becomes an avalanche of carry-on computers, shopping bags, and diapers from the overhead, wrench him over the three-across seating. His moaning rises to an air-raid level howl.

I lean over close to my son's ear and, as tenderly as possible, hiss, "Cut this crap out now!" The last passengers look back with alarm and scurry out the cabin door. I grab under his armpits and half-carry, half-drag him up the aisle, past the grim-faced pilot, the fashionably coiffed steward. By the time I get into the concourse, the boy is weeping. Some other time, I might've uttered something profound to mark our arrival. But my frazzled mind seizes on only the handiest cliche.

Lafayette, I mutter, we are here.

Fall

Two

What were sunsets to us, with the wild excitement upon us of approaching the most renowned of cities! What cared we for outward visions, when Agamemnon, Achilles and a thousand other heroes of the great past were marching in ghostly procession through our fancies?

Mark Twain, before his first visit to Athens,
in *The Innocents Abroad*

The first weeks are madness. Seven pieces of luggage—including air beds—don't make it to Marseille the morning we arrive. When they get dropped at the house the following afternoon, an apocalyptic rain has been pounding for hours; the drought-plagued region has become a flood zone, the dirt driveway a sea of mud. I run out, head down. A tarry, rock-speckled goo encases my shoes in dripping cakes 3 inches thick. I hump the bags and mud inside. The empty new place, five bedrooms set in the hills outside the village of Greasque, has wood shutters the color of lavender but no oven or dishwasher, no furniture, no curtains. Unlike corporate expats, I get no stipend for housing or schools, no adjustment for cost of living or an ever-weakening exchange rate. So it is that, within hours of our arrival in France, we become obsessed with Sweden. We try to be polite. But no local is safe from the questions.

"How far is it . . .

"Have you ever been to . . .

"Is this a good day for . . .

"Which way to . . . IKEA?"

We make three shopping trips, all absurd, all frantic. They blend together into one epic $3,400 spree, with two jet-lagged kids and an eight-month-old infant whiningly hooked to a shopping cart buried under so many boxes and bags that it resembles a garbage scow with a broken tiller, heeling forever to the right. The milling Saturday masses hustle out of our way in the French manner—pursed lips and averted eyes, as if the inanity flowering before them simply doesn't exist—because once moving, the scow is all but impossible to stop. After one look at the hundreds of shoppers, the snaking lines, the children already fraying under the pressure of inescapable, adult-imposed boredom, Fran and I instantly degenerate into yelping fools, skittering through the aisles, spouting out the carnival Swedish names—*Lack? Stefan? Roder?*—with unearned authority, Ingrid Bergman and Björn Borg unloosed upon the mall. "Do we want the Klackbo?" I yell. "No. Yes. Let's get two!"

Lights, paper lanterns, knives, forks, rugs, plastic side tables, hangers, office supplies, desk and chair, three beds, two couches, kitchen table, towels, candles, bathmats. It is, really, a new Olympic event: speed furnishing with kids. Then, after laying flat all the seats in the rented van and ramming in the once-pristine goods, there's the challenge of getting five people—three of whom legally belong in child's seats in the back—into a front seat fit for three. No chance. Fran and Jack shimmy into the 10 inches of space left between the boxes and the van ceiling, flat on their stomachs and unable to move. I slam the rear doors before they can protest.

But it's good. Our landlord Philippe, who lives next door with his wife Jocelyne and son Jean-Philippe, built our house himself, and it's forever about a week shy of being finished: no banister on the steep stairway to the kids' rooms downstairs, no motor on the automatic gate, no landscaping to pretty up the pitted and weedstrewn backyard. Moths, mosquitoes buzz through the screenless windows. From the start, though, we convince ourselves that this is the price one pays for grabbing the golden ring: inconveniences, risk, lunatic missions. We sing and laugh as soon as each episode ends, because we did it together and we know. Stories rife with tension get retold most of all. This will be part of the family lore, the stitching that binds us someday, when adolesence hits and sends everyone scattering, when illness comes and we need painful sweet moments to remember . . .

I had shipped seventeen boxes of clothing, supplies, Charlie's crib from Washington—three-day delivery, weeks before. None of it has arrived. When, finally, DHL unloads a half-dozen, the driver demands an unannounced, 388-euro ($430) customs charge—payable only by check. This is my first exposure to the French suspicion of credit cards, French circularity, and French graciousness. I can't open my checking account until I have a phone—yet can't hook up the phone without a checking account—and now the DHL man is demanding payment or he'll pack up the boxes and go. Philippe, a squat and bubbly Parisian who'd fled the chill winters there, has already taken to pointing out the blazing sun and exclaiming rapturously, *"Le Sud!"* (The South!) whenever he sees me. He gives the driver a Gallic shrug, scribbles out a check for the full amount, and tells me to pay whenever.

I hadn't been expecting this, of course. The war in Iraq has been going badly for a while now, and we're Americans, after all. Yet as our first days unroll, the French repeatedly prove themselves anything but the brusque ogres portrayed on both sides of the Atlantic. Everyone is smiling, voluble, eager to help. We aren't complete boobs: Fran is a month or two from fluency. We know enough not to demand Jerry Springer revelations, we try to speak the language, we whisper a courteous *Bonjour* upon entering any establishment, no matter that you're often greeting the new shoes or groceries more than the people inside. Always, we are taken warmly in hand, and when I remark on this to Philippe he gives what I'll soon know as his signature reply. *"C'est le Sud,"* he says, and then in a simplified French I manage to understand, "They're not as nice up north."

It takes months to realize how superficial this can be. A longtime resident from Paris declares one day that he can't live in the South much longer. "They greet you with open arms," he says. "But they never close them." Still, it's better than the alternative. No one greets us more coolly than Americans. In the early days of September, when we drop Jack and Addie at the bilingual school in Luynes, the women (and it's women who dictate such things; the men dropping their kids don't linger or cluster, just a hurried rush in, the drop, the quick walk away) avoid the obvious eyes of newcomers sending out get-acquainted signals. One makes the mistake of introducing herself to an expat American, married to a Frenchman, who cuts her off. "I can't make friends with Americans who are going to leave in a year," she says. "I don't give out my number, I don't want to do play dates, I can't be friends."

It's a fashionable school. The women are married to rock stars, soccer players, consultants, corporate nomads, men who spend their one working day a week trolling the Internet (actor John Malkovich, I keep hearing, sent his kid here); the thin women are always well turned out and drive new cars. Finally, it dawns: They've hit the lifestyle lottery; they've moved to the South of France. They came to realize one of the most common fantasies of middle-class American girlhood, to redo houses and flirt with the breadman, to practice high school French on the heavily made up dry-cleaning ladies. They don't want to hear about Kobe Bryant's rape case or failing U.S. public schools or the greatness of Target—except from an ironic distance, as a thing left behind. Meet more Americans? They could've stayed home for that. And who's to say that, secretly, the women don't understand the bilingual school as a small betrayal of their romantic mission, an admission that they couldn't dive fully into the culture? Each passing year here makes them undoubtedly cooler, and each year a new wave of equally cowardly Americans (speaking English!) roll in to remind them of who they used to be.

This is more than a surprise. It's a blow. We had figured the school for our haven. Every day you can park and walk up a quarter-mile dirt road, under the trees, flanked by fields with the sound of the morning train hooting by. Packs of kids run ahead, skip, dawdle, weighed down by massive backpacks, and soon you see it: The most charming little farmhouse, set against a foresty hill perfect for building forts and hide-and-seek and a quick rush of tumbling down when the teacher calls—the whole scene like every Doisneau photo, every New Wave film, every black-and-white vision of France you didn't know you held in your mind. And for the kids, well, it should've been perfect: half the classes in French, half in English, plenty of mates from England, Australia, and America. We were so proud of our decision to send Jack and Addie there. Yes, the school day stretched from 9:00 A.M. to 5:00 P.M., but the days are full of activities, and no homework at night. What could be better?

I spend September finishing a piece I'd started back in the States, but as October breaks a weird anxiety begins to build: No one from the magazine, least of all me, can really say what I'm doing here. All energy had been directed toward just getting us to France, on logistics and figuring what the magazine would pay for, and hurrying boxes to Mail Boxes Etc. We had never sketched out a plan for what kind of stories I'd pursue or how often I'd write. No one seems worried back in New York, but the first stories seem like so much busywork: Go to Frankfurt and watch the German women's soccer team play for the World Cup title on TV. Go to Athens for the Olympic Committee's inspection tour. So I hurry off to Germany, to Greece, and the tasks involved—flights, hotels, interviews, writing—crowd out the clamor of home.

And when I call from the road, the conversation is mostly about the kids, whether they're making friends, listening to their teachers, *adjusting*. ("So how are they adjusting?" is *the* expat question.) I had pegged Addie for the most difficult time, but then, I had let Jack's curiosity, his shallow attachment to Washington, his seeming embrace of schoolwork and new faces, fool me. I'm feeling pretty good about myself until I hear that the school's headmistress has sent Jack home, after a morning of crying. This goes on for ten days: Jack breaking into tears for hours, unable to stop—and worst of all for a boy who has an answer for everything, when I ask why he only says, too calmly, "I don't know."

Still, he seems to settle down. I reward myself with the thought that maybe Jack had just missed me; when I pick him up one afternoon, he gives me a huge grin and hug. I'm about to ask how his day went. A precious Asian girl walks by. "There he is," she smiles. "The boy who cried all day."

Then I have to leave again: a trip to Paris for a piece on American tennis player Taylor Dent. So I make an adventure of it, taking Jack on the high-speed TGV train out of Aix to Paris. I do my interview, we check into a hotel on the Seine, go to our favorite sandwich place with the hot apple crumble in St. Germain-des-Pres. We find a bottle of Sonia Rykiel perfume under the bed and toss it in the suitcase for Fran. We lay down and turn out the lights, and Jack sighs and says, as if coached by some child psychiatrist, "I love these father-son moments." We wake the next morning, and pop onto the still-damp sidewalk, and there, up the opposite side of the street, comes a scarlet-clad regiment on horseback, dozens of men and horses with plumes of feathers on their heads and little clouds of breath puffing into the crystal air. I turn to a shopkeeper we've just passed and manage a passable, *"Qu'est-ce que c'est?"* and he informs me that this is *Le Garde.* I don't say another word, elated that I've actually survived an exchange of dialogue. The procession clops past. The three of us stare.

Two days later, on Halloween, a couple we know from Miami—now working in London for the *New York Times*—roll in with their two young girls, and I figure that will help, too. But we're hardly the best of hosts. Already, the invasion has started in earnest: This will be our third set of visitors, another group of energized Americans expecting a taste of wine-and-cheese, a tour of the Saturday marche in Aix, a whiff of French country life while we're still trying to settle in. Don and Lizette, though, have made the fatal mistake of being extremely close friends; they've never been to Provence before, but with them we have nothing to prove. They wait, politeness slipping bit by bit, for a tour that never comes. We set up an air mattress in the empty, spare bedroom, not a picture on the wall. They barely hear a word of French all weekend.

I don't care. I'll be leaving for Athens again in five days, and I have a new mission. I can't leave the family unarmed. Early on, we had harbored a vague hope that we could survive the year without television, that we would be able to unplug the monster and spend nights reading and discussing the news of the day. *Isn't this the South of France? We can be transformed, civilized!* But that's over now. The next afternoon, rather than take Don and Lizette and their kids to some picturesque cafe, I pull up to the spotless DARTY appliance store. It takes hours to get waited on, to choose a TV and sign papers. Lizette loves travel, and here it begins to hit her that this trip won't produce even a dab of local color. She glares and mutters, kids flop exhausted to the floor, but I'm rolling now: *Oui!* to the full cable package. *Oui!* to sports, movies, CNN, a channel called JIMMY with every edgy HBO program dialed in from the States, the BBC, ESPN Classic, Al Jazeera, 400 channels of French, English, Spanish, Arabic, German TV. And most important: Cartoon Network. *Tom and Jerry, Scooby-Doo,* the *PowerPuff Girls.* In English.

The news hits Jack and Addie like the declaration of a new holiday. They scream and jump; their two-month exile is over. To everyone under ten, I'm a hero.

That night, we crack open bottle after bottle and laugh and gossip and listen to our tiny stereo speakers blast song after song, the sounds echoing off the tile floors, bouncing through the house. Through the windows comes a clatter and bustle from the home below, a much bigger affair; our neighbor Helene is celebrating her thirtieth birthday. She had come by earlier in the day to let us know it might get loud, and we shrugged and said, "Of course. No problem." Good friends, understanding neighbors, kids happy: all in all, a good day.

The wives go to sleep. Don and I sit in the kitchen, talking about people we know, newspapers we've worked for, books we'll write someday. Soon it gets too late and the wives tell us we're too loud. We try to be quiet. But the music from outside only thumps louder, bounding up the hill outside the kids' rooms. Lizette storms in, short but scary and with a voice that could crack glass, hollering that we must go talk to the neighbors. We try to protest, but she whirls out the door, Napoleon in a baggy T-shirt.

It's 4:00 A.M., and now Don and I step out, fuzzy-headed but content under dome of sparkling stars, slipping down the muddy path to Helene's house. I peek into one of her windows: An endless disco song blasts in a room cleared of furniture, one man fluttering his arms alone on the floor. I bang on the door, then again, then again. A smallish man answers. Don looms over my shoulder, 6-foot-4 and silent and hulking, looking for all the world like the guy ready to step in if words fail: my muscle. *"Desole . . . La Musique,"* I stutter, hoping it sinks in. I point to my ear. *"Les enfants dormir, s'il vous plait . . ."*

The man disappears. Helene appears, sweaty and glassy-eyed. I wish her "Happy Birthday," then repeat my idiotic plea. She smiles and nods and shuts the door. The path goes dark. Don trudges after me up the hill, our steps dogged by disco, the volume knob untouched. A half hour passes, Lizette yells, but just as we're about to go back down, the music stops. The night fills with mountain silence, broken only by barking. Don lumbers up the stairs to wife and air mattress. The muscle needs his sleep.

The marathon runner takes a gulp of ouzo. "Bush knew about September 11," he says. I ask him to repeat it, just to be sure.

"He knew," he says.

We're sitting at a windowside table. It's a week later now, a damp night in early November. Across the street, down past the rocks planted here in 600 B.C., the sea rolls out cold and black. I peer out at the streetlights, over the water. I haven't come for this. I flew to Athens because I have a big story to write at last, and it gives me an excuse to wade into history. So much of what rattles in the Western mind—philosophy, aesthetics, literature, mathematics, biology, democracy, sports, the very idea of civilization—can be traced to ancient Greece, and I know anyone writing about sports in Europe had best begin with the beginning. I've gone to dinner with Nikos Polias, because I knew no one could take me there faster.

It isn't just that, at thirty-two, Polias is the country's top distance runner, the latest in a line that predates Christ, keeper of the classic course pioneered by a soldier named Phidippides who, in 490 B.C., apocryphally raced from Marathon to Athens to announce Greece's bloody victory over the Persians. It isn't just that he can describe how Phidippides gasped, "We won!" and then keeled over dead. It's the fact that Polias, unlike most athletes or students for that matter, cares so much about the past that he makes it immediate. When he speaks of the naval victory over the Persians at Salamina 2,484 years ago or these rocks installed as a coastal defense, he points to the spot as if it all had happened last week. When he speaks of how, during the 1997 Athens marathon, he started off in 104th place, and then for the first and only time in his career felt possessed by the spirit of Phidippides, it comes off as anything but hokey. Polias ran that day at a 4:50 pace—faster than he had even run 1 mile in practice—so euphoric that it felt as if he floated above his running self, so overwhelmed that he couldn't stop crying. He placed 19th, but no race, not even the four times he won the Athens marathon, moved him as deeply.

"I remember thinking it was very weird," he says.

So, yes, all night, I've been getting what I need, and more: a metaphor. Writers love when someone reveals himself as a metaphor; it makes our job easy. Now here's an athlete haunted by the past and racing against time, embodying Greece's current travails as much as anyone. The Olympics are going home this summer, back to the place they began in 776 B.C., and were reborn in 1896; after losing three years of construction time to bureaucratic tussling, niggling lawsuits, and archeological slowdowns, organizers are rushing to finish the venues in time for the opening ceremony. The final event on the final day will be the Olympic marathon, an event invented for the 1896 games in Athens and won then by a lightly regarded shepherd or soldier or water vendor from the village of Marusi named Spiridon Louis. Polias, of course, knows all about Louis, how he had never run a race that distance before, how he wore shoes donated by his fellow villagers, how he came running into

Panathinaiko Stadium accompanied by two princes and a rapturous crowd screaming "Hel-las!" Louis never ran a marathon again.

Polias, too, will be running in his first and last Olympic games. "I feel very responsible for the marathon because it comes from our history," he says. "I will give everything." He would've been just as happy to speak of his studies in mechanical engineering, his electric guitar, his software company. But I'm not interested in Polias's modern ways; I'm like every tourist in Greece for the first time, head aswim in togas and hemlock. I can almost see the laurel wreath on his head.

In fact, I've become so happy that I drop my guard. We've eaten off a giant plate together, and Polias insisted on pouring my first-ever shot of ouzo and I drank and still feel that rushing warmth and I'm almost convinced we understand each other. But when I mention corruption and Greece's laxity on terrorism and Olympic deadlines, he bristles and leans back in his chair, face reassembled into the universal expression of *How dare you?* He declares that the Bush administration knew before-hand about the 9/11 hijackings and kept it secret to use as justification to attack Afghanistan and Iraq. Now he stares, waiting for what I, repre-sentative of a very large American corporation, have to say.

The conversation stops. It feels like one of those moments when you hit an air pocket after hours of smooth flying: that shocking split second of freefall, the floor dropping away from your feet. Now we are arguing. Polias wants to get his punch in—we are no more dirty than you—and a realization comes edging around the ouzo with alarming slowness. Now I'm an embodiment. While I've been fitting him for laurel, Polias was looking at me across the table and seeing a cowboy hat.

"For what?" I say. "Oil?" He raises an eyebrow: of course.

"But there's no oil in Afghanistan."

He smiles. His eyes assume a cynical glint, and the gracious amateur who picked me up at my hotel, denounced steroids, and seemed the Hellenic soul of moderation is gone. I have the uneasy feeling that comes when preconceptions die; my tidy metaphor has the gall to be far more interesting than I imagined. I've been warned about the dark strains of paranoia and extremism in the Greek character, but hardly expected to find it interwoven so tightly with idealism and tradition. Voice rising, I ask if he feels—as American officials had charged and many Greeks believe—that the Greek government had for twenty-five years protected the infamous November 17 terrorists before some surprisingly easy arrests in late 2002 had seemingly broken the cell. "No . . . Maybe," he says.

"No, I just can't believe an American president would do that. Three thousand dead Americans?" I say. "Too risky. Bush knows he'd be found out. Out of ten of your friends, college-educated, intelligent . . . how many believe that?"

"Eight," he says. "Maybe ten. My brother, he's studying philosophy in Germany to get his Ph.D. He feels that way."

Polias asks why anyone should trust the United States. In Greece, he says, no one his age does. They all grew up in the shadow of a brutal, anticommunist military junta known as "the Colonels" that, from 1967–74, ran a pariah regime with the support of the U.S. government. Only one foreign dignitary visited during that time: vice president Spiro Agnew, who in October of 1971, lauded the Colonels as if they were the modern incarnations of Pericles. But of course I don't know that, nor about the $549,000 that the Colonels had contributed to the Nixon-Agnew campaign in 1968; in America those kinds of footnotes had been overwhelmed by Watergate and Agnew's legacy as a convicted tax cheat. But as anyone who has traveled to Latin America knows, minor history in the States can be bloodily major elsewhere. The 1974 partition of Cyprus, the U.S.–led bombing of Kosovo in 1999, blunt accusations in 2000 by U.S. officials concerning Greece's alleged protection of domestic terrorists—taken together, all the footnotes add up, for Greeks anyway, to ongoing proof of American arrogance. It's easy to dismiss most European anti-Americanism as fashion, but what do you say when it's justified?

Cornered, I sputter on a bit, conceding cancerous moments like the assassination of Allende or support of the Shah of Iran. But the interesting thing, I say, is that there are people in, say, Warsaw, who think the opposite. There are people in Berlin and Rome, even Paris, who see the U.S., in the end, as a force for good. . . .

"It depends," Polias says delicately, "from where you look at it."

After that, we don't speak for a while. I pay the bill, and we tug on our coats and walk to the car parked by the sea. It's then, I think, that I begin to find Athens irresistible. I don't understand this at first, because I've been conditioned to hate the place. All my life I'd heard Athens described as a pit, filthy and gagging on a glut of cars, stray dogs, and cheap concrete buildings, and nothing in my first few days here has suggested otherwise. "I suppose that ancient Greece and modern Greece compared furnish the most extravagant contrast to be found in history," Twain wrote, and that was before five million people descended upon a town designed for 350,000, before the city fathers forgot to build a decent highway or subway system. All those gorgeous ruins, all that classical grace, brought in tourists but only shamed the present; history's most glorious legacy had been overwhelmed by a century of shit. On my first visit, a few weeks before, IOC members had flown in to check the city's progress. They were greeted by garbage piled shoulder-high on the sidewalks and had no shot at hailing a taxi. The annual series of autumn strikes sent the same old message: Athens doesn't work.

Olympic preparations aren't helping. Over the winter of 2003–04, a crippled city has segued into near-paralysis. The usual traffic snarls have been teased into hourly impasses by construction on seemingly every major street, by roads torn up by the new tram and subway systems, by the double- and triple-parked cars caused by the loss of sidewalks caused by the miles of scaffolding across the face of building after building. Now it's 10:00 P.M. and Polias is showing me around town, and we drive past caffeinated construction crews banging away in the dark, pinching traffic and nerves. "All night, everywhere," he says. "We suffer . . . but it's good."

It takes a few days of exploring, but I'm not sure he's wrong. The maddening inefficiency has a point now; Athens is undergoing a makeover unlike any city its age, ever. By the time the games begin on

August 13, 2004, Athens hopes to complete a new subway system carrying 400,000 passengers daily, a 32-kilometer suburban railway extending to the new international airport, 210 kilometers of new and upgraded roads, a congestion-busting ring road, and a new 23.7-kilometer Tramway system that, for the first time in fifty years, opens Athens to the sea. Installing so much infrastructure—while refurbishing and building Olympic broadcast, athletic, and housing facilities—so quickly in a city so tightly knit is a task about as easy as taking needle-and-thread to a buzzing beehive. It's a desperate urban gamble. But Athens, sinking under the weight of ever-growing traffic and pollution problems, seeking legitimacy as a new member of the European Union, has no choice.

Complaints abound in the weeks I spend here, a sense of exhaustion seeps into every conversation, but few dispute the central truth: The Olympics, as newspaper editor Nikos Konstandaras tells me, are "a God-sent crisis." The conceit of transforming urban areas through sports has its exemplars in Cleveland, Washington, D.C., San Francisco, and Baltimore, but then, reinvention is an American specialty. It's not as easy to raze-and-rebuild in Europe, and for such a notion to gain traction in Athens, where archeologists halt construction at the mere whiff of old crockery, is downright stunning. As it is, the Olympic projects collectively stand as the largest archeological dig in Greek history, the past boiling up to redeem the present. In a case of historical payback three millenia in the making, the city that gave the world the Olympic games now hopes to be saved by them.

"This isn't a second chance," Konstandaras says. "It's our first chance. This is the first intervention since the modern city took root."

With time winding down, the stakes involved give Athens a far different atmosphere from museum-piece cities like London, Rome, or Paris. It has the energized, sexed-up feel of a newsroom just before the presses roll, of a stadium before the first World Cup match, of the instant just after the dice are thrown. It doesn't matter, at those moments, if the newsroom smells like a grotto or the stadium needs to be leveled, or the casino surrounds you with scum. The game is on. Talented people pushing themselves beyond themselves, nerves scraped raw: You can taste the adrenaline in the air, the exhausted buzz of a city putting its reputation and future on the line. Who knows if they'll make it?

Most appealing, though, is the fact that Athens can't be controlled. Organizers and government officials keep trying to project an image of a city that has learned its lesson, and can now be expected to be safe and, equally important, predictable—because nothing turns off the big money from tourists, businesspeople, and TV executives faster than unpredictability. "There's been a change," Pierre Kosmidas, a press officer with the Athens organizing committee, tells me. "Because of the Olympics, there's been more '*filotimo*'—putting in a little extra personal effort, initiative rising out of goodwill. One thing that's changed in Athens is the teamwork, coordination, and commitment to timelines, schedules. You might have ideas that Greeks are laid-back and relaxed, like Mexicans sitting back and having siesta all day. It wasn't really true— and now the games will disprove it."

Maybe, but this isn't a city capable of staying on message. No profession has a more stained or justified reputation than the city's 15,000 taxi drivers; Athens's first line of welcome is unregulated and notoriously crooked. When one charges me $123 for a $6.50 fare, my Athenian companion threatens him with arrest and says, "They do this all the time." The driver shrugs, body language for *I'll just get the next sucker.* Any attempt by the government to crack down is met with yet another strike: so much for *filotimo.* Security? The day after security minister Giorgos Floridis insists to me that, with the November 17 terrorists on trial, domestic terror is no longer a concern, six buildings in downtown Athens are firebombed in twenty minutes by a group calling itself Revolutionary Solidarity. Prior to that interview, I sat chatting with our gray-haired translator, and within forty-five seconds he was laughing in my face about the U.S. military's struggles in Iraq and declaring, "Your country has no future!"

So no, I'm not surprised to hear, three days later, that a crowd of at least 10,000 marched on the U.S. embassy in Athens to commemorate the thirtieth anniversary of the November 17, 1973, student uprising that began the end of the Colonels rule and gave the terrorist group its name, or that forty-two people were arrested then for carrying concealed weapons and hurling sticks and stones and firebombs. I'm not shocked, later, when a poll reveals that Greeks, more than any EU nationality, believe that U.S. foreign policy damages world peace and only impedes the battle against terror.

Somewhere, in all this, preconceptions die: the idea of Greece as a quaint antique shop, the idea of Greece regarding the U.S. as some sort of cultural heir, the idea of Greece as an *idea*. In its place stands a complex, dirty, electric place, the smallest to host a summer games in forty years, promising nothing more than to bring the Olympics home. Unlike Sydney in 2000, Atlanta in 1996, and Barcelona in '92, Athens is genetically incapable of presenting an event scrubbed clean of divisiveness or uncertainty. Instead, in a nation where anti-Americanism is embedded in the cultural DNA, the first multinational event since 9/11 will open amid fear of attack. American athletes will wave their flag before an audience ready to burn it. The world will watch and vote in a subconscious referendum on American behavior, success, and, most of all, power. The Olympics have long grown bloated with hype and self-importance, increasingly guided by the natural impulse of gigantic organizations to bully their environment into unthreatening blandness. I like Athens because slickness can't survive it. I like Athens because nothing is guaranteed.

"Do you want to come see my mother?" Polias asks, after we had ridden around for a while. So we drive into his old neighborhood in Pireaus, hard by the once-polluted harbor where his father labored as a ship's carpenter and the Olympic cruise hotels will make port, past the gym where he first played, over the bumpy narrow streets where he won his first race barefoot. He takes me into the house where he shared a cramped room with his two brothers, and modestly shows off his trophies and medals, and his mother trots out a homemade liqueur called *visino* and a dish of fruit awash in thick syrupy sweetness. Our argument has been forgotten; his mother's eyes sparkle and we speak of family and work and the summer to come. Polias doesn't have to be so generous. That's the night's second surprise.

But the city isn't finished with me yet. A few days later, at dusk, I walk up to the Acropolis for the first time, not knowing the gates of the Parthenon will be closed, nor that all tourists will be gone. I climb some rocks—the same slippery, foot-worn rocks at *Arios Pagos*, it turns out, where St. Paul first spoke when bringing the Word to Greece—and upon reaching the top find two black-robed, bearded priests standing alone. The sea wind whips their faces. I move past them to the edge, below which Athens lies like a martyred body, broken and revered, and the barking dogs and screeching brakes, the rattling trains and jackhammer pounding, come drifting up muffled and gentle. Bells begin to ring. I turn, wide-eyed, but the priests don't notice. They're singing. Over my right shoulder, I see the spotlighted Greek flag flapping atop the Acropolis, atop the bleached columns and spindly scaffolds.

It's one of those moments: cinematic, choreographed by a master hand. The breath of the past settles upon your neck, and you shiver and whisper, "Thank you," because you made it, you're *there*; you're here at last. One priest kicks at the stones beneath his feet. One wipes his nose. Prayers rise into the darkening sky. The men in black sing, but the wind takes their words before I can hear. Their mouths move, and the chaos below looks like a gift.

Three

We were going to France for a year, to a village in the south, not far from Grasse, where we had rented a large, sparsely furnished farmhouse. . . . It had been occupied the year before by Robert Penn Warren and his wife, Eleanor Clarke. I wrote to ask if they recommended it, and a letter came from her in reply. It described a paradise, from the windows of which the sea could be distantly seen. You will have the most wonderful year of your life, it concluded, if you don't happen to freeze to death.

James Salter, *Burning the Days*

The nation we've adopted, naturally, has begun another slide into crisis. It's rarely easy to pick up the thread when you break in midconversation, but this time is different. Though still a month away, the fact that Starbucks will soon open a shop in Paris is already causing much media hand-wringing and the inevitable conclusion: another blow to French culture. The national dialogue seems to always come back to the idea of *Frenchness*, to ask what is France and who is French in the twenty-first century. If there's a country equaling the U.S. in self-obsession, in the desperate taking of its own temperature, it's La France—but with a key difference. Here, no one seems to have an answer pointing toward anything but decline; stores are littered with best-selling books full of recrimination: *France in Free Fall, French Arrogance, France in Disarray.*

Such a spectacle is odd and riveting: a country's self-worth erod-
ing before your eyes. Nine months ago, President Jacques Chirac
indulged himself in a revealing fit of pique when, in responding to
news that the ten Eastern European nations soon to join the European
Union—and thus diluting France's power on the continent—signed an
open letter of support for the Iraq War, he snapped that "they missed a
great opportunity to shut up." No one took his suggestion, and Chirac
came off like a man too arrogant to know that it wasn't the age of de
Gaulle anymore. With the largest Muslim population in Western
Europe and the largest Jewish population on the continent, France
these days finds itself serving more and more as an outsourced battle-
ground in the Israeli-Palistinian conflict and increasingly defined to
the world by dark faces and strange accents and elements with no
interest in French ideals or bistro dreams.

Winter is starting to edge over the South, temperatures at night in
the thirties but no snow. Every few days I wheel my bike out onto our
twisty street—*Chemin des Grillons*, Cricket Road—and whiz down to
the D46. I take a right, cross a bridge, and begin the climb. When taking
the route through St. Savournin and Cadolive, there's a landmark I use
to tell me it's time to stand up on the pedals and churn: a tattered *Le Pen
Président* poster plastered over the announcement of a coming circus.

Keyed by Marseille, France's second-largest city and the one most
inundated with North African immigrants, Provence spent the previous
generation sending out two wildly divergent images. Internationally, a
torrent of books made it a peaceable symbol of the chuck-it-all-and-
start-over life, complete with restorable chateaux and charmingly
cranky natives. But domestically it became known as a stronghold of a
panicked strain of ultra-right-wing, anti-Semitic, anti-immigrant
nationalism channeled through ex-paratrooper Jean-Marie Le Pen and
his National Front party. In the spring of 2002, Le Pen rose to an unexpected level of seriousness when he beat prime minister Lionel Jospin
in the first round of the presidential election before being smashed by
Chirac—and a suddenly aroused electorate—in the final round. When

we first arrived, the tattered Le Pen poster from that campaign was the only one around.

Lately, I find myself taking the high route to Mimet, the highest town in the Bouches-du-Rhone, where the incline lasts 3 miles but once past the cobblestone square and the war obelisk with chiseled dead names, once around the chateau perched on its highest point, there's a message hand-scrawled vertically on a rusted drainpipe with a helpful arrow: *Vallee de Luynes*. And if you follow the arrow, there, indeed, is the great Luynes valley spread out below, with the power station towers and Mont Sainte-Victoire set in opposing corners, as if the chosen champions of man and nature have, finally, decided to square off. A vast gulf lies between the two, and behind each stands massed armies: the power plant fronting the crimped roadways and dingy clatter of Gardanne, the mountain backed by miles of scrubby trees, broken stones, lavender air. I've rarely seen a more horrifying juxtaposition of natural beauty and man-built ugliness. For visitors, the plant's two towers are Provence's big surprise; after all, Cezanne painted sixty studies of Sainte-Victoire, not a pair of massive trash cans. Yet I always pause to take in the view, in part because I've never seen anyone else here. It's mine.

Still, Sainte-Victoire would be just another forgettable butte in, say, the American West, but its flat surroundings provide dramatic contrast, imbuing it with hypnotic force. Something in the fusing of limestone, light, and Mediterranean air alchemizes what should be simple rock into a regional jewel, a community mood ring, reading the area's physical state and broadcasting it daily: beige as a molar for the cool mornings, flushed pink and then purple for soft evenings. For days when the mistral blows, Mont Saint-Victoire hunches white and frigid, flanks ribby and unsoftened by snow, looking no more inviting than a mesa on the moon. I sneak glimpses through the pine as I zoom down from Mimet, and that's when the wonder hits: with the wind stinging eyes, the bike whirring beneath, a cry leaping off the tongue. Magnificence pierces calluses formed by age and hurry; magnificence makes time stop. When I finish, mud-spattered and sweaty, I feel oddly purified. Or maybe I just love going fast.

Sometime in November, I notice a new Le Pen poster on a bus stop up the hill. Then they start to appear everywhere: on the roads out of Marseille, on poles and bridge stanchions. New elections have been set for the spring, and here's Le Pen's happy face plastered over a subtly applied dig—"Our Region Deserves the Best"—at the South's inferiority complex. It's a brilliant slogan. Marseille's image as a Mediterranean cesspool bubbling with drugs and corruption has been proven time and again since *The French Connection,* and it wears its badness well. The port is undeniably sexy, in a way that Las Vegas, say, isn't—dark and vital and vicious, a gorgeous older woman drugged-up and loose and more than happy to wield a knife to get your wallet. As the gateway to Provence, it counters nicely the tourist theme of rural leisure. But it's also a second-class city, and feels it, forever coming up short when compared with the capital. "Nothing in Marseille—the politics, the universities, the culture, the economic power—is better than anything in Paris," Dinesh Teeluck, a Mauritius-born, Aix-based journalist for the magazine *L'Express* tells me. "Nothing except for football."

"So," I say, referring to the French national anthem, "Marseille has two things to be proud of, then: 'Le Marseillaise' and Olympique de Marseille?"

"No," Dino says. "Marseille has only Olympique de Marseille . . . and Olympique de Marseille."

In southern Provence, it is the inescapable name. France's oldest and most storied soccer team, L'OM commands its own TV channel and an all-encompassing loyalty; you cannot pass one day without seeing its powder blue-and-white colors, its logo, or the motto *Droit Au But*—straight to the goal—emblazoned on a shirt, scarf, hat, or rear windshield. The hated rival Paris-St. Germain has risen of late, but it's still a thirty-five-year-old upstart with just two national titles. Founded in 1899, playing since 1938 on the same, dynamically upgraded ground known as Stade Velodrome, OM has won eight French championships. After its fourth straight in 1993, Marseille clipped AC Milan, 1–0, to win the European Cup final—a feat unmatched by any French club and surpassing in emotional clout even the disgrace that followed. Just before that campaign had ended, it turned out, OM representatives—including at least one player and club president Bernard Tapie—had conspired to pay off French-league opponent Valenciennes to lose by a goal. An investigation into his ownership revealed that Tapie had spent some 100 million francs on secret player payoffs and match-fixing; it was slime without compare, the worst soccer scandal in the history of the European game. Disgraced, Tapie lost his position and his team, spent eight months in jail. OM found itself relegated to the second division, sentenced to a decade-long search for a road map back.

OM hasn't won a French championship since. Significantly, though, the city hasn't disowned Tapie; corruption is a fact of life in Marseille, and winning isn't. OM brought him back as general manager in 2001 to great applause, little moral outrage, and an unmistakeably clear acceptance of the Marseille way: Straight to the goal, indeed—even if you must cheat, bribe, and lie to get there. But Tapie didn't last. OM didn't win, so after a year and a half he, too, was disposable. Nonetheless, Marseille's glory years were his too; now an actor and commentator, he remains a hero here. Over and over I'm told that to castigate Tapie in the city, even now, is to invite a beating. In the end, the only complaint OM fans have about Tapie is that he somehow passed on Zinedine Zidane.

Who can blame them? In the winter of 2003, there's still no greater player in the game than Zidane, France's dashing midfielder and a man whose implacable reserve and blank face mask a fierce competitiveness. Zidane doesn't hesitate to play nasty, but it's his grace and timing that set him apart; he's the closest thing in soccer to DiMaggio roaming center-field. Just as important, though, is Zidane's role as cultural emblem: The son of immigrants from Algeria, site of France's disastrous colonial war, "Zizou" grew up in the ratty streets of Marseille's Castellane—a crime-infested slice of the world that Le Pen finds so threatening—worshipping OM. Even in November, when the thirty-one-year-old Zidane returns home for the first time as one of the glittering *galacticos* of the megarich, megastocked Spanish powerhouse Real Madrid, he admits that he can't play with his usual fire. His family will all be rooting for OM, he knows, and his own love hasn't quite died.

"To come back to the Stade Velodrome brings back memories of my youth," he says to the press the day before the match. "Indeed, I spent more time in the stands watching OM and its great players of the past, than playing on the pitch. I will probably never be an OM player even though it was my childhood dream. Now it is too late. My contract is too long and my career too short and nearing the end. Too bad they didn't want me when it was possible."

It was possible during Tapie's ascendancy in Marseille, when Zidane was not yet Zidane, just a talent developing in Bordeaux. But Tapie dismissed him as too fragile and slow to play in the Champions League, and who knows if Tapie's future troubles didn't include karmic payback for inflicting on Marseille so brutal a civic loss? Zidane went on to make his legend with Juventus in Italy's Serie A, and sealed it with France's improbable run to the World Cup title in France in 1998. Decidedly un-Gallic, populated by so many blends of African, Mediterranean, and white blood, that national team was embraced by liberals as a diligent, diverse, valiant emblem of modern France—and an unanswerable repudiation of xenophobia. Even Le Pen, who once derided the national team for its multihued cast, had the nerve to describe Zidane, the team's undisputed leader, as an Arab who had learned to be "a good Frenchman." More than anyone, he is the face of France's new, mixed-up world.

"Zidane is the foreign symbol France needed," says Dino, the journalist for *L'Express.* "The guy represents all minorities in Marseille and France. Most people think foreigners come to be here for welfare or that they cheat. But Zidane showed it wasn't like that; he showed immigrants can succeed. He's the symbol of immigrant success in France."

We are meeting for lunch a week before the match, on a cool and damp November 20 somewhere along Aix's famed Cours Mirabeau. I've had the morning to myself, one of those harsh days that foretell a long, dead winter, with metallic light blasting through the besieged plane trees and a relentless jackhammer echoing down what's widely considered the most perfect main street in the world. Christmas lights are strung in a web high above the Cours, and it's still, at 11:00 A.M. when the university kids are just rolling out and the scent of morning has yet to burn off, sweater weather. I sit on a bench opposite the Societe Generale bank. Over one shoulder, a mime poses in white-powdered robes; over the other a flautist plays a halting version of Pachelbel's *Canon*. The coffee had been hot and thick, and I have my *International Herald Tribune* in hand. For the longest time, this moment had been my exact vision of Europe.

The sidewalk behind me fills with cyclists, women with tiny dogs, hangover cases, vacationing seniors. A truckful of *forestiers* work tree-to-tree, chopping off every leafy branch with chainsaws, grinding the summer shade into dust. The air brightens; now you can see a vast stretch of sky. The flute begins playing *The Four Seasons*. I read the story about a firebomb attack on an unoccupied Jewish school in Paris. "Attacking a Jew in France is an attack on all of France," President Chirac declares.

Dino primes me for the game over a steaming plate of Provençal stew. It is, I figure, a high-tension week for Marseille. The city is competing with Lisbon and Valencia, Spain, for the right to stage the 2007 America's Cup and the announcement looms, but when I mention it Dino waves the topic away. No, what matters only is that OM is sinking into the mud of another second-rate campaign and, as it turns out, a loss to Real Madrid will drop them out of the Champions League, Europe's most prestigious annual competition. With its nine Champions League titles, and each position manned by a player of unequaled glamour—England's David Beckham, Brazil's Ronaldo and Roberto Carlos, Portugal's Luis Figo, and of course, Zidane—Real Madrid is everything Marseille wants and once saw possible for itself. "Understand: OM in the early nineties was like Real Madrid now," Dino says.

So Zidane is coming home conflicted, the favorite son angling now to deal his city a fatal blow. When I hop off the subway at the spiffy Stade Velodrome the night of the game, the psychic stakes have only grown higher: In the afternoon, Marseille learned both that Valencia had gotten the America's Cup and that Zidane—already twice named World Footballer of the Year—has been named a finalist again. The 58,600 seats are filled, with each roiling end punctuated by the banners of the team's infamous fan clubs—Dodgers, Fanatics, MTP, Kaotic Group, Winners, Yankees. A Confederate flag flaps incongrously in the frigid sea air. At 8:08 P.M., with AC/DC's "Hell's Bells" screeching through the sound system, the scent of marijuana drifting by, an animal roar rising out of the mass, Real Madrid comes trotting on field for warmups. Zidane lopes out, spotlights imbuing his balding head with a dim glow. He boots around a ball with Raul, then jogs off. The crowd whistles in the European salute of disgust, and Zidane and the rest of Real disappear into a tunnel.

Then the game begins, and everything Real Madrid *means* goes on display. Here are the cashbox boys, wielding a $350 million budget that dwarfs any other team's, sending out its roster of megastars with studied casualness. Real doesn't play so much as pay off, and all goes as it should: Of course Beckham opens the scoring twenty-one minutes in with a looping free kick, bent just like the movie says, to put OM in a 1–0 hole. Of course Real is dominating. Then Zidane collapses at midfield, left leg writhing. Stretcher-bearers scamper out, but Zidane finally hops up, limps over to the side, and lays down like a tired hound. A sourness, an understanding that maybe all the buildup has been a con, overtakes the Stade. For forty minutes, it looks like OM will go down without a whimper . . .

Then BANG!, that quickly, the place is transformed. OM's Ahmed Mido heads the ball with a crack into goal, and now smoke bombs explode, banners shake, people scream. We all feel the goal as much as see it: Yes, I'm on my feet too, there before I know it, yanked up by the roar of the crowd, its surging pride, the sniff of an upset. Throats yell, "*All-ez! All-ez! All-ez!*" and what has been a lethargic contest accelerates, the crowd and the play pulling each other along faster, faster. Beckham gets slapped with a yellow card, OM sends another header just over the crossbar, Ronaldo goes just wide with a header of his own. All around me, faces stretch into grins, mouths twisted by shouts and laughing. No one cares what they look like or who sees them; they've all gotten what sports can give: the chance to lose themselves. Back and forth, the two end zones of fans chant at each other, 40,000 voices booming across the field:

"*Aux Armes!*" (To Fight!), yells one.

"*Nous Sommes Les Marseille!*" (We are Marseille!), responds the other.

"*Nous Allons Gagner!*" (We will win!)

"*Aux Arms! Aux Arms! Aux Arms!*" (Fight! Fight! Fight!)

I'm hooked. *OM must win*, I think. *OM is going to win*. For the next eleven minutes, the stadium shakes, and I'm part of a collective vibe all but impossible to resist. But just as I'm getting happy about it, just as I thinking of my new life in the Bouches-du-Rhone and allowing the words *This is my team, too* to take shape, everything dies. Real is Real, after all, and Zidane is Zidane, no matter where he's playing. Who else to deliver the killing blow? Zizou sets up on the left wing, clips a perfect pass to Raul, who finds the charging Ronaldo to pop home an absurdly easy goal. Everyone is watching him now: There's Zidane hugging Ronaldo and smiling, because goals are gold and you're paid millions and you do what you must, without thinking. Love is one thing, and winning another; you grind your spikes into the opponents' neck. 2–1, and it isn't going to change. The fans know it, Real knows it, Zidane knows it, too.

So with eight minutes left, he shuffles off the field and the crowd of 60,000 that had whistled at him during warmups and when he was hurt and when he scored because *We Are Marseille!*, rises to its feet as one and applauds for a good long time, and then a chant rings out and grows as people begin to understand: "Zi-ZOU! Zi-ZOU!"

Afterward, under the stadium, a waiting blue bus chuffs out exhaust, REALMADRID.COM printed on its rear. Hundreds of women, kids, firemen, and men, of course, wait to see soccer's Rolling Stones walk one by one to the bus, and soon they come, walking up the concrete tunnel, hair still wet from the shower: Roberto Carlos, Raul, Figo, Ronaldo. Steel barriers hold back the staring people, the reporters with their cameras and digital recorders and pens. Beckham limps up, diamonds as big as a nickel in each ear. He is, still, the glamour boy of soccer; cut loose from his home with Manchester United, Beckham seems to be adjusting well enough in Madrid. The papers have been full of stories about supposed strains in his marriage, but Beckham still carries himself with little-boy sweetness, his high mushy voice full of nothing but patience. I stop him and ask about Zidane's night.

"It's special for Zizou because he's coming up to Marseille where he's from and the people love him here," Beckham says. "So for him, it's important that we won."

Another man, sweating, speaking rapidly, cuts in and blurts a question less journalistic than human, with all the desperation of someone overwhelmed by the existence of such talent, fame, and pressure. "How do you do it, David?" the man pleads. "How?" Beckham blinks, stammers. It's an excellent question. "I can't . . ." Beckham begins. "I just . . . " he tries again. "I practice and I work hard at my game and that's what I'll carry on doing until I'm finished playing."

The man just stares. Beckham moves on, signing scraps of paper, stopping for pictures. The crowd, then the bus, swallow him. Ten minutes later, Zidane emerges, eyes darting, a security man's hand grabbing his coat from behind like a parent guiding a toddler through the mall. He doesn't stop. He doesn't speak. Stunned by the sight of him, quieted by his quiet, the people just watch him pass.

I leave not long after, hurrying down to the subway, taking the number 2 line from Le Stade to Bougainville back to Marseille's central station. The train is crowded with fans, but none too upset over the loss; two bald fat men decked in OM gear sing "*All-ez! All-ez!*" and fill the ride with laughing. When the subway car pulls into the station, I walk out into the night and stop. There, in the distance, is the cathedral of Notre Dame, bathed in soft yellow light, glowing like a candle. The broad marble stairs, the Boulevard Athenes below, are both empty. Damp air fills my lungs.

I hear the chant stuck in my head, and let it set the pace for my footsteps—Zi-zou, Zi-zou—as I hurry toward the carpark. I see a bar, an OM sticker on the window, and step inside to take its temperature. Three faces turn to look, not a glimmer of welcome in any of them, then turn back to their glasses. The bartender is closing up, the city shutting down. I back out and pick up speed: Zi-ZOU!

The next two weeks bring endless rain. Marseille goes under water; the papers show pictures of cars awash in a rising tide. I fly to Athens to speak with Mayor Dora Bakoyannis, who survived the 1989 assassination of her first husband by the November 17 gang, who had survived in late 2002 a gunman's bullet fired into her car, who had interrupted her testimony during the trial in 2003 to ask the man who'd killed her husband, "Why?" "It was a very big shock," she says of the terrorists, "to realize that those people were so small." She's a big woman, 6-foot-2, and makes no effort to hide it: Her father had been an enemy of the Colonels, a prime minister after he returned from exile, and as a massively popular politician whom many believe will lead Greece someday, Bakoyannis has a calm sense of her own destiny. She smiles often, but when the smile fades her eyes look like black stones. "My life," she says, "was exactly the life of modern Greek history."

This is hard to argue. The day before, December 8, she had sat with her children in the courtroom as the November 17 terrorists were pronounced guilty.

"Everybody asked me if I felt . . . happy," she says. "No. A verdict cannot bring back the people you lost."

After our chat, Bakoyannis walks outside her office and points to the glass case displaying the Barbie-sized figurines of Athens's previous mayors, all men, all in dark suits. For decades, she had personally endured the blacker instincts of one of the world's most macho cultures, and now stands as the first woman mayor of Europe's oldest city. "They haven't made a doll of me yet," she says with a laugh. "I promised them: When I become a doll, I will wear a skirt."

From City Hall, I grab a cab to the airport. The car winds through the chill December streets, and then the driver takes a call on his cell phone, hangs up, and says into his rearview mirror, "Problem . . . mother . . . take bus?" He pulls over and nods for me to get out. I stand waving for ten minutes before another taxi stops. This driver looks vaguely menacing, and there's another large, glowering man next to him up front, but I need to catch that flight. As the car pulls away, I amuse myself with a headline: AMERICAN REPORTER KILLED BY N17 SYMPATHIZERS. The silent men drive for ten minutes. Then, without a word, the driver yanks the car to the curb. The door opens, and without a gesture a middle-aged woman lowers her butt unstoppably into my shoulder, my side, my hip, and—with my feet now plopped far to the right and my besieged torso leaning left only inches from full horizontal—shunts me and my bag to the other side of the car. I consider yelping, but she seems too preoccupied to care.

We drive for 2 blocks. I wonder if she's an N17 ringleader, Athens's version of Ma Barker. I feel embarrassed by a woman pushing me around until I realize that no one seems to notice I'm still in the car. The driver stops, the woman hands him a few coins and gets out. A mile on, the man in front hands him a few euros and gets out. Now I get it: I've hopped an unofficial jitney. For a moment I envision the entire city's taxi fleet, stuffed with three and four riders paying cash off the books, part of a phantom economy churning away so systemically, so brazenly, that it's almost admirable. At the airport, the driver cuts me a deal and grins at last. I should be outraged, I guess, but I find myself smiling. I kind of miss my fellow passengers.

I change planes in Paris, and on the flight to Marseille engage in the usual pointless, silent, unacknowledged but all-important jockeying for arm-rest dominance with the Frenchman in the next seat. Cheeks burning, the man stares at his *Le Monde* as if nothing is happening, and since we've gotten so close I feel free to start reading over his shoulder. TWENTY-TWO PERCENT OF THE FRENCH PEOPLE BELIEVE IN THE IDEAS OF THE NATIONAL FRONT declares the top headline, and underneath is a cartoon playing off recent flooding in the south: The symbol of the French republic, adrift in a rowboat, happens upon a tree that, in place of branches, sprouts a thicket of arms festooned with fascist armbands. All of them offering a helping hand.

I congratulate myself; I get that, too. Le Pen's men will be running in the regional elections and the South is up for grabs, and *Le Monde*'s poll indicates an exploitable ambivalance: Yes, 70 percent believe the National Front is *dangereux pour la democratie*, but yes, the republic is concerned about racial dilution, so yes, only 42 percent now judge Le Pen and Co. unacceptable.

I cede the man his armrest, and stare out the window and think of that game at the Stade Velodrome. I do the math, and wonder if 12,000 of those people in the stands actually hate everything Zidane stands for, and want him and his kind thrown back into the sea. I wonder whether he's a wedge into their fear, a way for the world to change peacefully, or an exception made palatable by his talent. I wonder if that standing ovation was real, or just a nice heartfelt lie.

Four

Scott told me about the Riviera and how my wife and I
must come there the next summer and how we would
go there and how he would find a place for us that was
not expensive and we would both work hard every day
and swim and lie on the beach and be brown and only
have a single aperitif before lunch and one before dinner.
Zelda would be happy there, he said.

Ernest Hemingway, *A Moveable Feast*

A few weeks later, I pinpoint the moment when human beings form national identity. At the age of three years, nine months, my daughter Addie sits at the IKEA playtable, scribbling with rare purpose. A massive thunderstorm is rolling over the Chaine de L'Etoile, rain hammering the roof loud and lovely. She picks up one colored pencil after another, red, green, lavender, orange, blue, black, gray, and brown, filling in an array of splotches and chickenlike figures and strange fish. She runs over and hands me the paper, a gift. I do the usual parent thing: Stare dumbly at the chaos on the page, murmur how beautiful it is, ask what I'm looking at. "It's the United States," Addie says.

I do a classic movie double take. "The United States of what?"

"The United States of Lots of Things."

I stare at her, feeling caught. Kids sense the slightest shift in parental mood, I know, but I didn't expect her to sniff out my quiet fit of . . . what? Homesickness? Nostalgia? Americosis? before I'd recognized it myself.

The news has been full of Bush's upcoming visit to London, and maybe we've been talking about that, but I suspect the scent rises mostly off me. I've been preoccupied with the U.S.A. lately, suddenly obsessed with all we've left behind. It's understandable, I guess. After twenty-four years of resisting it, I've wasted the week absorbed in a tattered paperback of Walt Whitman that I've hauled all over the continent, from New Mexico to Connecticut to North Carolina to Northern California, Miami, Washington, D.C., and now at last to France. I should have known that reading it, the last of a breed, would send me spinning. Everything I love about travel begins with that book.

By now, too, it has become clear that our French sojurn has no chance of conforming to whatever vague ideal Fran and I had carried with us. My reporting so far has no resemblance to Edward R. Murrow's broadcasts from the London blitz; I don't even own a trenchcoat. Worse, we've made enough expat friends to realize that our home is a disappointment: Everyone but us is living in some perfectly furnished version of a French farmhouse, with big wooden dining tables and broad lawns perfect for flying a kite. With throw rugs on the floor and the kids' artwork on the walls, our house feels only a bit more cozy than a warehouse. The quietest conversation bounces off the tile like a cartoon roman candle, ricocheting from room to room with deafening clarity. The one escape is a step out into the driveway muck.

But we wouldn't mind, not usually. It's just that we had such superb role models for how to do this right. A few years back, an American couple named Peter and Virginia Carry lent us the use of their home in the astoundingly picturesque hilltop hamlet they'd discovered in the Ardeche. We descended on it for nearly two weeks, three families with six kids under six, broke a lamp, and went swimming in the nearby gorge. I created a family legend by leaping into the river from a tree, but that wasn't the important thing. Peter refused any offer of money, and he could've charged thousands: magazine-perfect house, gourmet kitchen, spectacular view of the vineyard valley, cobblestone lanes, and a honey shop across the way. He was the executive editor of *Sports Illustrated* then, but his jocular generosity, coupled with perfect taste, revealed a man and wife who'd come as close as possible to the popular idea of "the good life." When we visited them in their Manhattan apartment later that year, that, too, was exactly as it should be: bookish, distinctive but not too edgy, like the set of a Woody Allen movie. Their kids had gone to Princeton, were getting married, embarking on fascinating careers. The Carrys brought us to an upscale French restaurant and had the grace not to take any of it seriously; when Fran slipped on the stairs on the way out, Peter cracked a joke, he and his wife giggling as if we'd somehow done the place a service. The Carrys, bless them, make it all look easy.

We come from different stock. "Come on, Dad," Addie has been saying lately, pouncing on me with her hairbrush. "Let's make your hair cool." An impossible task. Fran can be cool; she has a great eye and great bones. But she gave up on me long ago; I'm just not made for sure elan, for ease, and now Addie is beginning to see the deficiency. Part of it is biology, but part is also the usual case of suburban fraudulence, the secret terror all bedroom community wanna-bes feel about being exposed—Imposter!—by a coven of black-clad urban hipsters. In the '60s, *Time* magazine called Stamford, Connecticut, "a dingy factory town" and in the '90s *Rolling Stone* called it "The Big Empty." I grew up there in between, when development took off and corporate headquarters mushroomed across the landscape, drifting in a safe and discomforting dullness. We were small time in Stamford, and couldn't help but know it. What exactly was I thinking, moving to the land of coolness supreme?

Still, I've been reading the Whitman, a few pages a day. I have the time. It's gotten cold enough that I don't need to tend to the weeds that serve as our backyard, cutting them up with a one hundred-pound contraption that Philippe calls *Le Monstre*. All fall, I had ripped the skin off my palms while wrenching the vibrating beast through the mud. Now, though, the only thing to do is stand on the terrace staring at the firetower rising on the highest peak in the Chaine de l'Etoile, its rectangular, plate-glass eye reflecting the sun until it slides over the top, toward the

Mediterranean, and the hills darken as if coated with tar. The mailman on his yellow scooter delivers around noon, and if I'm there we'll smile and I'll pretend to understand what he says after *Bonjour*, and not point out that I'm getting mail postmarked two months earlier. I'll go lie on our bed when Fran leaves at four to pick up the kids, and maybe I'll read and maybe I'll dump out the week's load of magazines from the office: *Entertainment Weekly, People, Sports Illustrated*. This week, I thumb through a December issue of *Time*, and come to a story about a stirring in the New York art world: With his one-man show at the Whitney Museum of American Art, the painter John Currin has become a critic's darling, credited with revitalizing the art of the human form and indulging a misogynistic obsession with huge breasts.

Fran had been best friends with John's sister once, and we had all gone to high school in Stamford together. After years of dramatically despising my hometown, lately I've begun to wonder if maybe I'd just ginned up the Sensitive Young Man's cliched first conflict—the artist versus the provincial boobs. But here, filling half of page 79, is a painting called *Stamford After-Brunch:* Three young, wealthy women smoke cigars and clink martini glasses on an overstuffed couch before a picture window. It's winter. The women's eyes are narrowed from laughing about . . . a memory? A dirty joke? It takes a moment to understand. Two of the women's bodies are thin and oddly flabby, but the picture's focus is the third woman sitting to the right, her head wrapped in a pink knotted scarf, her body all wrong. Her ass juts impossibly; her legs stretch impossibly; one thigh bone looks as if it has been wrenched, ball and all, out of the hip socket. She is a freak and, laughing despite her freakishness, her friends are pale horrors too. I turn the page. So maybe, I think, it wasn't just me.

My father's father had been gassed during World War I, and his son, George, joined the Marines and served during the Korean War. Ours was a house of politics and arguments and slamming doors, fueled by the resentment of a promise never realized. My older brothers slept amid clouds of marijuana. We drove around in used Ford Pintos with the door handles snapped off. The money dried up, but North Stamford filled with huge homes and property values skyrocketed, and taxes too. We always paid them late, my mom borrowing from family, pleading her case to the bank with four kids in tow. My father quit his job, started a business that sounded special, "American Advertising Co.," but failed, began spending his days in the basement, filing magazine clippings into secondhand steel cabinets stacked around the walls, voicing intense, vague plans about a new venture involving etchings or engravings or something. We spoke a strange language to each other, couched in contests of historical trivia—*Okay, you might know the captain of* Old Ironsides, *but who won the Battle of Fallen Timbers?!*—but in the sharpening of minds against one another, in the smilingly heated banter, we knew each other best. In that ongoing exchange, me thirteen years old and lost and him pushing elsewhere for a success that never came, we had a rhythm that everyone else missed. I fell for America then, the idea of it anyway.

Taking high school French was intellectual luxury, the domain of those sure of college. The driving force was a rotund, bun-haired thrush named Mrs. Fenn, who inspired a cult of devotees that gathered about her after class and called her "Madame." Fran adored her like everyone else, and proved casually adept at speaking with that necessary French curl in the back of the throat; she was one of Madame's stars. I, however, had Madame Fenn just my freshman year, and with no ear, no work ethic, no potential to buckle down, barely limped through. And at that school, Apres Madame Fenn, Le Deluge: The rest of the department was a wasteland. First came Mrs. Fisher, a geriatric case who graded solely on the basis of some mysterious standard of personal deportment. If you were nice or polite or had a nicely shaped head, you would get your B and move on to French 3—no matter that you butchered the language with a dull knife. Next came Mr. Troisi, genial and scattered and looking like a cartoon Inspector Clouseau; to forestall any serious learning, all you need do was walk into class and mention some political controversy, and the forty minutes would fly by in loopy argument. Sometimes, he would have us close our eyes and meditate. Three years of the language, and I couldn't utter a sentence.

I didn't want to think too hard about what my failure there seemed to signal: I wasn't quick, I wasn't smart, I wasn't designed to go to some foreign place someday. And that wouldn't line up with the desperate dream then grabbing hold; I wanted my brothers, my family to disappear. I had to get out. I caddied, pumped gas, sold shoes, worked the usual part-time jobs, overdosing on Springsteen and books full of departure: *Huckleberry Finn, On the Road, Don Quixote*. I marinated at home for the first years of college, short on money, short on sleep, desperate to ace my courses, intoxicated by a melodrama of my own inventing. My father rarely left the house, and any trip required a paralyzing amount of planning and safety checks; he never just *went* anywhere. "Maybe," he'd say, "we should call the police in each state and give them your license plate number ..." I didn't break the news about Albuquerque until it was too late to stop me.

This was the summer of 1980. A friend and I hopped into a Plymouth Duster and took off, picking New Mexico by closing our eyes and pointing at a map, setting out for somewhere we didn't know. That was the point: to go someplace unfamiliar, to do that American Thing; to drive thousands of miles and reinvent ourselves, to be larger-than-life instead of two suburban no ones deep into New Wave music and Wiffle ball. This was the summer I was eighteen, had decided to write and left home for the first time. We came upon the city at night, unsuspecting, the world outside the car windows utterly black. We crested a ridge. There, laid out below us, millions of lights fleeced across the desert floor, a third-rate town transmuted by youth and darkness into gold.

We rented an efficiency, and ground through the listless days of a Southwest summer. Every night at six o'clock, the streetlights buzzed and yellowed and we'd tune into the oldies show on KRKE-AM, or eat spaghetti and Ragu. We got jobs in the mall, a newspaper, the minor-league ballpark. If we were anything but teenagers, it would've been a pathetic existence, but we found it endlessly cool. At the end of the apartment complex stood the shopping mall where I interviewed for a job selling knives, in which was planted a deserted shop called The

Paperback Recycler: trade in used books for used books. We hauled out dozens. I've added hundreds of others along the way, and consumed them obsessively, but in the end they were just great, good, or awful, something to argue about and put on a shelf. The Albuquerque stash was different, invested with a ridiculous, invented import that had nothing to do with the titles or authors involved. I hoarded those thirty-three cheap paperbacks like a miser, lugging them to each new town. I'd read one or so a year—even if I'd lost interest in the author—wanting to parcel out the feeling, the fuel I'd felt that summer, smelling it rising off the rotting pages. I told no one. Who could care about such a thing? It was mine.

In the winter of 1980, a few months after we got back, I went downtown to Bobby Valentine's bar. Bobby V. was Stamford's most famous son, the best athlete the city ever produced, once ordained by Tommy Lasorda as the next great Los Angeles Dodger. I walked in from the back parking lot, into the place where I punched a friend in the face once and Valentine served Fran a drink when she was fifteen. There was twenty-nine-year-old Bobby V., his once-sterling playing career shattered with his leg on the outfield fence in Anaheim, slinging beer and making nice with the only people who still considered him great. And I thought, Lord, if even *he* can't get out of here. . . .

I knew, then, that when I finished all those books someday, I'd be somewhere different, someone different, than I was when I first pieced it together. Twenty-four years on, the Whitman is the last one.

One night in December, Fran and I are making ready to go see a movie. This is a massive victory. At last we have found a babysitter, a Swiss woman named Tanja whom Charlie adores and who doesn't mind making the trip in from Aix where she lives with her French boyfriend, Christophe, so long as she can bring him. We love Christophe. He's a bartender at The Red Clover in Aix, one of the few French nightspots that radiates the charm of an English pub and carries games like an American sports bar, and he's sweet and curious and searching for some way to open a restaurant. Maybe he and Tanya will run one together, over in Switzerland. We talk about this as we rush into our coats. It's a half hour into Aix, but worth it: The hot movie of the year, *Lost in Translation,* is playing at the Mazarin, one of the few local theaters that show movies VO—*version originale*—which, in this case, means English. Which means we can relax.

· Fran's French has bounced back nicely, but it's not easy for her to concentrate when I'm around, interrupting just as she gets into a conversational flow with my panicky, "What'd he say? What? Don't forget . . . tell him that . . ." She is, then, not just the one hustling the kids into the car each morning to beat traffic on the ride to school, cooking dinner, getting up in the middle of the night with Charlie, but also the clearinghouse for all information. She translates each letter from the French government, makes each call for appointments or questions about bills, walks the point on any emergency. Who else would handle it when Jack decided to shove a bean into his ear?

This happened a week ago. There had been a Christmas pageant at school. Jack didn't want to hear any more carols, and got tired of squeezing his hands over his ears. He found a pod outside, cracked it open, shoved one of the pellets into his ear. Hours later, we were still mystified by boy and bean. We tilted his head sideways under the light. We peered at the side of his head. We flopped him on his side, alternating between outrage, fear, sympathy, and wonder over the limitless range of human dopiness. There, wedged in the opening, sat the bean, purple and smooth. Pliers, scissors, a corkscrew: Nothing could grip it. Poking with a pin, a fork, would only push it deeper. Jack lay on my lap, eyes fixed on the lime-green Klackbo. We stared down at the bean. The bean stared back. We couldn't let him sleep on it. We—no, Fran—had to find a doctor. The two of them drove off. Addie and Charlie went easily to bed. I turned on the TV.

Fran drove into a clinic in Aix. The doctor didn't have the proper implement. She drove the forty minutes over to Marseille, still awash in stormwater, through a series of dingy, unfamiliar neighborhoods, got sent to two different emergency rooms, both dimly lit and creepily unsanitary, both stymied. The car pulled into the driveway around 11:30. I turned off the TV and tried to act as if I'd been inconvenienced, too. The next day, a doctor in Aix found the appropriate tool and scooped the bean and, in a manner unfamiliar to lawsuit-fearing U.S. doctors but by now wholly welcome, scolded Jack for doing such a thing.

Two days later, Jack sidled up to Fran across the room. "Mom," he whispered. His urgency grabbed my attention; seven-year-old boys aren't usually much for intense conversation. "I'm really sorry you had to do all that." I didn't say a word. It's not often you're front and center for the dawning of conscience. It had been a while since I felt that close to something holy.

Still, such a moment can't last—not in this house anyway. One of the toilet pipes has snapped. The air smells of sewage. Philippe keeps saying he'll fix it, but then, the banister he keeps promising hasn't come yet, either. One night, carrying Addie downstairs to the basement for bed, I slipped on the slick tiled stairway, yelped, and landed with shoulder-to-toe bruises; soon after, Jack and Fran fell down the stairs, too. The front hall is perfect for our daily game of soccer in the front foyer, with the TV room as one goal and the basement stairwell as another. But when a shot sends the miniball bouncing down the stairs, whoever gets it must change instantly from foot-stomper to flamingo; one slip, after all, and the game ends in tears. So it is that one night's escape, for a movie in English no less, has inspired the kind of anticipation usually reserved for, well, a getaway to the South of France.

On the way to the movie, we hurtle down the windy roads to the A8, me swishing through the roundabouts as if I've been driving them for years, the two of us chattering like teenagers overdosed on hormones and processed sugar. I drop Fran to get tickets and park. Fran waves me up and grabs my arm, smiling at the fashionable French couple behind us. They smile back. She hisses not to let them get ahead; Fran has spent the entire time trying to keep them from cutting in, and now we find ourselves thrown into a scene out of fourth grade. It's all very civilized, of course; this battle always is. But coming from a people certain they set the bar for gracious living, the French disregard for lines is shocking. "What movie is this?" they will ask, looking perturbed, then anxious. Then it begins: the edging forward, chattering all the while with impressive preoccupation. Soon you are behind them, and you're not sure why. You look at the other French people who've also been cut, give a can-you-believe-this? roll of the eyes, and get nothing back. They don't know why you're making faces. They're trying to do it, too.

The line is long and moving, but the cutoff for seats can come any time. We push ahead, elbows out, keeping the couple behind us. They shuffle closer, chatting merrily. We buy our tickets, the last two; inside, Fran does a victory jig like a tailback after a touchdown. The seats are up front, far to the side. We can see about one-third of the screen, but the sound is good and our victory even better. We like the movie a lot.

For Christmas we decide to go skiing, three hours north at Pra Loup. A friend of Tanya's is a travel agent, and she insists the resort is *tres bon*. The winter ski vacation is as much a tradition in France as July at the beach; when we check in the place is teeming with families. Our apartment has neither heat nor hot water. We ski, play pool; the kids flop about in an ice-cold hot tub. Charlie doesn't sleep. We wake up Christmas morning and give each other some small presents, and feel good in spite of the hardship, a bit like you do after reading O. Henry's "Gift of the Magi." At midnight, Fran doubles up writhing on the bed: *Un Calcule.* Kidney stone. She doesn't sleep. The next morning she takes a walk and vomits in the snow. We drive the highway home in a state approximating shellshock.

When we arrive, the kids get happy; the TV room is full of presents. The dead zone between Christmas and New Year's produces two major developments: I discover I've overcalculated on an expense check, and have only $200 left in the checking account. Then comes a sudden yelp after dinner; Fran passes the stone while doubled over in the kitchen doorway. She holds it in her palm: a jagged monster, one-quarter inch in diameter. Maybe, she says, she'll have it made it into a necklace.

When Philippe and Jocelyne discover that we have no plans for New Year's—in France, St. Sylvester's night—they insist we come for dinner.

Wine, food, jokes: We meet another couple, a former professional cyclist and his wife. Jack plays video games with the couple's children. Addie and Charlie sleep soundly next door at our house. We sit for dinner, flushed and friendly. The conversation turns to Bush and Iraq; the cyclist politely demands an explanation. The table goes quiet.

Philippe looks miserable. "I vote for . . . Stalin!" he smiles, but nobody laughs.

Everyone looks at me. So I try—with Fran pressed again into service—to convince the French that, no, we all aren't power-drunk cavemen and that, no, we aren't the only nation impelled by irrational fear to act in strange, impulsive ways. Only half the country supports Bush, I venture, and when that sways no one, I mumble something about the Supreme Court's questionable ruling against Al Gore in the 2000 presidential election. Finally, in desperation, I burp out the impolite words.

"What about Le Pen?"

The mere mention causes a shift; it's probably as close as I'll ever come to the moment in *To Kill a Mockingbird* when Scout recognizes Mr. Cunningham and all energy drains out of the lynch mob. Everyone knits their brows and nods, and the cyclist says softly, "That was just a protest . . ." But they back off. I've made my point, unoriginal but good enough after four glasses of red: We are not so unalike, you and I. We both come from countries that, believing themselves exceptional, often can't square such arrogance with reality.

"I vote for Stalin!" Philippe says again, and we laugh this time, but it's late. No one even notices when the clock hits midnight.

Winter

Five

All told, more than 3,000 suspected terrorists have been arrested in many countries. And many others have met a different fate. Let's put it this way: They are no longer a problem to the United States and our friends and allies.

U.S. President George W. Bush, State of the Union,
January 28, 2003

I'm beginning to realize I have a problem. The phone isn't ringing. All around me, stories are happening: A mysterious Russian billionaire is transforming Chelsea into an English soccer power, Beckham and Real Madrid aren't quite clicking, racist incidents are mushrooming at Italian soccer stadiums, Russian tennis loon Marat Safin is down the road partying in Monaco. French handball, German rodeo, Israeli basketball—the whole continent bursting with stories portentious and quirky, emblematic and fun. I can't get enough. I pore over the *IHT*, stumble my way through the sports daily *L'Equipe*. I track the highlight shows. I send off ideas to New York. But the phone doesn't ring. Soon a panic, the classic writer's paranoia, kicks in: Why doesn't the magazine want pages and pages on this stuff? Why don't they care? The weeks pass, and I see my once-monthly "Letter from Europe" shrink to four tight paragraphs once in a while, maybe. I stare at the hills and run up to call my editor. Didn't they send me here? Didn't they agree that Europe was a smashing idea?

An absurd thought begins to nag me: Maybe I'm too far away. Well, yes, I think, but wasn't that the whole point? But then I also remember how it was in the late fall, when the Boston Red Sox endured yet another horrifying autumn collapse. I tried to watch the games, the biggest baseball story a Connecticut boy could ask for: the Yankees seeming to collapse, Grady Little's mesmerizing refusal to take out Pedro Martinez. I called Christophe and asked if The Red Clover would show the broadcast. "The base-ball American game?" he asked. Not a chance. I was reduced to paying $9.95 to get the netcasts piped into my Mac, lying on my office floor at 3:00 A.M. as play-by-play crackled, and the Fenway crowd screamed and prayed and melted into silence.

But then something strange happened. I gave it up. The World Series opened, but the six-hour time difference proved too daunting. I couldn't see the drama, couldn't live the games, and, most important, couldn't wake up the next day and read about it and bump into someone and rehash. Faster than I'd ever anticipated, sixty days in, I had slipped loose of the American context. Red Sox collapse, Marlins surprise, Patriots march to another Super Bowl, American athletes named in BALCO drug revelations? I'm interested, I guess. But what I really want to know is when Olympique de Marseille will fire its coach.

But even sensing that, I'm still not thinking clearly. I'm not seeing that what holds for me holds for my bosses in spades: Sports, like politics, is local. I smirk over the fact that *L'Equipe*'s NBA coverage revolves around French star Tony Parker in San Antonio, but can't fathom why its U.S. counterpart must be just as parochial. I just figure I'll go bigger, give the magazine the most dramatic sports story in Europe, in fact, complete with horrific disaster, astonishing comeback, humility lost and found. Arnold Schwarzenegger may be the most famous Austrian in the world, but a recent poll in an Austrian newspaper declared skiier Hermann Maier the second most important Austrian ever behind Mozart. And that was before he unspooled this season's larger-than-life adventure.

"Come to Kitzbühel, then you'll know: They are crazy about Hermann," says Austrian ski team coach Toni Giger, when I speak to him in

Switzerland in mid-January. "Everybody wants to talk to him. He is . . .
I don't know the word in English . . . special. You know: *Charisma*. Everybody thinks before, 'It's not possible he will win the next race.' In
Nagano he had a real spectacular crash and everybody said he won't be
able to win a gold medal—and he did. But now? This makes him really
a hero. You could do a movie about him, for sure. It's not an Austrian
story. It's an American story."

I know what he means. Realism, not "city on the hill" idealism, is
Europe's philosophical pose, and its class structures make rags-to-riches
tales as rare as dollar bills. Sports may provide the continent with one of
the few outlets where the poor can rise to spectacular heights, but its
most revered sports gods combine talent with stylish ease (Björn Borg,
Jean-Claude Killy), infectious *joie de vivre* (Alberto Tomba), or both
(Muhammad Ali). Europeans, it seems, like their stars best when they
achieve without too much effort; unfettered desire is acceptable when it
comes to food and sex, not success. The French loved Michael Jordan for
his spectacular looks and dunks. Americans, on the other hand, began to
love Jordan only when his hunger, that demonic work ethic, became part
of the lore: *No one wanted it more than Michael*. Yet now, in a place and
time when American values couldn't have less appeal, here's Maier, a
striver whose legend is rife with themes like "rugged individualism" and
"overcoming adversity." Here's Maier, with a story seemingly cooked up
on some Hollywood backlot—Herminator Returns!—resonating
throughout Europe. It would strike me as strange, except that I've spent
the past months watching French shoppers pack the McDonald's in Vit-
rolles. I've pedaled past French road workers washing down their
midafternoon baguette with Coke. I've seen my French satellite TV network air the '80s hit *Dallas* on a seemingly endless loop.

I've seen it. Despite the differences over Iraq and widespread
loathing for Bush, Europe retains a deep well of affection for a version
of America—the one, as Giger senses, that's about adapting to challenges,
coming back when no one thinks it possible, and winning. It's not hard
to understand: For all its vaunted liberalism on lifestyle issues, Europe is

hardly an open shop. It doesn't embrace cultural tumult. You see no black faces in leadership positions anywhere on the continent, and few women. The U.S. may be a far more conservative place politically, but it's socially elastic, built to absorb the tremors of immigration, civil rights, women's rights, gay rights. Rapid progress is part of its DNA. Europeans view Uncle Sam as an unsubtle bumbler whenever he straps on army boots, but there's grudging agreement that he can be light on his feet otherwise. This attitude—summed up by the conversational throwaway "I love America; I just hate your government"—may seem schizoid. But it's the only way to explain how, in the days when European editorial writers and cartoonists are delightedly caricaturing Bush as the apotheosis of the most negative American type—shoot first, ask questions later—that archtype can still command immense popular appeal.

Because in the winter of 2004, there's no bigger cowboy in Europe than Maier. Throughout his career, the thirty-one-year-old native of Flachau, Austria, had acted like someone auditioning for *Sergeant York*, not *All Quiet on the Western Front*. The former bricklayer crashed the gates of his country's skiing establishment, bulled his way to the top by dint of ability and a near-oblivious optimism, came back from the Nagano crash and won Olympic gold. Then, in August of 2001, Maier got blindsided on his motorcycle by an elderly driver and nearly saw his right leg severed at midcalf. He landed in a ditch, sat up, and held the bloody thing in his hands. He saw the bones poking through his torn jeans. "I was there in the grass and some people came there," Maier tells me. "I told them, 'I need a doctor. I need the leg. I need the leg for the future.'"

So I sell the magazine on a Maier story, and catch up with him and the rest of the Austrian team at the World Cup circuit stop in Wengen, Switzerland. But as I speak to Giger and Maier and the rest at their hotel, it becomes clear that, indeed, I'll have to go to Kitzbühel—and not just because, a year earlier, Maier stunned everyone, including himself, by winning his first race since the accident in the Super-G, and shed uncharacteristic tears at the finish line. No, Kitzbühel is the heart of Austrian skiing, where Maier's roots burrow deepest and, most important, the most traditional, most coveted, most dangerous prize in the sport. Besides, I figure, you should try everything at least once in life, and when's the next time I'll be able to surround myself with fifty thousand drunks?

Every year in January, the alpine ski season peaks at the event known as Hahnenkamm, turning one tiny and tony village in the Alps into a hybrid of the Super Bowl and Mardi Gras. The Friday in Kitzbühel is devoted to the Super-G—the Super Giant Slalom race—and Sunday is devoted to the slalom, but Saturday matters most. Saturday is the Hahnenkamm Downhill, the race revered by Austrians as the pure core of alpine skiing, the race won by every skiier—Franz Klammer, Karl Schranz, Killy, and Maier—who matters. As American downhiller Daron Rahlves puts it, "You reach legendary status in the ski world if you win at the 'Buhl."

It's not just the skiing that's mythic. Packed trains chug in early from all over the country, and when the doors slide open it's no surprise to see some inebriate tumble into the snow by the rails. By midday, bottles litter the streets and people stagger about blind, and come sundown they aren't just spectators. Tradition sends every downhiller who survives the legendarily harrowing Streif course into the Londoner pub, where they hop behind the bar and drink themselves into oblivion. After he won the Hahnenkamm downhill in 2003, Rahlves drank so much it dented the rest of his season. "I was sick for three weeks after Kitzbühel last year," he says. "I couldn't speak. I couldn't even breathe."

When I tell people connected to the race I'm thinking of bringing my family with me, they insist that's a mistake. "But if you do," they say, "make sure not to bring the kids on Saturday."

But I'm not prepared to listen. My forty-second birthday will fall the day of the Super-G, and I can't leave them behind. Our run of luck has been so bad that only a frontal assault will do. We have to get out of that house, all of us, try a trip, an adventure, *something*, and dare the fates to take their best shot. I hustle up some rooms next to Kitzbühel, in the village of Oberndorf, book a cheap flight, and figure I'll pay for it somehow, someday. It's such a stupid move, so lacking in common sense, that it makes me kind of giddy. Everything, I say, will work out fine.

The inn at Oberndorf, the *Gastehaus Dallarosa*, turns out a gem: A foot of snow drops our first night there, and we wake in a chalet surrounded by postcard-quality mountains and air so crisp I want to snap off a piece and eat it. I race into town for a cocktail party hosted by Atomic skis: Maier might be there, I'm told, and that's reason enough. Coming into this, his first full campaign since the accident, the Herminator had been looking only to regain form. He still has just 70 percent of feeling in his right leg; for the last three months, in effect, he has been racing on one and a half legs against the best skiiers in the world. Yet Maier has been winning. In December, he won the downhill and took second in the Super-G at Beaver Creek and won the Super-G at Lake Louise; he amassed enough high finishes since to crash the top three of the overall World Cup standings. Including his operatic return a year ago, Maier had never lost a Super-G at Kitzbühel, so now he's in the confusing position of being both underdog and the man to beat. "I'm feeling that I've reached my goal," Maier told me the week before. "So now it's hard to create a new goal and keep the motivation. Now, I have these victories, it's really hard. It was maybe too easy."

Maier never shows, so I troll about, plastic cup of champagne in hand. I bump into Rahlves. It has been months since I've talked to an American athlete, and with the elfin features of actor Michael J. Fox and a surfer lingo worthy of *Fast Times at Ridgemont High*, the thirty-one-year-old skier is a particularly classic version: one more strangely boyish man from California. He finished third this day in a makeup downhill— a last-minute addition thrown in to make up for previous races lost to bad weather—and as reigning champ of the Hahnenkamm Downhill is well worth chatting up. Yet it's strange: Rahlves can't seem to break out as anything but a supporting player. American skiers get famous only in Olympic years, and Rahlves never got close to the podium at the 2002 games in Salt Lake City, disappearing into the powder while the brilliant, erratic Bode Miller became a star. Though Rahlves established himself as the greatest American downhill racer ever with two downhill wins and five other top three finishes during the 2002–03 season, his name isn't even a blip on the media radar. Even last year's win at Kitzbühel held the taint of the second-rate; fog had shortened the Streif in 2003, and plenty of skiiers, especially the Austrians, regarded his breakthrough as illegitimate. Hours before, sitting next to Rahlves at the postrace press conference, Norway's Lasse Kjus casually dismissed that '03 downhill as "Mickey Mouse."

So Rahlves, too, has come to Kitzbühel with stature and something to prove. Even today, when he's edged Maier off the podium by .28 seconds, he's getting overlooked. I may be from an American magazine, but I'm like everyone else. I ask about the Herminator.

"It's awesome," Rahlves says. "It's not like he just blew his knee out; his leg was *mangled*. I saw it in Bormio last month. He had his boots off, and I was shocked. I hadn't seen it close up before." I ask if Maier is the same intimidating presence. "There's times where he's the old Hermann and there's times when he's not," he says. "Before he was so dominant, he had so much confidence, that other guys were thinking 'The only way I can win this race is if Hermann goes out and makes a huge mistake.' It took a huge hit like that, physically, to even the playing field."

I start to ask another, but Rahlves cuts me off. "But I beat him in worlds before he got hurt . . ." he says, and pauses. I don't say a thing, just let the words hang there; people get uncomfortable with silence. Rahlves can't help it. His ego pushes him through the thought: ". . . So if there's ever a time now when someone says, 'You beat him now because of his injury,' Well, I got him before—when he was *the* guy."

I like this. Rahlves's need to impress, his insecurity, moves so out of step with the usual slick images of American jocks cooked up by agents and ad men, that it's endearing. Something else: It's a relief to talk with him. I hadn't realized how much I've missed chatting with a cocky Yank. You don't banter when you're struggling with a foreign tongue, when the conversation's only laugh is on you, struggling. Rahlves talks about growing up outside San Francisco, vacationing in Tahoe, how he owes his career to "my mom and dad"—all standard stuff. Yet it feels fresh. His parents have come this weekend, he says, and that's a change; Dennis and Sally Rahlves have never seen their son win before. Every time they've shown, he's lost, and his mother has gotten so spooked that she blames herself. Daron isn't sure she's wrong. "I can sense it if somebody feels uncomfortable like my mom," he says. "She's always worried about saying things, trying to be too careful. That's what gets me more off track: being too careful around me. It's easier to have friends around because they're used to just hanging. I haven't been around my parents a lot."

But 2004 is different. Rahlves has been gaining confidence all season from the work of his new ski tester, Willi Wiltz. He has faith now in his equipment, and he has also cut down on drinking. "Now I'm feeling good, I know what I can do," he says. "When you're younger, you can bust though that stuff, no big deal, but it's more important to me now to be consistent everyday. I enjoy waking up feeling good. Better than having a hangover."

We shake hands; he walks off. I turn back to a room filled with the sound of German and French and Italian chatter, and instantly miss him.

Friday morning dawns clear. The *Gastehaus Dallarosa* squats on the edge of Oberndorf's quaint downtown, and the family sets off: crunching past the newsstand and restaurants and hotel, winding by the town cemetery toward the railroad station. Then the buildings end and the walk breaks open, a half-mile down an empty road surrounded by a snow-blanketed plain. We cross a covered footbridge, feet thudding across the timbers and drowned out by the freezing river below, to the tracks. We watch the air puff out of our mouths, feel the cold pinch our cheeks. Soon, a clean and quiet train pulls up, not a drunk on it, and ten minutes later we hop down in Kitzbühel. The race course rises to the sky. We're just a few hundred yards from the finish line. We split up: Fran's taking the kids swimming.

Loudspeakers pump out Austrian oompah songs, fans hold up banners emblazoned with Maier's pink pig symbol; the sun shines down on a stage set perfectly for another Maier triumph in the Super-G. The first skier of the day, a Frenchman overwhelmed by the course's stunning speed, a sixty-degree drop known as the Mousetrap, and his 75-mile-per-hour pace, crashes as if to remind everyone just how treacherous this party can be. The public address announcer yells out times, and to American ears the repeated exclamation of the words "Der Fuhrer!"—the leader—before a cheering Austrian crowd sounds eerie. But Rahlves blocks it all out. Starting eighteenth, he bombs down in 1:23.08 to take first place, checks his time, and instantly finds Sally's face in the crowd of thousands. "Pretty cool," Rahlves says. "My mom was right there." He then stands with a frozen grin as ten racers attack his time and fail.

Now Maier, snorting and huffing, hurtles out of the start gate, beating Rahlves's run on the first two splits. But when he hits the final *Hausbergkante* corner, all of it kicks in: Maier's long layoff, his lack of concentration, his infinitesimally small but magnified weaknesses. He comes in too hard at the turn and nearly misses the gate; he leans left then right, but it's too late to recover. Maier races into the finish, face crimson, head shaking no. For ten minutes, steam rises off his shoulders. Goggles, skin-tight outfit: He looks like something from another planet.

He has come maddeningly close to Rahlves—3/100s of a second—but not close enough. The crowd sags, goes mute: The Herminator's run is done. For the second day in a row, Rahlves has taken down The Man on his own turf, beaten the master of the Hahnenkamm Super-G. Just as sweet, Rahlves has broken the Austrian stranglehold on the event; all previous five Hahnenkamm Super-Gs had been won by the home team. Yet he still isn't getting any respect. Dwarfed on the podium by Maier and Austrian third-place finisher Michael Walchofer, Rahlves has his first-ever win in a World Cup Super-G saluted by a song declaring, *"All I wanna do is get drunk here with you . . . "* Maier's first words to Rahlves? "I made a mistake." Then, just to make sure he gets his point across, in his press conference Maier laughs and dismisses Rahlves's win last year as "not the real downhill."

It's about now that I feel the story shifting on me. I had come to write a comeback tale, but here's the food sportswriters really love to feast on: Conflict. Trash-talk. Bad blood. Told of Maier's feelings, Rahlves dismisses one of the great skiiers of all time as a "sore loser." As for anyone else who has questions about his win in the 2003 downhill? "I'll just make them eat their words tomorrow," he says.

It's late. I hop the train back to Oberndorf, and crossing the plain back into town see the mountain range that had been at our backs in the morning, jagged and gray under the moon. Someone has set candles before the headstones at the cemetery, dozens of flames flickering in the darkness, hollowing out cups in the surrounding snow. The wax drip-drips to the earth beneath. Around the corner, amber light fills the windows of a restaurant, warm with dinner's chatter and clink. I walk into the inn jazzed by the day's events. Fran and the kids are wiped out by a day of swimming; we head out for pizza, everyone content.

We take the train again Saturday morning, and the family returns to the pool without being exposed to one bare breast or puddle of vomit. But, then, it's early. The narrow streets bustle with adults of all ages staggering about; the streets fill with beery trash; cows laden with huge bells lumber clamorously by. By the time he hits the starting gate for the legendary downhill, Rahlves is operating under almost no pressure. Maier has already bombed out with what will end up a ninth-place run, and Rahlves, starting twenty-eighth, skis the Streif—the whole Streif, unfogged and all the way from the top—to perfection, passing Kjus, passing Bode Miller, passing Maier to take first place with a time of 1:56.69. When he hears Rahlves's time, Austrian Stephen Eberharter, the 2003 all-around world champion, thinks, *You devil. You're fast.* "He was just skiing in another league," Eberharter says after. "He was just perfect."

Really, only the next two racers—Walchhofer and Eberharter—have a chance to catch Rahlves. Walchhofer falters, and it all comes down to the last and oldest Austrian, thirty-four-year-old Eberharter. The only way he can win, Eberharter knows, is to ski the tightest, fastest line down the hill, no mistakes, and the question now becomes the most basic: Do you have the guts? "The one who takes the most risk, has the most courage, usually takes it away," Eberharter says, and he does and he has and he takes it away—easily. Crushing Rahlves's time by over a second, Eberharter careens down the course in 1:55.48, sending the Austrian crowd into a frenzy of cowbell shaking and screams. Rahlves doesn't seem the least bit upset. He greets Eberharter with a hug because, he says, the Austrian had been one of the few to treat him well. Besides, his second-place finish gives him a one-two-three sweep of the speed events—the best showing ever by an American at Kitzbühel.

Not that many back in the U.S. will know. It's not an Olympic year, after all; Rahlves's accomplishment will rate a mention barely above bowling in the American press. The Austrians, though, have already begun celebrating and repeating the legend about Eberharter's dramatic finish, so even after the performance of his life, on skiing's biggest stage, Rahlves finds himself overshadowed. On the podium, he has only one place to go. Rahlves again finds his mother in the crowd. This time, she's crying.

Maier, meanwhile, has never had a worse performance at Kitzbühel. In his prime, nothing summed up Maier's icy rampages better than that nickname for the killer cyborg—half-human, half-machine—played by Schwarzenegger in *The Terminator*; in the last two years, though, it hadn't really fit. But losing here seems to reawaken the machine. When asked if Rahlves's performance had proven anything to him, you can almost see that infamous red eye glowing back to life.

"No," Maier says, laughing. "No, nothing."

When he hears, Rahlves is not pleased. He shakes his head once and snaps, "So it's going to keep going? I'm going to keep crushing him then."

In other words, the 2004 Hahnenkamm has had something for everyone: Rahlves gets the weekend of his career; Maier regains his fire; the Austrian crowd gets an Austrian champion in the downhill. Even I'm satisfied. Nothing about the story itself has gone according to plan; the wrong Austrian and the wrong American have won. Sunday, Bode Miller will collect the combined title, but neither he nor Maier have performed as hoped, killing any hope of a blowout piece in *Sports Illustrated*. Still, it's the unpredictable elements that make sports compelling, human. A writer can't ask for much more.

On the Monday after, we pull out of town buoyed by a rare sense of triumph. The inn was perfect. No one got sick. We make the two-hour drive to the Munich Airport with time to spare, return the rental car, and I get so cocky that, when I see a Burger King, I suggest lunch. The kids haven't had Burger King since we left the States: Here's a reward for a trip well done. I get in line to pick up plane tickets. They go off to order.

The airline agent is mystified. Our reservation has disappeared; I get sent to another agent, then another. Half an hour passes. It's 1:55 P.M., forty-five minutes from our scheduled takeoff. I'm not worried. I find the family, my cheeseburger still warm, and we sit and eat. We gather our things and meander to security. There's only one person ahead, but somehow that takes a while. Now it's 2:15. The gate's farther away than expected. We begin to race down the hallways, yelling at the dawdling kids to run. We reach the gate sweating. Where's the plane? The passengers? The lone Lufthansa gate-agent glances at our tickets and glares. "Where were you?" she demands. "The bus taking the passengers is gone. You missed it."

She sends us imperiously away. The man at the Lufthansa ticket desk stares as if I'd ask to borrow his toothbrush. "Why were you late?" he demands. No, he says, it's not our fault that your reservation had been botched, or that you'd been sent to three agents, or that nobody told you the bus would leave for the gate twenty minutes before departure. Nothing we can do: Those tickets are nonrefundable. You must buy new ones and, by the way, you can't get a direct flight back to Marseille now. The flight that was going to get your family home by 5:00 P.M. is now going to get you there, after a stop in Frankfurt, at 1:00 A.M.

I pull out my credit card. My stomach feels like the Herminator is standing on it in skis, jabbing his poles into my ribs. Yes, I figure, I'll be able to pay for it somehow, someday. But we all begin to pay, actually, while still in the air. Around midnight, Jack and Addie lose all control.

He begins to fall asleep, and she wants him to draw a picture, and in the dimmed cabin his eyes flutter as she shrieks, "Sleep in home! I want to see your handwriting!" Then she weeps, too deeply and too loudly through landing, debarking, and the walk through the terminal. Disturbed passengers scowl from all directions. Nice going, I think. Sure! When in trouble, why not bury yourself deeper with a trip to the land of the $1,300 Whopper?

Yet in a perverse way, it's satisfying to see that our bad luck can be so stubborn, so hardy; this is *our* luck, after all. We've raised it, we've nurtured it, and it's good to know it has such staying power. When we get home, the smell of sewage meets us at the front door.

Our terrace lies on the western side of the house, facing the Chaine de L'Etoile. I go out there each day about noon, after the *Herald Tribune* arrives, spilling coffee on the tiles. No matter how cold it is at night, the sun blasts this end all afternoon, sending temperatures soaring; so I hang the laundry that will be dry within an hour, and peel off my shirt. To the left of the firetower, I can take in the string of rockfaces we've claimed and named: Dinosaur Backs, Mr. Rastapopoulos, Chateau D'If, the Point, Blockhead. Usually, when I slide open the glass door, the grizzled face of Tommy, Philippe's ancient German shepherd, will pop up behind their wall and he'll trot over to say hello. Maybe today our new babysitter will come. Tanya has gone home to work in Switzerland, and ever since someone firebombed The Red Clover, Christophe has been working construction in Marseille. Or maybe the FedEx guy, or a college girl taking the French census, or Philippe coming to drop off an unexpected case of unlabeled rosé—one dozen bottles that, when the sun catches them, blaze like rubies.

It's too bad about The Red Clover. No one knows if it was a grudge crime or an insurance scam or some race-related act, but Christophe says it's not an unusual event in Aix. Still, most of the town's bars are ill-furnished, too-bright rooms with no music or crowd. To see the Clover shuttered up now is the most depressing part of being there.

In the afternoon, I'll usually take a ride up to Mimet, and on some weekends I'll hook up the trailer bike and bring Addie along. We always cause a minor sensation, drivers twisting their necks, kids waving and laughing, and I suppose it's quite a sight. I've never seen anyone here riding such an ungainly contraption; no matter their age French bike riders are always male, always serious, and always turned out in the same ad-filled, skin-tight lycra outfits you see in the Tour de France. They zip past in packs on tires the width of a pencil, calves bulging. Me? If it's warm enough, I wear an old pair of gym shorts, a pair of running shoes, and a thick sweatshirt, and my stumpy mountain bike has no business being on the road at all. My helmet looks like something worn by a Welsh miner, and with Addie on back, her Tweetybird helmet in place and the bike's flourescent orange hazard flag flopping about, it's obvious we're not locals.

Jack never liked the trailerbike much, but Addie pedals with ferocious intent, and when I stand for some particularly steep incline, she screams, "Chick-chick, chick-chick chicken, lay a little egg for me!" as a means of encouragement. It works, too. One Saturday, we come gasping and singing around a turn and startle an older French couple. Their mouths drop, turn into grins, and as we chug by they clap and yell, *"Bravo!"*

One of our first contacts in town was the Pizza Man, Gerard, who parks his truck, Chez Gerard, complete with flaming wood oven and chrome counter, on the road into Greasque; you call him on his cell phone and twenty minutes later drive by to pick up a perfect pie. Soon after we arrived, Jack suggested a party. The first person he thought to invite was Gerard, but my favorite is the Chicken Man who occupies a semipermanent tent near the Intermarche, selling succulent roasts for less than the price of an uncooked bird. For her part, Fran loves chattering with the Fruit-and-Vegetable Ladies who greet her by name, and ask with concern if she has a cold. Fran will roll in the driveway with the kids around 6:00 P.M., when it's dark and the wind rushes through the olive trees; and after dinner we sometimes go out on the terrace and I lift up one-year-old Charlie and point at the moon. "Booon," he says.

Late in February, we make the drive back up to Pra Loup. My friend, Dale, a sportswriter in Houston, has a house in the nearby village of Barcelonette, complete with hot tub. Driving there, we feel like insiders, like we're taking advantage, for the first time. But Charlie is touch and go and the *garderie*—the resort's child care—only has room for him on the days he's sick, so Fran stays home while I slide with Addie down the bunny slope. On Sunday, they stay home and I drive Jack in for that morning's ski school. To kill time until he's done, I clomp into an empty bar and pick up the local newspaper.

It has already been a volatile month for France: On the eleventh, the National Assembly, in an attempt to shore up the French ideal of *laicite*—secularism—approved a controversial ban on Muslim headscarves in public schools. Four days later, the president of Israel visited to protest the recent wave of anti-Semitic attacks. But now the headlines scream the biggest surprise: Suddenly, Le Pen is battling for his political life. In a move comparable to getting Al Capone on tax evasion, an administrative tribunal—citing Le Pen's lack of the necessary taxpayer status in the Provence-Alpes-Cote d'Azur region—has barred him from running in the March elections. Today, a Marseille court will hear the appeal no one expects him to win.

The weekend's other big story is about the strange wind sweeping our region. It came up out of Africa, the paper says, rising from the Sahara and crossing Morocco, Algeria, and Tunisia, a sirocco carrying sand and a grainy red dust that has settled on cars and houses, seeped through seams in the walls, covered all the gorgeous Provençal homes. There are photos of people driving with lights on, squinting against the darkening of the day. I can't get past the coincidence. It's a message from nature, I'm sure, for anyone willing to see: Le Pen is out, and trying to stop the immigrants from coming, from changing France, is like trying to catch grains that come riding on the wind. The red dust—the *sable rouge*—lays like a thin blanket over Philippe's beloved *Sud*.

I put aside the paper and go to meet Jack. We head up to the top of the mountain, and it's something to see your seven-year-old son flying so fast without fear, carving down the slopes in a way you wouldn't have dreamed at his age. I'm an intermediate skiier at best, but Jack doesn't know that yet. To him, I'm still faster, cooler, more daring than he, though really it's just that I'm bigger and know a few tricks. We yelp over jumps and I zip in front of him, knowing I've got a year, maybe two, before he leaves me behind. For lunch, we stop on the sun-splashed deck near the top and wolf down hamburger and pasta with mushrooms, bragging about our flawless runs, perfectly warm until a shadow slides near. Two guys, hanging out.

When we get home the next day, the news is still full of Le Pen: how he lost his appeal, speculation on the National Front's future. It seems a clear victory for French liberals, for tolerance, but who can say? We check out the damage from the *sable rouge:* The red dust is everywhere, caked on the railings, the terrace. A mere broom can't clean it; you need soap and water and muscle. On Tuesday, Osama bin Laden's lieutenant, Abu Ayman al-Zawahiri, in a taped message broadcast on Al Jazeera television, lambasts the French—anti-American, anti-Iraq war as they might be—for the headscarf ban in French schools, calling it "new evidence of the extent of the Crusaders hatred for Muslims, even if they brag about democracy, freedom, and human rights."

"France, the country of liberty," he rages as the tape goes on, "defends only the liberty of nudity, debauchery, and decay, while fighting chastity and modesty."

So with winter fading we scrub and rinse and brace for the attack, and when the sun begins to bake the ground we scrub some more. But it really doesn't help. The red dust has become part of the household, deep in every corner and crack.

Six

Hold onto yourself, Bartlett. You're twenty feet short.

Steve McQueen, in *The Great Escape*

On the morning of March 8, I head up to my office and start skipping around the Internet when an item catches my eye: John Henry Williams, son of Red Sox hit genius Ted Williams, dead of leukemia at thirty-five. He had been ill for a while, and even from France it's easy to see that death hasn't softened the prevailing sentiment back home. There aren't many unforgivable sins in America anymore, but apparently freezing your dead dad is one of them. Reaction to John Henry's passing boils down to one sentence: Punk got what he deserved.

I try that stance out for a few minutes, but it just won't fit. I had been appalled, too, when John Henry, citing a crumpled, oil-stained revision to Ted's will found in a car trunk, shipped his father's corpse to an Arizona cryonics lab in July of 2002, where the corpse and head were frozen, stored separately. But I had also seen the two men together back in 1996, not long after I'd learned that relations between fathers and sons are never simple. One October morning I stood next to Ted Williams, poolside at his house in Citrus County, Florida. He was seventy-eight, half-blinded by three strokes, but had perched himself on the edge of a chair to cheer a seventeen-year-old local girl named Tricia Miranti who, confined to a wheelchair since youth because of a brain aneurysm, laughed as she went through the paces of therapy. Williams often gave over his pool to Tricia, paid for his personal trainer to work with her. He had made calls to get her into college. But here Williams spoke of how he begged God to let him do more, *something*, to make her better, and cursed the higher power that could hurt a child. His ten-year-old Dalmatian, Slugger, lay at his feet. Williams worked his hand through the dry fur on the back of its neck.

"I absolutely pray to that c————ing Jesus Christ," he said, glancing up at me, "that I die before my dog."

I looked down at his cragged face, the pair of incisors ground to nubs, tufts of gray hair springing off his head. The day outside was full of rain. It's a bit breathtaking to watch a man take on God that way, especially a man standing on His doorstep, and I edged back a step. Years of Catholic church had instilled the instinct of metaphysical self-preservation; if the bolt flew, I wanted it clear that I was only a bystander. But I also scribbled down the quote. It's why I was there, after all. We sportswriters love characters, those profane, goofy guys who don't measure their words, who don't care how the world views them, who speak odd sentences minted from the heart, and in the second half of the twentieth century no one fit the bill better than Teddy Ballgame. Ted Williams was modern sports Ur-character. He warred fiercely with the Boston writers when he played, called them derisive names like "knights of the keyboard," but that was long ago. Old jocks are like whores and politicians; all become respectable with age, especially if they can fill a notebook. Then they're forgiven anything.

It helped that Ted remained Ted in an age of spin. Year by year, as television made sports less human, Williams's humanity became only more appealing. "You don't need to spend a year to know him," John Henry said of his father. "He's not like a chameleon. You get him full force in the first hour." With time Ted's voluble cursing, vile as a sailor's, became part of his charm, and his curiosity and tempestuous outbursts became less a mark of instability than a sign of passion, of life lived large. His longtime disregard for his three wives and three children evolved from inhuman coldness to artistic license; as William Faulkner drunkenly said to his daughter, "No one remembers Shakespeare's son." Williams was one of the greatest hitters and fishermen of all time. Williams had served his country twice and nearly died in a plane crash. If the price for his he-man skill was a few pouting kids, what of it?

No decade since he retired in 1960 had been free of a major Ted Wiliams profile. The public loved reading about him no matter how long he'd been away—loved it more somehow—and he made the writer's job easy. You couldn't write a bad piece about Ted Williams. Not only did he tell you how much he hurt and loved and felt, he showed you those things, and you couldn't help but feel you'd captured his essence. He guilelessly rattled off opinions, but even better: He peppered everyone with questions, demanding opinions on the world, sports, politics, the famous. He wanted to know. If you paid his price, he didn't mind being captured.

"You know anything about baseball?" he shouted at our first meeting. It was a Saturday morning. John Henry stood in a doorway. His live-in aide, Frank Brothers, stood at the stove making breakfast. "Number 1: I'm not Willie Mays. Number 2: I'm not Joe DiMaggio. Have you got that? THAT's good. Where'd you go to school? North Carolina? You know a guy named Orville . . . Orville somebody with the paper down there? North Carolina fan . . . Oh, Je-SUS. Orville, he ran for politics. *Helluva* guy. He was in the Navy, one of those publicity guys."

Frank appeared at the table, with one plate of eggs, toast, and sausage for Ted and another for me. "Now, I want you to eat this toast, because this is special right here," Williams said. Williams had been a pilot with the Marines in World War II and Korea, and I asked him about a story I'd heard about John Glenn being his wingman, sending him off on a classic Ted tangent full of odd stresses, John Wayne cadences, and the intermittent shout, as if an infant stood nearby twisting his volume button for fun. "That's BULLSHIT. I flew with John Glenn. You talk about ROLE MODELS, and great AM-ericans . . . I did fly with John Glenn one time, several times. I was on an early-early with him one day, and the weather was SHITTY, foggy, and I didn't want to lose him because my navigation was never that good. I kept right in on him. The hairiest trip I ever had, I was with John Glenn. I got hit with small arms . . ."

Then he talked about his thirty-nine missions, that famous crash, and how he had never flown a plane himself since. "I realized how lucky I'd been," Williams said. "I said to hell with this. DAMN right."

John Henry piped in then with a story about Neil Armstrong, the first man to walk on the moon. Ted didn't seem to notice. He was concerned with the most effective method of placing eggs on toast. "Now here's the way I eat it," he said. "Here's the way I want *you* to do it . . ."

"Come on, Dad, let me finish this story," John Henry said. "So as he's getting back into his craft, he's talking to Houston and he says, 'Good luck, Mr. Gorsky.' On the moon, he's talking to Houston. And everybody just figured Mr. Gorsky was one of those Russian guys trying to do the same thing. But there never was a Russian in a space program named Gorsky; and they never get an answer from him on it. 'Til recently. Armstrong said, 'Well, where I lived . . .' "

But Ted was fixated on the mess on my plate. "See what I do, and I just want you to look at this, and this is what adds to that toast . . ." He stared for a moment. "But you got to get at the egg PROPERLY." He cocked his head toward John Henry.

"Sikorsky?" he said.

"No, Gorsky," John Henry said. "He'd had an argument next door. And the wife came out and they were screaming back and forth at each other, and she said, 'Oral sex? You want oral sex? When a guy walks on the moon, you get oral sex!' "

His words hung out there for a second or two, the punchline dissolving into silence. Frank bent over something at the stove. I looked at Ted. Ted didn't smile. "The story is a little confusing to me, because I'll tell you why: When I was a young cadet, after we'd solo'd in Cubs, we went to a biwing plane, much more powerful," he said. "And he was from Sikorsky and his name was Si-KOR-sky. He was a helluva pilot and when you started all this all I could think of was Sikorsky . . ."

He stopped. My plate still bothered him.

"Now you're going to love this bread," Ted said. I tried to slip the egg on my toast.

"You can't do THAT! Just dip that, and break the yoke a little bit. Alright, now you're on the right track," he said. He took a bite himself. "Oh, yeah, that is good. Um-hmm. And that bread is made special here, Frankie made it; got a little cheese in it, a little jalapeño. Now, don't be AFRAID to dip your egg in there. And you don't have to SLOP all over the place. See that? My egg is not slopped all over."

John Henry stood fidgeting in a doorway. We finished eating, then sat and watched a fishing show on TV. I asked Ted some questions, and each answer seemed hilarious, interesting, smart; the man had that kind of force. When John Henry finally spoke again it came as a shock. It had been so long you'd swear he had disappeared.

My father didn't like Ted Williams. It wasn't that he was a Yankee fan or hated the Red Sox; it was Williams himself—his rages, his spitting in the direction of the press box, his refusal to tip his hat to the crowd after hitting a home run in his final at-bat. My mom and dad would occasionally drop everything and dance around the kitchen grinning and singing from the old '40s ditty "Joltin' Joe, Di-Maggio!" because the Yankees center-fielder was still considered, even in the 1970s, the epitome of public grace. Simon and Garfunkel didn't sing about a nation turning its lonely eyes to Ted Williams, because he wasn't gone. By then Williams was all around us: in the nonconformist pose of quarterback Joe Namath, in the acting styles of Marlon Brando and Al Pacino, in the Me Decade self-centeredness of a society rebelling against itself. Williams made my father nervous.

I liked that. DiMaggio was always too static, too corporate, too buttoned-down, too old by the '70s to be known as anything but the Mr. Coffee pitchman. To an adolescent overly vigilant for any sign of fraudulence, Williams was never calculating, dynamic to the point of hyperactivity. He was, to borrow the phrase, "pure act." He didn't seem to need anybody.

I liked that even more. I arrived in Chapel Hill in August of 1981, not long after dawn, alone and pleased. Once you discover the salvation of travel, the way it allows you to escape the old, escape yourself, it's a habit as tough to kick as any narcotic. But it wasn't the thrill of the exotic that got me hooked. It was the pleasing shock of becoming exotic, too. Arrive from somewhere 600, or 2,500, miles away, come without parents and school ties, come as a stranger spouting certainties, and now you are no longer a bland suburban boy, heir of nothing. Now you awake suddenly imbued with unearned mystery, now you are like that Czech exchange student who transferred into high school. Now you are different. You have done nothing but come from far away, yet to the people you come upon it's a distinction. You were like them once, restless and stuck. Not anymore. You *moved*.

The heat lay over the town like a tarp. Sleepless and sore, I stepped off the Trailways bus, collected my suitcase and trunk, and hopped in a cab to the dorm. The brick tower on South Campus swarmed with chattering freshmen and the parents they desperately wanted to shed, girls squealed over faces they recognized from high school. I was older, a junior transferring in, exhilarated by the thought of arriving unclaimed. I threw the stuff in a grocery cart and rolled in, sure I was as hard as stone.

My mother came to visit that fall, but I didn't want her there. One brother moved to Florida, but when I went there for spring break, I didn't call. It wasn't their fault, of course, but I didn't want a mother, a brother, a family, a memory of life before North Carolina. I was sure I needed isolation, like someone recovering from a dread disease. I wanted only to be around the family I'd collected; for the first time, I felt sharper, funnier, smarter than I am. The most valuable friends put you at the top of your emotional, moral, intellectual game, an alchemy that can make a person better. And I knew: I needed to be better or I was done. I don't think my family had understood all that before. They began to see it in Chapel Hill, and backed away, taking offense at a coolness that has never completely passed. I wasn't displeased. I thought I needed them gone.

Money ran out, and by the end of the semester I had my first job as a dorm janitor, toting trash and delicately scraping up shriveled condoms. By the spring of that year, I was writing for *The Daily Tar Heel*. I took dictation when skinny Michael Jordan hit the jumpshot with 17 seconds left that beat Georgetown and began his legend. The football team was ranked in the top ten and I began writing baseball. I lost twenty pounds on a diet of Ramen and canned beef stew. That summer I stayed in Chapel Hill, bartending at night, cleaning dorms by day, increasingly desperate because I had no idea how to pay for my senior year. I'd stop in at the office of the summer dorm manager, a graduate English student from New Jersey. We'd talk books, about Dos Passos and the rest of that generation and a professor we knew. I was terrified of leaving, sure that if I went home the noisy failure would suck me down and never let go. Come August, with the days dwindling and classes about to start, he called me in.

"You want to be a resident assistant?" he said. "I'm in charge at Morrison dorm. I'd like you to be one of mine."

RAs got paid. RAs got a room to themselves and a salary that would cover the year. Later, I asked him the question I would ask so many friends: "Why did you help me?" He grinned. "You're like me," he said. "You remind me of that line in the Stones 'Street Fighting Man': 'What else can a poor boy do?'

My senior year, I covered basketball for the *Tar Heel*, sitting courtside at Jordan's dawning. None of us, especially the student journalists who had grown up with the North Carolina stars—James Worthy, Sam Perkins, Kenny Smith, Phil Ford, Walter Davis—thought that he would be anything but the latest link in Dean Smith's glittering chain. By midseason, though, the 6-foot-6 sophomore had unleashed so many last-minute heroics, so many astonishing dunks, and lorded his authority over the best competition, that it was clear he was something rare. Indulging a taste for bombast, I described his "frying-pan hands and puppydog feet" and then went for broke and called Jordan "the best guard in the country." It was the first story I ever wrote that I felt good about; I drew off his energy, and for a few minutes it made me feel in control, buzzing and light.

North Carolina lost to Georgia in the tournament in 1983. That year belonged to North Carolina State, and Jim Valvano's Cinderella run to the national title. It was an appealing tale, and Valvano's ebullience, his gabby New York con man act, contrasted so appealingly with Smith's stern nasality that even UNC fans couldn't help but pull for him when State lined up against Houston in the title game. By then, I had a rooting interest, because Valvano taught me my first unwritten rule of journalism: Follow the scene to the absolute end. Earlier that spring, at the end of the regular season, Valvano's Wolfpack tore up the Tar Heels in Raleigh's wonderful ramshackle Reynolds Coliseum—his first win over Smith—and after all the dull, polite compliments in the press conferences, I happened to follow Valvano as he walked outside. He didn't know I was there. After a few steps something struck home, and Valvano laughed and shouted to the sky, "I knew that once something good would happen in my goddamn life!"

I landed an internship at the entrancingly named *Memphis Press-Scimitar*, an afternoon daily long on quirky talent and short on cash. I had applied so late that the only job left was aide to the newsroom aide, with the promise of a story or two. A friend handed over the keys to his oil-spewing Volkswagen; I loaded up the trunk with clothes and Quaker State. The car chugged heroically, but as the rain turned to torrents and darkness fell, gears began to shudder and smoke. I downshifted to 40 miles per hour, made the mountaintop town of Monteagle, Tennessee. With visions of *Deliverance* thrumming through my head, I stopped at a phone booth in front of a dead-faced store and embraced my first unambiguous moment of adult cowardice: I dialed home. Voice shaking, I talked to my mom and dad, trying to sound casual, as if calling them while driving through hillbilly country's worst storm in decades in a shuddering jalopy was a normal act. They were hopeful and didn't scold and, kindest of all, didn't ask why suddenly, after years of that *attitude*, I needed to hear their voices so badly.

I was sure I would never make it out of Memphis alive. Even allowing for my penchant for melodrama, I'm still not convinced that I wasn't
fated to emerge at least brain-dead; my immediate boss was the half-wit
newsroom aide who regaled the nearest unfortunate with long and
complicated stories about his lawnmower's "master-leg" or the merits of
returnable bottles. For weeks I was given sympathetic looks by the editors and writers passing the mailroom window as I cut and pasted each
writer's article from that day's edition on a piece of paper and slid it into
their slots. Then I earned my first promotion. "Come in at 5:00 A.M.," I
was told. "Call up the dead people's families to find out their details."
Now I would be the obituary writer's assistant.

I woke the next morning at 3:30 A.M., cutting down the empty
highway into town. The newsroom sat downstairs from its A.M. counterpart, *The Commercial Appeal,* just past the small, threadbare Sun Studios
office where the Elvis Presley tale began, and in the humid chatter of
insects, the crumbling buildings, the lank black men who wandered the
hazy streets with plastic showercaps on their heads, I sensed only confir-
mation of my dread. Memphis had the high rhythm of melodious rot.
You could almost hear the termites chewing away, and for that I am
thankful. Unlike sparkling and faceless new South towns like Nashville
and Jacksonville and Charlotte, Memphis thrummed with a soul of
untameable originality, howling the blues and only half-disappointed
that progress had passed it by. A loon calling himself Prince Mongo drove
around town in a Volkswagen Thing, scarf trailing, running endlessly for
mayor. You drank at Huey's, had a burger, served your time. Memphis
was out of the mainstream; big city newspaper editors didn't troll for talent there. The writers wrote how they wanted. No one seemed in a
hurry to leave.

The obit writer was a tight bearded man plagued by a pressure that
had nothing to do with the job. "Don't worry," he told me. "Most families will *want* to talk about their dead guy." Each morning at about 9:00,
after scanning police reports and funeral home lists, I started dialing and
sometimes there were tears and sometimes a story, but mostly I just

checked spellings and addresses and the ages of Lervell or Bobby or whoever. The sports editor, George Lapides, whose motto on writing style he summed up with the toothy declarative—"Awww, you ain't no good if you don't steal . . ." —threw me a story about old black caddies and I did another on the rain that went unpublished and one on warring blood banks that made the front page. When I drove into Chapel Hill sixty days later, the trees and streets, the people themselves, popped with this strange luminesence; I felt like I'd emerged from a deep sleep. Three months later, the *Press-Scimitar* died.

The money ran out for good my final semester, so I fled North Carolina owing thousands. Needing to pay off the debt to get my transcripts and diploma, I headed home again, wondering if I'd ever leave. I waited tables. I crossed the New York border for Port Chester's late-night bars, romanced an older bartender, sent out clips. Fran Brennan dropped back into view. I had dated her sister and she had dated friends in high school. We trained into New York for the museums and bars, split up for the night at Grand Central, and then met again the next morning and rode back to Stamford chatting about the cute pickups we'd made. One day, I came home from a lunch shift with my polyester black vest stinking of grease, shirt stained yellow at the armpits. "This editor called from Sacramento," my mother said. "He wants to know if you'd want to cover the San Francisco 49ers."

I allowed that, yes, I think I would.

Seven

The forces of history have accelerated the growth of
friendship between the United States and Pakistan.

George W. Bush, February 13, 2002

March trudges on, each day marking a numbing escalation of fear. It's
one of those rare times when the news overwhelms all routine, when
nowhere seems safe, when it feels like civilization's superstructure is
cracking amid a rising jackal howl. The first week, the entire French rail
network shuts down for a day as workers walk every mile of track in
search of bombs. Someone has threatened to blow up the trains—our
high-speed TGV to Paris, the tracks that line our daily route to school—
unless paid millions. On March 11, Al-Qaeda terrorists blow up three
commuter trains in Madrid, killing 200 people and wounding 1,400, dis-
lodging the Bush-allied Spanish government, and undermining the increasingly shaky US occupation in Iraq. A hotel blows up in Baghdad,
Palestinians blow themselves up in Israel, and as the one-year anniversary of the U.S.–led invasion of Iraq approaches, terror gossips speak of
the next target as London or Paris or Lisbon.

The air outside grows warm and bright, but there's no room in the
psyche for the rites of spring; who knows what the shadow will touch
next? Neutrals, neighbors, allies: All of them are suspect. Even without
Le Pen, the National Front has hardly disappeared. Someone may have

scrawled "Fuck Nazis" in English over the FN logo and *Je Nique le Fashos*—"Fuck the Fascists"—on the public school in our town of Greasque, but the Front still received a robust 23 percent of the vote in Provence-Alpes-Cote d'Azur. In the third week of March, I read, a poll notes that 61 percent of Pakistanis feel suicide bombers are justified in their attacks on U.S. troops.

I think about that number often, first when I call the U.S. embassy in Lahore for information on traveling there. A cheery woman with a voice as wholesome as Iowa milk advises me not to make appointments with anyone, not to advertise my whereabouts—and, well, "just to be safe," she adds, I probably should identify myself as a Canadian. Pakistan is where U.S. journalist Daniel Pearl had been beheaded, after all; Pakistan had supported the Taliban in Afghanistan and swarms with militant Muslims. For decades, Pakistan had been at war, hot and cold, with India over Kashmir, the disputed territory Bill Clinton once called "the most dangerous place in the world." I take all that in, mix it with the panic of the day, and keep it to myself. But at some point, as our jet barrels across Europe and flies around Baghdad, as night turns to morning and the map monitor in the cabin starts identifying the countries below in Arabic, I think, *Well, you're really heading into it now, aren't you?*

We're going to Pakistan, two of us—me block-headed and fair-skinned and afflicted by that jabbering American obviousness, and Bob Martin, a pink-faced giant of an English photographer with blond curls and a fearsome gut. We arrive in Lahore at 6:00 A.M. Friday, eve of the one-year anniversary of the start of the Iraq war, buzzing with that red-eye-induced combo of intense fatigue and hyperawareness: senses gone woolly, nerves jangling as if you've lost six layers of skin. The feeling only gets magnified when you're paranoid to begin with, when it's the West's worst month since 9/11, and you arrive, for the first time ever in an Islamic land, and notice you're the only Western faces there. The crowd is thick, pushy. The unspoken limits of personal space shrink to mere inches. No one else brushes the flies away.

You clear customs and the airport doors slide open and you walk into a blasting sunlight and a gauntlet of brown faces, and you and the massive Brit inch into a world where nothing—clothes, music, alphabet, religion, food—is familiar. After a night's sleep, all that will be a plus, interesting, *an adventure*. But now your ride isn't here, and you're wandering aimlessly while faces look at you with . . . pity? Indifference? Calculating murderous rage? And you don't have a number to call and Bob wanders away and now, over the public-address system, a cold male voice begins reciting the call to prayer.

But, then, we've come for good reason. We've come here, of all places, for the world's only spot of hope. India and Pakistan have decided to play cricket.

Sometimes a game is just a game, a showcase for athletic prowess. Sometimes a sporting event serves as the stage for personal drama: the comeback from injury or illness, the culmination of a family dream, the settling of a score. Sportswriting usually boils down to excellence—the youthful rise to it, the aging fall from it—or character study, but it becomes important only when the game's boundaries shatter, when politics or race or sex intrudes and the ultimate manufactured event becomes something else. The most stirring moments in sports have always been tribal, differing only in scale: If you're white and have the luxury to chart the progress of the human race, you have Edmund Hillary scaling Everest and Roger Bannister breaking the four-minute mile; if you're black, you have Joe Louis versus Max Schmeling, Jackie Robinson versus major league baseball, Muhammad Ali versus the U.S. draft board. If you're a woman, you have Billie Jean King versus Bobby Riggs.

But the end of the Cold War diminished the role of sports as a vehicle for cultural tumult or political stands. With the Olympics now serving mostly as a tool for urban regeneration, only the World Cup provides a regularly scheduled platform for tribal pride. Everyone plays soccer, everyone knows it, everyone cares. To cover a World Cup is to feel as if you're at the center of the world. To be caught in a soccer riot, bricks and bottles flying, riot batons flailing, the stink of beer and sweat and tear gas in the air, is to inhale an unwelcome whiff of zeal, the contagion of a crowd as passion whirls out of control. It's terrifying—and, truth be told, exhilarating. After living through my first in Italy in 1990, I found myself forever searching for the intersection of sports and national character. I went to Cuba and saw Cuba's boxers destroy the Americans. I went to Colombia and saw the drug cartels infect and kill the nation's once-mighty soccer team. I went to Liberia and saw how soccer star George Weah could serve as his country's lone source of light.

So, really, I had no choice when my editor called. I'd complained for months about the magazine's lack of interest in foreign topics, but when, in February, the news broke that India's cricket team would tour Pakistan for the first time in fourteen years, everything changed. They knew it mattered. You could simply characterize India-Pakistan cricket as the planet's supreme sports rivalry, but the phrase "sporting event" can't contain the sick brew of extremist religion, unforgiven deeds, and jingoistic pride that swirls around any meeting between the two. The air is haunted by battle dead, and charged by rage over Kashmir. The U.S. and the Soviet Union used sport as a proxy battlefield, but subcontinent cricket involves two nations more than willing to uncork the real thing. Hindu-majority India and Muslim Pakistan have gone to war four times since 1947, and the two nuclear powers nearly did so again in 2002. "It wasn't a game," Pakistan cricket legend and current member of Parliament Imran Khan tells me about his contests against India. "Losing wasn't an option."

Always, India-Pakistan matches seemed just one madman away from chaos. When the two met in a 1999 Cricket World Cup match at Manchester's Old Trafford, fights speckled the stands and flags were set aflame in the outfield. That followed Pakistan's visit to India amid death threats from antipeace extremists, when rioting fans in Calcutta forced police to stop play, clear out a stadium of 70,000 people, and finish the match before empty seats. In India's last tour of Pakistan in 1989, a Pakistani fan ran on the field in Karachi and grabbed the Indian captain by the throat. If anything, things had gotten worse since. In 2002, New Zealand cut short its cricket tour after a suicide bomb blast outside its Karachi hotel left fourteen dead.

When tickets went on sale for the opening match of the five-day series on March 13, Karachi police dodged rocks to subdue a rioting crowd. Some 3,500 security men swarmed the grounds when the two teams entered National Stadium, and you couldn't blame the India players for being nervous. A few days before, Pakistan greeted their long-awaited arrival by launching a test of a nuclear-ready Shaheen 2 missile, capable of incinerating any corner of India.

Obviously, the story is a natural: games desecrated by blood conflict, playing fields overwhelmed by street fighting, the risk of unprecedented war. No sporting event in 2004—not even the Olympics—could be more important. If the Indian team or even one Indian fan were somehow harmed, the fallout could be disastrous. The first three matches had been held before shockingly welcoming crowds, but only a relative handful of Indians traveled to the distant cities of Karachi, Rawalpindi, Peshawar. Lahore would be different. Thousands of Indians were already making their way into the city, the core of Pakistani cricket, the Punjabi capital so many Hindus had fled in the bloody partition of 1947. Each passing hour only increased the chances for conflict.

I didn't tell Fran any of this. I got my visa from the Pakistani embassy in Paris, made my reservations, paid off every outstanding bill with a studied casualness. It was more than not wanting to worry her; I didn't want her talking sense, saying that I had three children to think of, because then I couldn't go, could I? Here was the ultimate parachute job: Drop in, become an instant expert on Pakistan-India history, the cultural-religious subtleties that had killed millions, the intricacies of a game no one at home had any patience for. I had been asking for this story my whole life. Now it was mine.

■　■　■

Each night in Lahore, I ride the hotel elevator up to my floor. The door opens, I swing left and there, at an intersection of two hallways, sits a uniform man with legs splayed, submachine gun lying in his lap. The first few times, he had deadened his eyes and I would walk shyly past, but now we smile and nod. Yes, the desk clerk downstairs tells me, one of these guards sits on every floor, all day and night. "We're probably overreacting," he says. "But there are Indians in the hotel now."

Each night in Lahore, I go to sleep in a bewildering state of cognitive dissonance. All day, I've walked the grounds of Moammar Gaddafi Stadium, marveling at the fact that Ronald Reagan's "mad dog of the Middle East" could be a hero somewhere; but then, Libya's tyrant did help out Pakistan during the 1971 war with India. I've passed a casually massive array of official bullying—security crews cased in riot gear, black-clad commandos with "No Fear" stenciled on their backs, sweat-suited Punjab police, Pakistan Army rangers—passed the 3,000 hard men fingering Kalashnikovs, sawed-off shotguns, Mausers, MP-5 machine guns, Uzis, or, for those who like their brutality up close and personal, the 3½-foot bamboo *lathis* that are surprisingly effective at beating back a riot. I've zipped up and down the staircase past the stadium's mosque, where soldiers and officials go to pray. I've ridden back to the hotel, sidled past my armed guard and his gun, felt his eyes on my back as I recede down the hall, wondering whether I should be reassured or shaken. But once in my room, I flip channels between CNN, Indian music videos, a stern Muslim cleric intoning endlessly, Hollywood movies like *Old School, Pulp Fiction,* and *The Great Escape* in English. One night, at 2:30 A.M. exactly, the bedside light goes dark and the air-conditioning unit stops in a simultaneous negation of sight and sound. My stomach hops. I think, *Well, here we go* . . . When the power hums back to life, I feel like a fool.

All is weirdly well. Pakistan is leading the series 2–1, and it has never lost a series to India at home. In the days leading to this upcoming fourth match, there have been no reports of violence. It has been a year since India prime minister Atal Behari Vajpayee began a series of peace initiatives with

Pakistan president Pervez Musharraf, and before the Indian team left for Pakistan in this stab at "cricket diplomacy," Vajpayee presented it with a bat bearing the inscription: "Play the game in the spirit of the game, and win their hearts." On the drive to and from the stadium, you can see the banners hanging off streetlights. *Jeet Lo Dil,* they all say in Urdu, in what has become the slogan of the series. "Win the heart."

My first few days, I told anyone who asked that I came from Toronto. But something about that made my gut twist, so when an Indian writer asks me just before Game 4, I tell the truth. The woman laughs. "At least you're not like that writer from, I think, *Esquire,*" she says. "He came for the first match in Karachi, and kept saying he was from Canada! But everyone knew."

"Huh," I say. "Really."

Pakistan bats first. Behind its captain, the rotund and bearded Inzamam ul-Haq, Pakistan rolls up a score of 293 with nine lost wickets. I barely understand what I'm seeing, but survive by wedging an extremely complicated game into the narrow context of American baseball. This version of cricket—the one-day international—is basically one six-hour inning played in the center of a field. The batter protects the three sticks stuck in the ground behind him—the wickets—from the man hurling the ball, the bowler. Two sets of wickets are placed on each end of a 20-meter-long, greenlike pitch in the center of a large oval field. Runs are scored by running back and forth between wickets, and the equivalent of a home run—a six—flies over a fence standing no more than 4 inches high. Batters stay in until the bowler hits the wickets. At times some better batters can score more than 100 runs. When Pakistan ends their at-bat, the teams take what is, in essence, a dinner break. I stare at my notes, recognize my handwriting. I have no idea what I'm looking at.

I wander to the back of the press box. Some things are universal: The Pakistani and Indian writers, like journalists everywhere, gather for the break in loose clots to talk over what they've seen. I don't dare say a word. On a stairstep, a perfectly made-up Indian woman—black pantsuit, beige piping, patent leather purse, scarf fluffed over her shoulders—sits talking on a cell phone. She scans her manicured fingernails and speaks into a device connecting her to the stars. Not 10 feet away, a guard squats on his knees in a corner, forehead on the floor and pointed toward Mecca. His dust-caked shoes and beret are placed neatly behind him. My head swivels back and forth: him praying, her jabbering away. No one else looks twice.

I go to find Imran Khan. I need some clarity. While India, the world's largest democracy, chugs on, politely culling U.S. telemarketing jobs with its outsourcing centers, Pakistan's place in the world is nearly impossible to pin down. Any place that names its premier cricket stadium in honor of Gaddafi has a lot of history to overcome. Pakistan's post–9/11 emergence as an antiterrorist bulwark has been nearly as confusing as the news, in early 2004, that Pakistan scientist and national hero Abdul Qadeer Khan, "father of the Islamist bomb," peddled nuclear secrets and material to Libya, North Korea, and Iran.

Only in cricket has Pakistan proved itself a consistent force, its image burnished over three decades by Imran's steady hand. Intolerant of losses, corruption, or excuses, Imran Khan nearly single-handedly transformed Pakistan's program from colonial vestige to world power, capping his twenty-one-year career with the '92 World Cup title. Then, the devoutly Muslim, Oxford-educated Khan retired and became his nation's best advertisement for tolerance. He spurned protests from fundamentalists by marrying a British Jew, built a cancer hospital in Lahore in honor of his dead mother, became the spearhead of a new and struggling political party called Movement for Justice. He criticizes extremists from East and West, calls Musharref an American puppet. He apologizes for nothing.

"There are ignorant people everywhere who don't understand their religion properly, and they go into this negative nationalism—which is a disaster," says Khan, once I've moved past my few cricket questions. "I never had any illusions on that. I was always going to marry someone I could live with, no matter what race or color she was."

We're sitting in the back of one of the broadcast booths at Gaddafi Stadium. Seven other men are there, seemingly ignoring our conversation, but as Khan begins talking about the dark state of the world, something strange happens. He has always considered it his destiny to be president of Pakistan, and though he hasn't yet come close—and many say he never will—his words carry the enormous weight of deeds dared and done. Rumors circulate about the health of his marriage, but no one doubts Khan's integrity. As he speaks, sentence by sentence, one by one, the other men let their conversations lapse. By the end, everyone in the box is silent, pretending to watch the action on the field.

"This is the only good news right now, because we have been caught in this mad war on terror—which is a never-ending war, producing more terrorists than ever before," Khan says. "The world is getting more unsafe, because it's being fought very foolishly: War on terrorism should be fought on two fronts. One is of course dealing with the terrorists, but the other is the causes. Coming up with these stupid statements like, 'They envy our freedom, they envy our lifestyle; that's why they're throwing themselves out,' you're not going to end it. If that was the way to end it, Putin would have finished it in one week in Chechnya as he promised, Sharon should have squashed it very quickly with his iron-fist policy in Israel—and yet Russia and Israel are less safe than when they started this carnage.

"History tells us: If people are prepared to die for a cause and they are treated as heroes among the people, it's not going to die. The more you kill, the more you're going to produce. Of course, people who commit crimes like the Twin Towers, you've got to go after them. But you must also start thinking, 'Why are people blowing themselves up?' Ask yourself the question: 'Why are young people, educated people, doing it?' I'm afraid the reason is very simple. If they have no stake in living, they'll keep doing it. And there's a whole new generation coming. It's a never-ending problem."

I return to my seat in the press box, next to our roly-poly driver, Abad Nagi. Abad is dark and mustached, polite to the point of obsequiousness, and yet as the match progresses he forgets I'm there and begins to grunt and moan, hitting the desk with his hand. Pakistan didn't score enough in its own innings, he says, and nothing can shake his darkening mood.

Now India is at bat, and here's the showdown everyone has been waiting for: Pakistan's Shoaib Akhtar, the world's fastest bowler, versus Indian batsman Sachin Tendulkar, the 5-foot-6 "Little Master" acclaimed everywhere as the greatest batsman alive. The two have been tied together for five years now: In 1999, during that wild test in Calcutta, Akhtar, legs shaking with fear, blasted his first ball past Tendulkar to claim the legend's first-ever duck. Then, in the second innings of that match, Tendulkar collided with Akhtar while running and was called out; the crowd rioted, India collapsed, Pakistan won the series. "Pretty much changed my life," Akhtar tells me.

Every other cricketer insists that nothing about the sport is one-on-one. Not Akhtar. He considers Tendulkar the best and his philosophy, delivered with a cartoon leer, is simple: "Go after him," Akhtar says. "Hunt him down." So, with 25,000 fans howling on this night, Tendulkar, just getting warmed up with seven runs, steps in. Now comes Akhtar: racing in from the outfield, twenty paces at full speed, the music of the crowd pushing him along. At full gallop, he slings the ball back over his shoulder, hits the line, and then, after jumping as high as possible, snaps it back like a catapult. Tendulkar swings, slices the ball back into Pakistani hands. The umpire signals out. Tendulkar's head drops; Akhtar flashes his teeth. What could be a better omen? I turn to Abad. He nods, but he's still wary.

Shoaib takes another wicket, but now India starts chipping away and Shoaib can't or won't step off the gas. His bowls fly faster but spray wildly, and soon he and the rest of Pakistan's bowlers are not only getting pummeled, but giving away unforgivable "extras"—bonus runs for errors like stepping over the line or bowling wide. The collapse is so total, and India's run scoring so steady, that suspicions of a fix start circulating before the match ends with the series knotted at 2-all. The logic is so twisted—somehow twenty-two players, two hostile governments, and a crew of international umpires have conspired to give India its first-ever win in Pakistan, to improve relations, to foster peace—that within hours it becomes impossible to find a Pakistani who doesn't believe it.

"It's the *Jeet Lo Dil* series," Abad all but spits as the match ends. "Win their hearts."

Forty-five minutes later, I walk onto a platform overlooking the still-jammed streets outside Gaddafi Stadium. I look down. There, under a crescent moon, Imran Khan walks toward the gate. A Pakistan cricket official standing on the steps sees Khan below and, unprompted, says, "He gave this nation such confidence in itself, playing against the British and Australians as an equal. If there's one role model in Pakistan, it's Imran Khan. He made it big in the West, and he did it on his terms."

Khan walks into the street, looking for his ride, and the milling crowd finds its focus. It surrounds him like ants on sugar. *"Imran Khan!"* someone shouts, and the rest answer, *"Zindabaad!"* Long live Imran Khan. The match went rancid; the series smells wrong. But now here's the man who had beaten India in 1978 and '83, who takes on both Musharraf and Bush. Hundreds of bodies crush in from all sides. Face blank, light-blue blouse and robe billowing behind, Khan walks as if alone, staring off into the distance. The chanting grows louder, more men racing over to join in: Someone to believe in. Someone to cheer.

"Imran Khan!

"Zindabaad!"

"Imran Khan!"

"Zindabaad!"

The people throw their right hands up to the sky.

Late the next morning, we go out for a drive. Bob needs to photograph some street cricket, and I have nothing better to do. There are still no reports of bloodshed or tension in the city, even after India's win, and I'm left to wonder how to write a story about the world's most insane sports rivalry when no one wants to cooperate with a riot, a bomb, or even a few harsh words. There's a reason war draws the most ambitious writers: Peace is not sexy. Calm isn't as easy to write or read about as catastrophe. Yet now I'm hearing how the Indian players are feeling safe enough to walk the streets of Pakistan, even go shopping, and though that's news, it's not what I came for. Abad Nagi steers us into the ancient heart of Lahore. My heart's not really in it, but what else am I going to do? I ask him what has changed.

Like nearly everyone in both countries, Nagi's family had been scarred by the partition of '47—the post-British creation of India and Pakistan that sent Hindus fleeing south on the subcontinent into India and Muslims fleeing north into Pakistan. Some ten million people moving at once, inflamed by religion and displacement and fear, fell upon each other along highways like the Grand Trunk Road outside Lahore, and the butchery, the savage atrocities, claimed perhaps hundreds of thousands of lives. "When I listened to all the stories about the migration I wanted to kill all the Indians," Abad says. Just a few years ago, he made a point of repeatedly taking his seven-year-old son to the border crossing at Wagah.

"Baba," the boy would ask, "that is ganda India?" *Ganda* is the Urdu word for filth. "Yes," Abad would tell his son. "That is ganda India."

Abad shrugs. "But if I think the same like that now, we cannot live in this world," he says. "I'm looking at the future. Everything is very expensive here in Pakistan. We have a lot of taxes. Why? Because 80 percent of the budget goes to defense. Because of the relationship between India and Pakistan."

I ask his son's name.

"Osama," he says.

For a minute, my mind spins off into a weird calculus of linguistics, time, terrorism, and identity. His son was born in 1997. Was bin Laden a popular figure in Pakistan then? Do Muslims name their children for living heroes? Is this as common a name as, say, José in Latin America? Should I ask? If the answer is yes, does that mean Abad, in revealing his sympathies, suddenly will feel compelled to drop his sunny obsequiousness, jam on the brakes, turn with a sudden pistol, and shoot us dead? I want to ask, I don't want to ask; the words climb up my throat. The moment begins to recede. I grunt a reply, and find something to be distracted by outside.

It doesn't matter where he takes us. On every dusty street, every free patch of grass or dirt, a wicket has been fashioned out of stones or bricks or chalk marks on a wall. Balls ricochet off cars and the collapsing tombs of moguls. I have never seen a sport anywhere—not baseball in Cuba, not ice hockey in Canada, not even soccer in South America—that inspires a more pervasive devotion. Everywhere we go, all day, we see the poorest kids, the most devout Islamic students, even blind men, playing cricket. India won the World Cup in 1983, Pakistan in 1992, and England has never won, and one big reason is that for the two former colonial outposts, cricket has become a true national pastime. Some 450 million television *sets* in both nations have tuned in for the five-day series, and hardly anyone watches alone.

We chug past chicken stands swarming with flies, past the barbers cutting hair on the sidewalks, past the street vendor selling posters of Osama bin Laden, past railroad tracks and parkland, and over dirt-caked rubble, cricket games wedged into every spare space in between. Bob click-clicks away, men in robes, men in beards, boys everywhere swinging the thick flat bat, more local color than he can possibly capture.

Abad turns into a warren of narrow streets worse than any American slum, full of hungry faces and piles of filth. "I don't think I want to get out here," Bob mutters.

Abad doesn't hear. "This is my neighborhood," he announces. "This is the middle-class area." He pulls up alongside a boy negotiating the narrow cluttered sidewalk like a wirewalker. "Osama!" he cries, and the boy comes to the window and smiles sweetly and shakes my hand. Abad beams, his pride as thick and inescapable as the afternoon dust. "My son," he says.

Over and over the next few days, I hear Abad's sentiment echoed by Pakistanis: Enough is enough. The parade of generals, dictators, and seemingly democractic Bhuttos that has dominated rule for the past half-century did Pakistan no favors by devoting most of its budget to missiles and tanks, and the behavior of the cricket crowds is the clearest signal yet of a cultural exhaustion. One morning, I ask Abad to drive us out to the

Wagah border, where in 1965 the Indian army came pouring through in a surprise strike at Lahore, and where every August 14 since, on Pakistan Independence Day, it has been customary for Pakistanis to mass and scream, "Death to India!" Now, before my eyes, dozens of Indians are coming through again, on buses, on foot. No one tries to stop them.

"We're sick of it," says Akhtar, Pakistan's star bowler, late one night. "Sick of war, sick of terrorism, sick of Kashmir. We've had it, mate."

Every night on CNN, the cricket series is overshadowed by reports of how Pakistani troops are teaming with U.S. forces in cornering Al-Qaeda leaders at the Afghan border, or the news that the U.S. has now declared Pakistan—the one-time terrorist sympathizer—as one of its key allies in the war on terror. It takes a while, but I begin to see it as all of a well-calculated piece. Musharref, the latest general, comes off as an extremely clever practitioner of *realpolitik*: Pakistan, its tour industry all but erased by 9/11, needs investment. Pakistan needs the kind of money that only trade with India and U.S. protection can bestow, and what better way to refashion its image than an incident-free tour with India?

"Because, in the twenty-first century, there's no point," Akhtar tells me. "It is time. It's very stupid to say we're going to go to war for this, or do that. Look at other nations—the Chinese, the Americans, the Japanese: They want economic war. We should be playing economic war rather than with missiles. It's time to make money rather than enemies."

To hear Akhtar, of all people, serving as a voice of reason may be the oddest sign of a sea change. Most conversations with him revolve around speed, fun, and, well, Akhtar. He brags about beating a ticket for driving 120 mph or the feel of his face cutting into the wind on a bungee jump. He celebrates his wickets by spreading his arms and gliding around the field like a happy jet plane, hair cascading into his eyes, and Pakistan old-liners grumble over the spectacular instability of the country's No. 1 problem child: Shoaib Akhtar is just not cricket enough. He has little use for coaches, revels in his celebrity, and, as Pakistan's venerable cricket writer Omar Kureishi puts it, "sees himself as a free spirit who enjoys immunity from mundane rules of discipline." Translation, courtesy of one high-level Pakistan cricket administrator: "He's a spoiled brat."

Not that Akhtar is too concerned with his reputation. At twenty-eight, the "Rawalpindi Express" is one of the sport's biggest names, and he gets paid plenty for playing what he calls "relaxed cricket" in England, toying with the idea of testing his wondrous, double-jointed arm against the New York Yankees. The perfect Shoaib story? After he was quoted last year criticizing some former greats, a fan sued him for defaming Pakistan and causing "mental torture"; but once the series with India began, the suit was dropped. More than money, the fan said, he needed Akhtar to focus on India.

"Defame Pakistan, my country?" Shoaib says, laughing. "Don't I look like a reasonable person to you? I don't do anything intentionally to make myself famous; I do things that I enjoy. I fly around, it's my style. If someone scolds it, that's their job; if they don't like it, I don't care. What I do, I run in and I feel the music from bowling. Running and bowling fast? I *like* it. Getting wickets? Flying stumps around? Yeah. You've got to make emotion when you're playing. You're young, you're the fastest—what else do you want from the cricket? You've got to chill out, you've got to go out and have a good laugh, play hard for the country, take the pride on yourself—and after you've got to enjoy it. You can't just *stand*. You cannot be boring."

The eternally serious Imran Khan, of course, is the emotional opposite of Akhtar, and he views his antics like an indulgent father. "He's a showman, he laps it up," Khan says with a shrug. "He also wins." But he agrees with Akhtar that now, suddenly, "cricket has made the ground ready for the politicians." A peacefully played series, Khan says, is vital to peace on the subcontinent. Taken in that context, with so much at stake, it's inevitable that the India-Pakistan showdown would fall under suspicion.

Two nights before the deciding match of the series, Bob and I go to the hotel's Japanese grill. A teenager with a Linkin Park T-shirt sits across the room. Sitting nearby is a man and his pretty, well-turned out wife, and their young son. He introduces himself as a businessman, part of the

Servis shoe dynasty. "Yes, I think it was fixed," he says of the series. His wife, Shaheen, bored with the subject, asks about my family and wife, and introduces me to a new term. "So it was a love marriage?" she says.

I ask how they met. Shaheen grew up in Morocco, her husband says, but is Pakistani. His mother had met her, and arranged a meeting. "We got engaged one hour after we met," he says. So I dive in, with a glance at the six-year-old boy with Spider-Man boots and one missing tooth. "So," I say. "Was yours a love marriage?"

"Yes, I think so," he says, and at that Shaheen smiles.

"So . . . love at first sight."

"Yes," he says. "I had more hair then."

Now comes Wednesday. Now comes the fifth match, a showdown so absurdly crucial that one Pakistan newspaper describes it straight-faced in a front page headline as, ARMAGEDDON ON 24TH. In the hours before, I wander outside Gaddafi Stadium. More than 8,500 Indians—the largest legal influx since 1947—have flown, bussed, even walked into Lahore, and now they're passing crowds of Pakistanis, shouting and singing. I keep expecting some sign of tension. It doesn't come. I bump into a man in a turban. The savage March sun hammers his face, but he's smiling.

His name is Davinder Singh. He is a Sikh and an Indian citizen, but fifty-five years ago, at the age of five, he and nine members of his family deserted their home near Lahore and fled to a new life in India. Until yesterday, when he boarded a morning train in New Delhi, Singh had never returned. But when he heard that Pakistan would open the border for this day, Singh got himself ready. He was scared. As the train appoached the border, Singh felt like singing or crying or both, his chest churning with emotions he'd thought long dead. He was processed through immigration at Wagah, expecting anything but welcome. Yet one after another, Pakistanis stopped to thank him, Pakistani shopkeepers refused to charge him, Pakistanis kept welcoming him home. "We got so much love we didn't expect," Singh says.

Kids stream past, one cheek painted with the Indian flag and the other with the Pakistan moon. Groups of men wave the Indian colors, untouched. "I've never seen this happen before," Singh tells me. He isn't alone: Every recent train and plane unloading in Lahore from India has produced some older woman or man returning for the first time since 1947, shocked by the reception. "It's a lifetime dream for me, now a dream come true," Singh says. "I want to come every year."

Still, in sporting terms, he has every reason to expect disappointment. While it's odd to think of India—with a burgeoning economy, a 10–1 population edge, and a history of military success over Pakistan—as prey, the paradox of the India-Pakistan cricket rivalry is that the smaller nation has always been the bully. Again and again, Pakistan had proved itself not just better, winning nine of the fourteen test series between the two and fifty-two of the eighty-six one-day internationals, but far tougher: Despite death threats and hostile crowds, since 1986 Pakistan has been able to step on Indian soil and win. India, meanwhile, has never won even a single test match in Pakistan, much less a series, and the players come into this decisive day dragging a fifty-year-old body of disgrace.

As the Indian team's wealthiest and most photographed face, Sachin Tendulkar has also been its most conspicuous failure. Though, at thirty-one, he is well on pace to become the most productive test run-scorer in history, Tendulkar has consistently come up short when it has counted most. Legendary batsman Donald Bradman may have rightly anointed Tendulkar as the world's best a few years ago. But Little Master, many say and write, can do everything but lead India to the big win.

If any of that plagues him, Tendulkar knows better than to show it. A master batsman, by necessity, cultivates a defensive cool; emotions, grudges, "confrontations" can only cause trouble. Told that Akhtar all but salivates over the thought of facing him, Tendulkar won't bite. "I would block that out," he says. "I want to maintain a stable line graph." He's everything Shoaib isn't: modest, secure, winningly dull. Still, the detours against Pakistan have marked him. Tendulkar made his test debut at sixteen during India's last test tour in 1989, and against Pakistan since, he has struggled: His body would break down—mystifying him as much as anyone—and his test batting average sagged. This deciding game in Lahore, he knows, will either confirm that legacy or reverse it.

"It is different," Tendulkar says. "In '89 I just wanted to play and establish myself as a permanent member of the side; I was too excited to play for India. Now I'm playing under control altogether. This tour is taking place after fifteen years, so it's not only cricket. Both the teams are getting closer this time; we met the prime minister and he said not only to win the games, but also to win their hearts. It means much more than cricket to everyone."

How much becomes clear after Davinder Singh and thousands of other Indians move through the gates Wednesday afternoon. Inside the stadium, the unthinkable is happening: For the ultimate match, Indian and Pakistan fans find themselves sitting down together, side by side for the first time in history. Fearing violence and chaos, Indian officials had pressed before the series to seat the two camps separately, but the large Indian contingent made that impossible. Now Sikhs and Hindus and Muslims, men and women and kids—many with memories of war, all of them wary, have combined for a mix unimaginable a year ago. Security is even tighter: Musharraf, dressed in camouflage, has come to watch and meet the eighty-five-year-old daughter of Pakistan's founder, Quaid-i-Azam, a woman banished by her father for marrying a Christian Parsi—and now returned from India after fifty-six years.

"This," she tells the Pakistani press, "is the happiest moment in my life."

Below her, Indians wave their flag next to Pakistanis waving theirs, all without rancor. Early on, when the final follows the same familiar path of Pakistani dominance, there's little taunting and no fights. With India batting first, Akhtar and the Pakistan bowling attack reduce their extras and dismiss India's Big Three—Tendulkar, Saurav Ganguly, and Rahul Dravid—without major damage. India puts up a 293—the same Pakistani target India so easily overcame just three nights before.

I venture out into the stands. No one here is foolish enough to think a cricket match can cement peace. But, "it's a beginning," says Jasmeet

Singh, forty-eight, a New Delhi resident here to see his mother's home for the first time. "I think there's a change in mind-set. I don't think we look at each other as different anymore. Enough is enough, isn't it? Maybe this is a good time."

Down on the field, India's Dravid looks up at the fans sitting together. *This is fine*, he says to himself. *This is good.* Down on the field, Pakistan manager Javed Miandad looks up at the stands. "They were sitting together: India and Pakistan *together*," Miandad tells me a few days later. "I haven't seen this before. I played thirty years for Pakistan and played so many times against India in India and I never saw this kind of gesture, and never saw this crowd behavior. The top political people, they just shake hands, but look at the public: They respond beyond that."

But now comes the moment of truth, because Pakistan is about to lose in Pakistan, badly. India's bowlers, led by Irfan Pathan, nineteen years old and a Muslim at that, mows down the Pakistan batting order, scattering stumps, squeezing Pakistan's windpipe. Then, with four wickets claimed and Pakistan gasping, ul-Haq, its captain and greatest batsman, begins chopping away. If he can just duplicate his last performance, score massively, Pakistan has hope. Ul-Haq scratches out 38 runs, and then, suddenly, launches the ball high and deep, a sure six over the boundary, the kind of Kirk Gibson stroke that changes everything.

Tendulkar makes his move. Ul-Haq had cracked a similar shot in the previous match and Little Master had been watching and waiting all night, thinking, *If he plays it today, I'm going to be the one to catch.* The ball sails, Tendulkar races to meet it. He has to jump, he has to extend his little frame and short arms and get both hands on the ball and make sure to keep his feet clean inside the boundary, and somehow Tendulkar does all that, spectacularly. When he lands, ball in both hands, he yelps and his teeth gleam, prey turned predator. Ul-Haq is done.

The Indian fans roar. Everyone knows now: It's over. Playing against type, Pakistan has choked. India has won. As the home team spends the next two hours wobbling to a 40-run loss, the only question is how the Pakistan crowd will respond. But when it finally ends, and the Indian team gathers on enemy soil to celebrate its first-ever series win, the fans play against type, too, filing out quiet and quick. Fireworks explode over the field. In one corner of the stadium some two dozen soldiers, fingering unused bamboo and steel, stare up at the pretty bombs.

On TV, only Imran Khan seems puzzled: "Embarrassing for Pakistan," he says. "Bizarre . . . The team went down brainlessly . . . senselessly." But to the fans, it makes perfect sense. *"Jeet Lo Dil,"* Abad mutters. *"Har jao match."* Win the hearts, lose the match.

An Indian man holds up a poster: INDIA WON THE MATCH, BUT PAKISTAN WON THE HEART. A Pakistani holds up another: WE LOSE TO WIN FRIEND. In the streets, Pakistani boys race motorcycles and scream, "I love India!" and it's obvious something strange has occured. Cricket is a game, sometimes a game that means too much. But on the night when the game should matter most, it's impossible to say who has lost.

I don't need anything else. I have my story—PEACE BREAKS OUT— but plane reservations have me locked in for another five days. The tour, all anticlimax now, moves into a best-out-of-three series of five-day test matches, with the first to be played in the desert town of Multan. On Thursday, March 25, we board a small, vintage Fokker airplane for the rattly flight out of Lahore, and as it creaks up and away I swear I can see the sky through the window seams. I scan *The Nation*, with news of the cricket defeat topped by a headline worthy of World War III: TAME SUR-RENDER. The plane skips over the air for an hour and lands with a bang. Legs jellied, I walk across the tarmac and glance up at the roof of the tiny terminal. A soldier sits behind a mounted machine gun, pointing it straight at us.

"Congratulations," grins an Indian journalist after we pick up our bags. "You're still alive."

True, but Multan compares with Lahore like Oshkosh with Boston; again I get hit by that overwhelming feeling of dislocation, multiplied tenfold. BEWARE OF THE TERRORIST warns a yellow notice posted on a wall outside Arrivals, and as we walk out the airport mosque issues its tinny call over a loudspeaker. We ride into town and the driver speaks of Multan's claim to fame: Here, he says proudly, was the place where thirty-three-year-old Alexander the Great received his fatal wound.

"Is it known for anything else?"

"Cotton," he says.

As we wind through the streets, whizzing past familes of five perched insanely on motorbikes, past unfinished highway stanchions and roaming livestock and peeling posters advertising nothing, past narrow shopstalls with couches piled high behind and the mealy wares out front, Multan feels dead, forgotten, used by history and abandoned. The evening air, thick with refracting dust and billions of flying bugs, softens the electric lights, making the drive seem as if it's taking place underwater. We turn a corner, and I literally blink twice when I see the sign ahead. There, out of nowhere, in the middle of nowhere, gleams a mass-market mirage: KFC. We have to get closer to see the wall holding it up, but yes, it's a Kentucky Fried Chicken outlet out here on the edge of the Thal Desert. As we get closer and the plate-glass windows grow in length and the Colonel's face looms over a massive playground, I realize that it's the biggest, newest, most sparkling KFC I've ever seen.

We pull up at something called the Sheeza Inn. At the door, a man looking both exhausted and grim sits with a shotgun in his lap. The women at the desk acknowledge our reservation, but seem surprised to find that we actually want a room. Abad, after a day of driving Bob's equipment in from Lahore, tries to take charge, but the staff can't be more oblivious: Brown water flows out of the taps, the towels are streaked with mysterious black stains, the phone doesn't work, the air conditioner is broken. The toilet smells like a septic tank. I lay down on the bed, a light cloud lifts off the spread, and one by one, an army of bedbugs creeps down my collar, up my sleeves, my pantlegs. I jump at every sound. My eyes feel like they're melting. The crawl on Fox News reports that Ayman al-Zawahiri has called for the overthrow of Musharraf for his alliance with Bush.

I dial my cell phone for home and get a nice dose of the family I'm not there for: Charlie has bitten Addie on the cheek in the bathtub, the kids are sad, and when am I coming home? Jack takes the phone, and I recite my usual bedtime litany about how I miss him and he's my No. 1 bug and "I love you," to which he invariably responds, "I love you, too." But this time he doesn't, asks a vague question instead, and I hang up startled and sad.

At 4:30 the next morning, I wake to the sound of someone sweeping madly outside my door. The hotel hallway is carpeted, but who has a vacuum? I fall back into a half-sleep, but then a door slams; the air conditioner rattles to life. Someone outside guns a motorcycle into a fading whine, and what had been an oddly vivid dream about Stamford fades into nothingness. I lay there short of breath. I turn on the TV, clicking through fifty-four channels of HBO, Sky News, Indian music videos, some Islamic channels—"Be grateful to Allah, if he indeed is the one you worship"—to one showing footage of mountains and a bee pollinating a flower. I lay there, in a 5,000-year-old town and it hits me for the first time. *It's 2004, twenty-five years since I graduated high school.* And all of it taken together: The dream, the remoteness, the fact that I have, in the manner of a vain fool seeing a photo of himself, realized I'm nibbling at middle age, softens me up. *God*, I think. *Maybe I'll die in Multan, Pakistan.*

To cricket purists, five-day test matches are the real thing, the only way to play. But with the end of the fevered one-day series, all energy has drained out of the tour. When both teams practice at the stadium— where, once, play was halted because of a sandstorm—barely anyone shows up to watch. Abad drives us back to the hotel, and just as he turns into the driveway, I hear a massive thump against my door and turn to see a man's balding, pop-eyed face hover for a split second outside the window before being yanked down out of sight. Abad brakes, leaps out, and the genial man with olive skin and a sweet smile, the man who patted his belly and said his wife wanted him to lose weight, who had driven us for ten calm days, transforms into a volcano of invective. Half a bicycle, and three-quarters of a man, jut out from under the tire. Abad keeps screaming.

"Okay, I'm sorry," says the cyclist. "Can you move the car so I can get my leg out?"

We get back into the car. The man and the bike disappear. "It's okay," Abad says. "The car is not damaged much: just a little dent."

But the incident leaves him rattled, and at first I think it's because of the man, his leg. At lunch, Abad is about to order, then he shakes his head. "You see," he says "Our country is very hard. If I didn't yell first, he would've yelled at me." The car has no insurance, he explains, no official papers: If Abad had lost the argument, he would've lost the car, his job, been sent scrambling for survival. I ask what happened to the cyclist. "He got up and drove away," he says.

That night, I don't sleep much: At about 3:00 A.M. dozens of feet start stomping on my ceiling. The next morning, when I ask the woman at the desk about it, she smiles and nods and murmurs a few words before drifting away.

India runs away with the first day's play. Pakistanis shrug it off as just another example of *Jeet Lo Dil*, but crying fix also proves an easy way to avoid a more troubling thought: Maybe Pakistan stinks. Maybe the Pakistan players simply can't muster the goods in the most important competition of their lives. I go and find Imran Khan, who bats away any idea of a fix. "These India players have more mental toughness," he says.

In the middle of that night, I awake to a tremendous crash, followed by minutes of high-pitched jabbering. For the next few hours the sounds of thick wood furniture shoved across tile comes screeching through the wall. The next morning, when I ask the woman at the desk about it, she smiles and nods and murmurs a few words before drifting away. When I tell Abad, he seeks out the manager. I'm sorry, says the man, but our workers are sleeping in a storeroom next to your friend.

On Day 2, India runs away with the Multan test match after scoring a massive 509 runs. There are fewer than 1,000 fans in the stands. I make some calls, and nab a flight to London for the next morning. I fly from Multan to Islamabad, this time on a decent 707, and arrive in my room in time to turn on the TV and see Tendulkar, the one who had beaten Pakistan in the one-day series with a superb fielding play, now stick the knife in as a bowler. At the end of Day 3, with Pakistan holding a score of 364 with five wickets already gone, Tendulkar races in with the ball and whips it past the dangerous Moin Khan. Nothing could be more embarrassing, and it sums up the entire tour for Pakistan; standing there with just 17 runs on his bat, Khan watches in shame as Tendulkar's bowl swirls untouched through his legs. He's done, and so is his team.

At dusk, I open the windows in my hotel room, and in with the golden fading light rushes a blast of humid air, that chilling voice calling the world to prayer. I'm an infidel, of course; I am, I guess, everything Osama bin Laden wants to destroy. But my flight out is booked. I'm going to make it home, I think. Now the voice sounds peaceful, beautiful even.

In line at the Islamabad Airport the next morning I notice a handsome man, twenty-five or so, with a ponytail and an up-to-the-second black suit. I pigeonhole him at the speed of thought: poseur, nouveau riche, fan of boy bands and inane music videos. Then I forget him. Nearly half a day later, our flight lands at Heathrow. When I emerge I find myself walking side by side with the same man along the moving walkway. Our pace, our strides are exactly the same. We aren't, we both realize at the same subconscious moment, going to lose each other any time soon. Finally, he breaks.

"Long trip, eh?" he says.

The conversation lasts no more than three minutes. But in that time, propelled by our lockstep synchronicity and the odd traveler's honesty that makes one spill thoughts to a total stranger, he reveals he's a Pakistani living in Liverpool (sounding, as does everyone from Liverpool, like a Beatle). He confesses his love for Manchester United. I ask what had sent him to Pakistan, and his face changes, his voice softens; he says that he had gone to get married. He met the girl on the Internet, he says, and never spoke to her once before the ceremony, and as we whiz along he pulls out pictures of his bride, gorgeous and delicate, and his faith in himself and a no-doubt perfect future, his sheer happiness, hits me like an infection. "Congratulations," I nearly yell.

We talk about his father, and how happy he had been that the old man had gone all the way to Lahore for the wedding. We talk about how he now had to leave his bride behind for visa reasons, and his sorrow at suffering through another six months before seeing her again.

The end of the walkway approaches. With perfect timing, like some musical's over-the-top rendition of a random conversation in an airport, we shake hands and nod and wish each other luck. He turns left. I continue straight on, resisting the urge to click my heels. That awful film from eight hours aloft drops off my skin, the impersonal weight of the off-ramp, the walkway, the gray and faceless terminal falls away; for this day, this moment, anyway, travel feels new again. I walk the terminal grinning like a lunatic. One step too slow or too fast, and I would have missed it.

And that's how Pakistan—harbor for terrorists, suspect Islamic republic, military dictatorship—wins me at last. I know how I'm supposed to feel; I know India is the world's largest democracy. But it's out of my hands. The next time they play, Pakistan is my team.

Eight

I wish I'd never come back home
It don't feel right since I've been grown
I can't find any of my old friends hangin' 'round
Won't nothin' bring you down like your hometown

Steve Earle, *Hometown Blues*

Jack isn't doing well in gym. No father likes to hear this, of course—the male pecking order begins on the playground—but I'm distressed for a different reason. It's not that Jack can't play; it's that he won't, and he won't because the game is soccer. It doesn't matter how many friends at the school in Luynes are involved. It doesn't matter if they beg, and it doesn't matter if I beg. If play involves France's—and the world's—most popular game, Jack will simply opt out, stalking the sideline in sullen disdain. What can one do with such a boy? *Dommage* reads the note sent home by the French PE teacher: Pity. But I'm not about to force the issue.

I've been on the teacher's side. I've seen the Japanese family playing its fierce Thursday night badminton in San Francisco, the pale Englishmen playing Sunday rugby in Miami, the fields in Corona Park filled with Spanish oaths and the thunk-thunk rhythm of *futbol*. I'd always wondered about these subcultures moving beneath the American sports radar, and as a kid had felt uneasy: The sight of those beefy Italians kicking, always kicking, on that makeshift soccer field in a Stamford public park hinted at a world I'd never penetrate and felt almost like an insult, as if my games weren't good enough. I didn't know the outsider's need to regularly evoke home, to reaffirm roots, if only in a pair of shorts and sneakers. I don't know still, in fact, until it gets warm enough and I dig the baseball gloves out of the garage. Jack and I set up some 20 yards apart and start to throw.

The backyard isn't ideal: too narrow, too many ruts. Every errant toss runs the risk of getting lost in a thicket of rosemary, the impenetrable weeds. Still, Jack loves baseball. We'll loft the ball back and forth, high pops and grounders and the occasional line drive, and soon Charlie will hear and come giggling back and forth between us and Tommy the dog will hop over the dirt hump and sniff and Philippe's head will rise, too, eyebrows up, from behind the driveway wall. Now we're those foreigners playing some bizarre game, baseball under the olive trees, grunting with each snap of the wrist, sweat breaking under the shoulder blades, both of us yelping over each great catch. Jack's a lefty. He can fire it in there, too, when he wants to.

For that, I credit Fran. She's got this odd motion, left leg ramrod straight, pivot turning almost entirely off the back foot, but her arm is a gun. She played Miss Softball America in Stamford, and though hardly the thick-legged jock, her face sheds two decades whenever she puts on a glove. Jaw set, she's all earnestness and apology: determined to throw strikes and begging pardon when even slightly off. She likes to do a lot of things well and does, but I suspect that throwing a baseball is near the top of the list. Fran would throw for hours, really, if we'd all just leave her alone long enough.

Sure, we're trying to blend in. Addie is taking ballet at a local studio; Jack has learned to treat his teachers with Gallic deference. I've managed to create a pseudolanguage with Philippe: a mélange of hand signals, grunts, eyebrow wiggling mixed with various butchered French nouns and verbs. He's always patient and says I'm coming along, and one afternoon I actually make it clear that, yes, the neighbor up the hill *is* an asshole for not paying for the damage his fallen tree did to Philippe's fence. We nod and glare up at the man's house, united.

But then every few weeks we'll feel the urge for a catch, or feel ourselves drawn inexorably into the parking lot of the McDonald's in Gardanne. One Sunday, we make the two-hour drive to Montpellier's
planetarium for a day of high-minded science only to find it closed.
None of us bothers to pretend disappointment. Next door is a restaurant
called Route 66, a kitschy nod to American pop culture that looks like
it was dragged off the set of *Pulp Fiction*. The food is horrible, portions
greasy and huge but in no way tasty, yet the family sits in a retooled old
scarlet Cadillac, munching away. We drive back singing oldies—Elvis,
Gladys Knight, etc.—everyone elated by what should go down as a perfect waste of a day.

But the happiest of all may be me, and that's a shock. I'm not supposed to need any of this—music, baseball, American touchstones. I've
always avoided the places abroad where Americans congregate,
immersed myself in the culture at hand, cockily informed my parents
that I have no use for nostalgia or homesickness. Yet here I am now,
skimming past the French programming and studying CNN; who knew
Larry King could be so fascinating? The Jimmy channel shows *The
Sopranos*, *The Shield*, *Curb Your Enthusiasm*, commercial free no less, but
I'm suddenly not picky. Back in the States, the appeal of the saccharine
comedy *Friends* was lost on me. But now I get irked whenever I see Joey,
Monica, Rachel, and Ross dubbed over in French. Come Wednesday
night, Jimmy plays back-to-back episodes in English, and we're there,
couchside. When did this show become so hilarious? I wonder out loud.
That Joey!

There's a spot on Interstate 80 between San Francisco and Sacramento,
somewhere past the prison in Vacaville, where on spring nights the smell
of earth rises out of the fields of the Central Valley, dank, turned over by
steel, breezing through your open car window with a presence as strong
as smoke. You know then that you're not in California anymore, not the
mythic California of surf and movie stars and coastal cool, and as you head
east toward Dixon and Davis it's hard not to be afflicted by an increasing

sense of gravity. Coming out of the Bay Area's self-congratulatory haze—"Isn't this the greatest place to live? Ever?"—it's as if the farm-land, the widening space itself, conspires to settle the psyche. Your feet touch ground. More than any other place, I told myself once I'd left for good, it smelled like home.

I arrived in Davis in the summer of 1984, driving the wrong way down a one-way street. I began as a backup writer on Giants and A's baseball, then Sacramento State football and, because I had covered big-time basketball in Chapel Hill, landed the beat covering the newly arrived Sacramento Kings. I was, as everybody there can attest, an instant master—at overwriting, at missing deadlines, at trying to invest my sto-ries with an importance they didn't deserve. But with another daily paper in town, I had to hustle or lose, and fear of humiliation was only one reason I got better. The fact is, battling on a beat is one of life's few, clear-cut, postathletic competitive venues. Each morning, readers open up a newspaper to see who won the game. Each morning, sportswriters open up a newspaper to see which writers won the battle for the best lead, best quotes, best information, best kicker, best assessment of that game. I lost often and won some, too, and spent a bit of each day won-dering if I'd be fired.

There's a reason sportswriters get fat. The work occurs at night, the deadlines are crushing, the editors have no idea what it takes to jam that 18 inches of copy into a misbehaving computer, not to mention the fact that you've got twenty minutes to juggle words because the locker-room guy didn't open the doors on time and the players took long showers and said nothing and now the desk is saying hurry up and, Christ!, how do you say anything interesting about a 24-point blowout in February? By the time you filed for the 11:15 P.M. deadline, your stomach so twisted, your hair standing on end, you knew you couldn't sleep for hours unless you drank and, well, why not some nachos, too? Why not an entire meal? I did that for a while until I was twice pulled over and tested for drunk driving, and then began hopping the fence at the Cal-Davis field at 12:30 in the morning, running laps until I'd sweated out most of tension. The rest stayed, though, until I could compare the two papers in the morning. Then it started over again.

I would see Michael Jordan a few times a year, in Chicago or when he hit the West Coast, and by then he'd already become a national phenomenon: There was the autograph horde losing control in Houston, the surreal moment when a woman stopped his car by laying herself in front of its wheels. We weren't friends, but he always made a point of remembering me. I didn't understand why for years. The loyalty Carolina players have for Coach Dean Smith and Chapel Hill is a rare thing; it's as if all of them—Billy Cunningham, Larry Brown, Mitch Kupchak, Phil Ford, Mike O'Koren, Walter Davis, James Worthy, and dozens of others—had been convinced they would never again experience anything so special. Once, I stood in a pack of reporters interviewing former Carolina center Brad Daugherty in Cleveland. We had shared a psychology class during his freshman year four years before, one of those surveys for hundreds of students, but sat nowhere near each other. Yet midway through that mass interview, without me ever uttering a word, Daugherty glanced at me out of the corner of his eye, stopped in midsentence, and said, "Wait. I *know* you."

Jordan, though, took it further than any North Carolina athlete I had ever seen. As his fame exploded and he went from Chicago icon to one of the most recognizable faces on the globe, Jordan insisted on wearing his Carolina shorts under his Chicago or his Olympic or his—much later—Washington Wizards uniform, and whenever our paths crossed he'd insist on catching up on news with the latest Carolina gossip, lingering well beyond politeness. He granted me far more interviews and candor than a reporter from Sacramento should have ever expected, but I just chalked it up to Carolina loyalty, a bond with the old school as natural to him as winning. I found the trait admirable, but about as explicable as the mores of a fourteenth-century saint. Such a connection to home was beyond me.

I found myself then, in that place, living in Davis, working for the *Sacramento Bee,* racing down to San Francisco in my '60 Plymouth, and cranking music loud to compete with the wind. I had come into North-ern California with nothing but my name, made friends, a reputation, a life. I had pulled, I was sure, a Gatsby: complete reinvention, with a past I never mentioned and a future I would make on my own. After a year, I happened to mention something about my family, and my closest friend in town stopped the conversation cold. "It's so strange to hear you have a mother," he said.

I had fallen in love with newspapers, journalism, writing, sports. This is not a fashionable thing to say, especially among sportswriters; the spoiled athletes, the ever-manipulative agents, the double-talking own-ers had long been a staple of the industry, and Jordan's rise, fueled as it was by an unprecedented commercial sophistication, served as the lodestar of an age marked by money chasing from every angle. The fate of franchises, stadiums, players, and fandom in the '80s could all be boiled down to the bottom-line mentality that afflicted every area of American life, and made it fashionable—even wise—to strike a pose of weary cynicism. The smell of the grass? The roar of the crowd? Please. No one could ever sound wrong declaring that sports had gone straight to hell.

I loved it all. This has nothing to do with prime seats or access to athletes; what television—in its popular portrayals of sportswriters on shows like *The Odd Couple* and *Everybody Loves Raymond*—intentionally misses is the fact that sportswriting is a job. Oscar Madison and Ray Romano never bother with interviewing or transcribing hours of tape or waiting by the phone for someone to never call; Oscar and Ray don't work until 4:00 A.M. on a long feature; Oscar and Ray don't troll empty player lounges in search of that one compelling scene. Instead, they're your basic high school wiseasses fast-forwarded a decade or two, and though that's actually close to true about many of us, it still misses the best part, the quality that keeps us coming back. Sportswriters take the ephemera of a few lost hours and, juiced by coffee, adrenaline, and alarmingly deep neuroses, somehow infuse the seemingly unimportant act of hitting a puck, a ball, or a face with a fist with something approaching significance. Sportswriters are sometimes asked how they can waste so much time and energy on mere games and overgrown boys in short pants, but more often they're told by those who know no better that theirs is a dream profession. But then, this is only because people care so much about games and boys in short pants. We all know that too much money and time is spent on pro football or soccer, but only popularity separates it from more "dignified" pursuits. Ballet aficionados are just sports fans in formal wear. They, too, are obsessed with a physical act, honed by a manic devotion and years of repetition, transformed by the force of one moment, one crowd, and one serendipitous confluence of circumstances into something beautiful.

If you're any good as a writer, you'll be able to grasp and channel just a bit of that; if you're really good, you can do it night after night. But sometimes, you get it all: The dramatic home run, the perfect quote, the most perceptive take on what everyone saw, and then, if you're even luckier, you see the story clear in your head and get time enough to hammer it into your keyboard. The crowd's fever, the joy and misery of winners and losers, the running down the dank arena hall to the press room somehow alchemizes into a rhythm in your head and you're lining it all up, paragraphs gliding off your fingers like freight cars on greasy rails, and when you're done your stomach is rattling and you're as high as any drink will get you. You captured time. You bottled passion. It will be gone the next morning, but you saw it, you got it, you wrote it in a way that sounds close to true. Most likely, no one will know. Not the readers just looking for the score. Not the editors consumed by press runs. Maybe not even your competition, obsessed with getting beaten. It's a secret glory, and you must cherish it because it never lasts. You go to breakfast the next morning, and buy four newspapers and eat eggs and bacon and hot coffee and take your time reading. You wake up later than the rest of the world. That's the reward.

But there's also the electricity of walking into a packed arena, the boarding of an airplane for a story no one else will get, the landing in Paris, Medellín, Sapporo, Rome, Monrovia, and Santiago de Cuba on someone else's dime, in places a boy without money never dreamed of getting to go. Forget the exotic: There're also jewels like Portland, Oregon, at dusk in winter; Scottsdale, Arizona, on a spring night; and French Lick, Indiana, on a sticky summer morning. There's the dawning understanding that, maybe, you actually have a talent in this life. People told me things, right from the start: the ruined phenom whose father took him to a Reno whorehouse, the mother whose distance-running son had been molested, the coach who wanted to quit and couldn't help but say it. They told me things, I think, because once we started talking I had to know. The assignment, the interview, dissolved into conversation because I wanted to know. It was never a job. I had to know what moved them. It excited me, and it just so happened later that a tape had been running the whole time.

"I don't know," then-Mets manager Bobby Valentine told me one night in 1999 outside a Philadelphia hotel. "I wish we didn't come out here. I don't like to talk about all this stuff. I've had a couple of beers, knocked down my guard a little. It's going to be tough on you to write this story properly. You know a little too much, and probably not enough."

I'll take that, every time. Because when you don't know enough— and most always you don't—you make the extra phone call, scan the extra document, rewind the tape again. And if you still never find out everything, that's okay too: Mystery can make for better reading, and sometimes you get something you didn't expect. You reveal yourself to yourself along the way.

In January of 1989, I went to New Orleans to cover the 49ers in the Super Bowl. The first night there, my hometown friend Bruce called to say that one of my English professors had died the week before, on my birthday. He was forty. I hung up the phone, lay on the bed, and stared at the ceiling until I heard a noise. It seemed to be rising out of my chest. I jammed my fists against my eyes.

It turned out to be a good week. I wrote some stories that seemed important, and the day before the game I drove up to Baton Rouge with another reporter from Sacramento to see Huey Long's grave. The last time I'd been there was in 1980, with Bruce, and nine years later I had had enough success to know that Bruce had, without knowing it, helped pull me free. We had spent that summer chattering about history, girls, sports, books, Huey Long, had driven into Baton Rouge and seen the state capitol steps that Long built and where he was killed in 1935. I showed my colleague what I'd seen years before, and in a public bathroom in town we started babbling about former LSU running back Billy Cannon, how he'd won the Heisman Trophy in 1959, and later went to jail for something like running the nation's largest counterfeit ring. I wondered what year Cannon graduated.

A man in a wheelchair backed away from a urinal. "He played from 1957 to '59," the man said. Then he flushed, turned and rolled out the door, adding, "He's back in town. He's a dentist here now."

The 49ers won 55–10, and I couldn't get a flight out for days. I decided to waste Monday by driving up to Baton Rouge again, alone this time. It's one of the great things: an 80-mile stretch of highway, bad AM radio, time to kill. Bruce had called again, this time to tell me his mother had a spot on her lung, and as I drove I remembered the stories he'd tell of his sister and mom and him driving all over the West; I remembered his mother's electric embrace of the new, and that she'd given that to her son, who gave it to me. Halfway to Baton Rouge I looked over: Alongside the highway, the Goodyear blimp zoomed along, silver and huge and not 25 feet off the ground, morning sun glinting off its flanks. I drove alongside for a few miles, singing and craning my neck at such a grand and dopey thing.

Cannon's fame boiled down to the LSU National Championship team of 1958, his Heisman-clinching, 89-yard punt return to beat Ole Miss in '59—and now his crime. In the mid-'80s, he'd organized the counterfeit ring, got caught, turned state's evidence against his partners to reduce a five-year jail term to two. I called from a pay phone and got an answering machine: *Hello. This is Doctor Billy Cannon. I'm with a patient right now, but if you'll leave your name, etc., etc.* . . . I called a few more times. At 11:00 A.M., he picked up.

"You've heard of people keeping a low profile?" he said. "Well, this is a no profile. I'll be glad to talk to you, but not for any story." I figured the conversation was over. I tried to say good-bye. But Cannon kept wanting to talk: about Joe Montana, about ending his career, about the lure of being an outlaw. "For some it's hard not hearing the roar of the crowd," he said. "Most people adjust fine after football. It's just a few like me who fuck up a little." He went on for about fifteen minutes and I pictured a balding Southern dentist, standing with a still-warm drill in his hand, a bit lonely, a waste of time. I hung up, went to lunch, but couldn't let it go.

I found his office tucked back at the end of a parking lot past two nondescript restaurants. The place felt as if no one had visited in days. It was outfitted in mid-'70s suburban doctor: magazines, plastic covers on the waiting room chairs. A broad man stood alone at the reception desk, sifting papers. "I'm Billy Cannon," he said. When I said my name he boomed, "Scott, how're you boy? Come on in!" His voice was jovial and welcoming, eyes darting around at the papers, at the empty room, at me when he thought I wouldn't notice.

The handshake was like frostbite. He was balding, but at 6-foot-2 and about 250 pounds looked anything but the kindly Southern gent. His gut blew out over his belt. The wedding ring on his left hand was bounded on each side by mounds of flesh. On his desk were pictures of his three daughters and son, Billy Jr. He offered half his hamburger, a cold Whopper from Burger King, pulling out a white plastic knife and sawing it in two. He found a plastic cup and poured in more than half of his vanilla shake. My first mistake was to say something about him being a dentist. "Orthodontist," he said, bored.

I tried to fly past that by asking any question I could think of. It didn't matter: Cannon never asked why I was there; he acted as if strange people visited him every day. I asked about his son, about choosing to put a pressure on his boy by the mere act of naming him "Billy." Cannon got this odd look in his eye, then a gleam that never left, and I could see that, yes, here was a man who could be a criminal. "Hell," he said, "I *wanted* him to be me.

"I had only about two or three talks with him about it," Cannon went on, "and I told him that people were going to be after him just because of that, that he had to always be ready for it. What do we have here? I knew. And I remember when he was about nine or ten, I was at a friend's house and Billy was outside playing basketball with some of the kids and they were beating up on him pretty bad. They threw him in a bush. And in the car on the way home I said to him, 'They were pretty rough on you, huh? You know why? Because they want to be able to walk around and tell all their friends that they kicked shit out of Billy Cannon's son. That's goin' to happen to you from now on. Now you tell me if you can handle it.' And you know what he said? He said, 'I can handle it.'

"I told him it was okay. I don't care if he starts it or not, it was okay. One time, he was telling me that he was in a pizza place once with a bunch of friends and some guy came up to him and said, 'Cannon, I want a piece of you outside.' And as the guy turned to walk out he hit him. The guy went down. And when he told me, I asked him, 'Did he get up?' and he said, 'He tried.' And then he looked at me and he said, 'You know, the pizza was still warm.' "

He looked at me smiling, not caring a bit whether I liked the story. I asked Cannon what his son was doing. Billy Jr. had been a linebacker at Texas A&M. Drafted by the Cowboys, Billy Jr. injured his neck and never played a down in the NFL. He was about to sue the club for the second time. Cannon said his son was working somewhere in Texas, laboring in the dust to turn a tract of land into a nuclear waste dump.

The phone rang a few times: *Hello, this is Dr. Billy Cannon . . . ,* but he waved it off. At one point I was trying to make some brilliant insight and said, "I played some football . . ." and as the words left my mouth I knew I had made a mistake. Cannon shook his head, no, his lip curled slightly, and I could almost see the thought: "Don't give me that shit. One look at you says you never came anywhere close to playing big-time ball." I'd treaded on his turf.

We heard the outside door open, childish voices out in the waiting room. Cannon thanked me for coming and invited me to stop by the next time I was in town. My last picture of Billy Cannon is of him putting up his fists and barking to his little patient, "Come on in, boy, I think I can handle *you*." The kid put his head down and waded into Cannon's stomach. I got in the car and drove toward the State House, feeling like I'd missed something and would never know what.

It was about a quarter to five when I walked past Huey's statue, the best time to see it. The sun washed the Capitol with a fading gold, and the air had cooled; most of the workers were long gone. I walked through a side door and took an elevator as high as I could go. The capitol tower was off-limits to tourists, but I tried anyway, climbing up the stairways until I reached a locked door. A dirty window opened out onto the dusk, and I stood on my toes to get a glimpse of the Mississippi. I heard voices coming closer, but instead of janitors they were two guys like me: lost and looking to get to the top. We hurried off in different directions. The elevator came and I rode it down, twenty-four floors. When I hit the lobby, the lights were off, the place hollow and dead.

I got out quickly then, slid into my rental car and turned the key and found the highway. Then I drove down to New Orleans listening to the radio, not singing at all.

The houseguests have shuttled in and out: Fran's aunt, mom, sister, a few good friends. To get to the South of France requires effort, so the visits are also an unspoken roll call of kinship; if you come you care: about our lives, our adventure here, how we are now. My family, though, hasn't made any noise about flying in, and I don't expect it. Money is an issue, but they also need a welcome more heartfelt than my half-baked invite. Too much distance has built up over the years; though my disregard for Stamford has, with time, been downgraded to something of a family joke, the sting of the slap hasn't entirely faded.

But then, in the end the joke will always be on me. Because Fran is from home, from one of the more prominent families in Stamford, truth be told, and the fact that we're together remains my daily dose of irony run amok. Home doesn't let you go. I fled the place, then I ended up marrying it.

Fran's father, Don, was one of four kids, some successful, some not. On its best days, the family fancied itself Irish-American royalty in the Kennedy manner, and if Fran's generation generated more bar owners than doctors, some still managed to carry themselves with an alarming fillip of entitlement. Don bounced around colleges, struggled, drank, everybody's best friend in a tavern or a pinch, leaving her mom nightly to fend with the seven kids alone. She kicked him out, finally. I first met these Brennans in high school, when I went to their house in midwinter and shivered on their couch in my coat. There was no heat, and no money to pay for it. Maggie raised the kids, worked full-time; any vestige of Brennan arrogance got burned off in the struggle.

But Fran, the second oldest, had every reason to lord it over anyone: Gorgeous, whip-smart and funny, she had, by virtue of five brothers and a family premium placed on rapid-fire wordplay, something even more rare. She could give guys shit. What I mean is the bantering, aggressive verbal jousting among male friends, the secret language of men that almost no woman cracks. Fran looked like Mariel Hemingway, but engaged like every male actor in *Diner;* she's tough, and if you weren't looking closely then, you'd almost believe she was a hard-eyed bitch in the making. But Maggie wouldn't allow it. Scratched, every wisecracking, poor-relation Brennan bleeds sentiment and loyalty, all more comfortable giving than taking. Had Fran been brought up rich, I never would have had a chance. Come wedding day, her dad supplied the limo. It caught fire on the way to the church.

We moved to San Francisco, survived the '89 earthquake and, later, in Florida, Hurricane Andrew. Fran worked for the *Miami Herald* then, covering news in South Dade. When the storm hit, she was the only reporter who knew the lay of the land. We shared a byline once; she writes faster and easier than anyone I know, and her nose for nonsense—mine especially—is unerring. *People* magazine offered her a job as Miami bureau chief in the mid-'90s, and Fran almost bit. But the idea of keeping Jack in day care haunted her, and she turned her back on a career. Yet she's a journalist still, and there are days when three bickering kids leave her wasted. And then I'll go off on some intriguing, seemingly significant story—alone, out in the world, in the action. She resents it. She has never said a word, but I know. That's how writers are. I would feel it, too, but I wouldn't be able to stay quiet.

That's why I pushed for France back when we were deciding where to live. I wanted to let myself off the hook. The French life had been Fran's teen dream, not mine, and I could ease my guilt each time I'd travel by reassuring myself that she has that now. She can chat with Jocelyne, Philippe's wife, and Philippe is suaver than I'll ever be—cigarette dangling just so, Jean-Paul Belmondo with a hammer, a charming and funny counterbalance to an American husband consumed with frivolous words. Philippe is a contractor: He's always in the process of producing something solid. There's the condo he's building on the sea west of Marseille, the pool he's digging in his backyard, the little apartment he's adding onto his house for his twenty-something son, Jean-Philippe. Addie, of course, runs over to see Jean-Philippe whenever she can. When I tell her he has a girlfriend, I get my first glimpse ever of a four-year-old burning with jealousy. It's almost frightening.

When we sit on the couch now, sometimes I'll look at my wife knitting away and wonder about the bizarre mind-set that deemed it necessary for me to be with her. We'll laugh about someone we know. We'll speak of our children. It's not easy being married to someone smarter, funnier, more gifted, and kinder than you, unless you prize intelligence, talent, humor, and compassion above all. Then it's different. Then you're like a thief, and you've pulled off one of the century's great steals.

Spring

Nine

I can get on with you; you are practical. I understand
you. But talking to Wilson is something like talking to
Jesus Christ. . . .

French prime minister Georges Clemenceau
to Colonel Edward House, 1918

Woodrow Wilson was the apotheosis of a type: the American who
arrives in Europe sure that he has come from a better place, who
speaks as if charged with a holy mission, who sees his country as the
hope of the world. This type of American can be a politician, though
it's not a prerequisite. The mass American tourist widely regarded as
the turtle of the European circuit, toting its belongings, language, and
comforts around in a stunted effort to make everywhere just like
home, is generally the same man or woman who regards the continent
as a place where America's most generous impulses get repaid with
ingratitude, even betrayal. Wilson went to Paris in December 1918
looking to transform a shattered Europe with his Fourteen Points, and
the French, especially, never got over how this idealistic, arrogant
American tried to tell them how to live. That Wilson was broken by
the experience, the avatar of American exceptionalism undone by
European wiles, has become one of the most threadbare pieces of
received knowledge in American history. Europe has been suspicious
of crusading Yanks ever since.

The American set loose in Europe, setting his "innocence" against the ancient and corrupt, is a plot far older than Wilson. Ben Franklin, Thomas Jefferson, Washington Irving, Mark Twain, Henry James, James Whistler, Ernest Hemingway, and General John J. Pershing lived out the cultural cliche. Jake Barnes, Isabel Archer, a Connecticut Yankee, and Gene Kelly's American embodied it in fiction. Thousands of American troops took it to illogical extremes, surrendering their lives in the continent's rich old mud. When President George W. Bush, the most polarizing American in Europe since Reagan, came to London in November of 2003, to no one's surprise thousands jammed the streets in protest. It wasn't just because Mr. Bush's war had been sold on rumors of weapons never found. Bush's unilateral sense of mission, his advisor's dismissal of "old Europe," smacked too familiarly of Wilson's way; the United States, Bush liked to say, "was the greatest force for good on this earth" and his war a life-or-death struggle against "evildoers." Through the European lens, he was not a politician, not even a president, but a self-deluding boob. It was only right that he stayed in Buckingham Palace, the first U.S. president since Wilson to do so, ignoring anything that distracted from the song in his head. What Europe might have wanted for Iraq was irrelevant.

It's this Wilsonian hauteur, this disregard for any but his way, that makes Bush the figure everyone from the States has to account for now. He's there, in the first few seconds of introduction, those neutral moments when Americans, especially, are intent on making nice. The only variable is whether the question is spoken or not: *What about this man? Explain him, please. Explain yourself.*

"As players, we're not making decisions that change the outcome of the world," Tim Howard tells me in late February. "I love America; I'm American and I'd never change that. I believe in America. Does that mean I agree with all of our president's decisions? No. But he is our leader. I'm not going to shy away from that, but people here have to not be so ignorant. I'm not the leader of our military. I'm just an American."

Not quite. Howard lives in England, and in the spring of 2004 he may well be the second most recognizable Yank in the Old World. He is, after all, deep into his first season as goalkeeper for England's soccer powerhouse Manchester United, the most famous football club on the globe, an institution despised and worshipped beyond all reason and "built," as manager Sir Alex Ferguson likes to say, "on bigger foundations and history than any club in the country." In other words, Howard is living out the fairy tale life of, say, 95 percent of the planet's young men. Ignoring Howard's Tourette's syndrome, his status as third-string keeper on the U.S. national team, and the fact that they had never bothered with American talent before, in May of 2003 the Red Devils plucked him out of the relative obscurity of the U.S.'s Major League Soccer circuit and tapped him to be their starter. It's far more than the twenty-four-year-old could ever have hoped for. When the Man U goalkeeper coach phoned just to say that the club was interested in him, Howard says, "I could've lived on just *that* the rest of my life."

But the fairy tale keeps getting better. Though Man U has struggled through a fitful 2003–04 season, Howard hasn't been the problem. Teammates marvel at his consistency; English fans love his humility, serenading each save with his name set to Mary Poppins music: *Tim-timminy, Tim-timminy, Tim-Tim Terr-ee!* By the end of the season, Howard will more than prove he belongs; he'll be named the English Premiere League's goalkeeper of the year. "To come straight into the Premiership and to a club like Man United? Nobody could expect what he's done," says teammate Ruud Van Nistelrooy. "He's up there with the best in the world already." Europe rings with endless debate over the comparative primacy of Spanish, English, or Italian football, but Howard's achievement and timing are undeniable. At a time of virulent anti-Americanism, an American has become a star at the sport's highest level. At a time when Europeans wonder how to hold off America's cultural backwash, here's its opposite: an American embracing one of Europe's core passions, testing himself at its pinnacle, and thriving.

So I fly EasyJet up to London to write a piece on Howard, churn out paragraphs on his skill, his illness, but it's the subtext—tossed off in my story in a line or two—that stays with me. As I move on to other subjects, do other interviews, cover other games throughout the spring, at the slightest opportunity I find myself compelled to ask the American question—yet it's never so much about Bush as it is about us. What does it mean to be an American in Europe now? What are we looking for? What do we look like? It would be easy to fall back on cliches like the Bush-loving cowboy, but the most prominent Yanks ranging across the continent these days don't pop out of that mold. More often, they're like Howard—harder to pigeonhole, tougher to dismiss. Because in truth, for every rube who wanders off a plane at Charles de Gaulle, there's another American dazzled—if not intimidated—by Europe, eager to embrace its nuances, and desperate to fit in. For them, in fact, fitting in is the ultimate goal: to be considered a "good" American like T. S. Eliot or actor Johnny Depp, to navigate the traffic circles with that certain *je ne sais quoi,* to walk about and not be instantly recognized as Cleveland's own—such are the true expat prizes. These Americans aren't looking to import U.S. hegemony. They're trying to escape it.

"The best part is living in a different culture than we're used to, living outside our own country," Howard says. "A lot of Americans have never been outside the country, let alone lived outside it. It's a life experience you'll be able to lean on and cherish."

The presence of such Americans only validates Europe's limitless self-regard, of course. Something about the challenge of the other, about Europe itself, speaks to them in a way America doesn't. Maybe it's the cafes. Or the always-stylish women. Or maybe, as in Howard's case, it's crashing the biggest stage in the world's biggest sport. Because in the warm days of 2004, Howard has actually revealed himself as an example of a third American type: respectful, open, but determined to beat Europe at its own game. He's not anything new. Sidney Franklin in the 1930s and John Fulton in the 1960s tried with varied success to penetrate Spain's labyrinthine world of bullfighting, and cyclist Greg Lemond's success in the Tour de France during the 1980s set the stage for the coming of Lance Armstrong. But with Rahlves's performance at

Kitzbühel and Bode Miller's fourth-place finish in the World Cup over-all ski standings, Armstrong preparing for his record-smashing sixth Tour de France title, and Howard in goal for Man U, this is shaping up as the greatest American season "Over There" ever. But Howard's achievement may well have the most impact, because it comes in the sport Europeans live and breathe. And he isn't alone.

In the spring of 2004, seven Americans are playing soccer in England, six in the Premiership, more than at any time in history. Goalkeeper Kasey Keller began the tide in 1991, and fellow stopper Brad Friedel followed after years of work permit snags. But the biggest breakthrough for U.S. players in Europe actually happened in 2002, half a world away. The U.S. team, after bombing out miserably just four years before, stunned experts when it made the quarterfinals at the '02 World Cup in Japan. Since then, the U.S. has ranked among the world's top ten—higher, even, than Italy—killing off the dusty notion that American men can't play with the best footballers on earth, and dealing a blow to Yankee provincialism.

"The problem with Americans is that we invent sports and call our-selves *World* champions," Keller says one afternoon in Amsterdam. "Indy Car racing is the red-haired bastard child of Formula One, and the rest of the world doesn't give a fuck about Indy Car; Formula One is 150 times bigger. But we just have to do our own thing. That's the scary part. The problem a lot of old-school American guys have with soccer is, 'How come we aren't winning?' Well, we're in competition with more than just ourselves now. It's not just us against us, and then you get to say, 'We're the best in the world!' Now that we can compete with the best, people are starting to realize that it's more than just us against *us*."

In England, of course, the Americans have much to prove. Though they haven't won a World Cup title since 1966, the English still fancy themselves the inventors and keepers of the world's game, and Man U, Arsenal, and Chelsea have spent insane sums of money on players the last few years to ensure their primacy. A few years after the '98 World Cup, Keller was speaking to England goalie David Seaman and another

England player, and the two Brits laughed and said, "Oh, you guys were in the World Cup?" Keller snapped back: "Yeah, we lasted almost as long as you. You got knocked out in the second round, we got out in the first; wow, you won one more game. You guys must be World Champions." Years later, the memory angers Keller still. "Shut the hell up," he says, as if talking to all of England. "It's not 1966 anymore."

Not even close. For more than a decade, domestic leagues all over Europe have been debating the role of foreign players: Are we letting in too many? What's the right balance to improve the quality of play, but at the same time keep it English . . . German . . . Italian? But if anything, "the impressions of Americans is continuing to get better and better, almost month by month," says Eddie Lewis, who has played in England since 2000. Because Americans are better than expected—and cheap. "When I came in, it was more difficult for a foreigner from another country," Lewis tells me. "But it's no longer, 'I'm not even sure Americans play soccer.' Now it's, 'An American is probably a good value for money.' "

And he brings something else, too. "A very American style," Lewis calls it. This has nothing to do with the derided rogue behavior of U.S. athletes abroad: the Fuck-the-Nobility rages of John McEnroe at Wimbledon in the 1980s; Charles Barkley's bullying elbow in an Angolan's chest during the U.S. Dream Team's roll through the 1992 Olympics; the preening arrogance of the U.S. 4x100 relay team at the 2000 games in Sydney. Howard, in fact, makes every effort to deflect attention because he doesn't want people to focus on his Tourette's symptoms. He acts more British than the Brits. But athletically, he's the exemplar of an American boy raised on basketball and football and baseball, multitasking sports that demand complex combinations of running, catching, throwing, dribbling—a coordination between hands *and* feet that soccer doesn't call for. If it were up to Howard, he would have played basketball; he lunges for the ball like a small forward leaping high for an alley-oop.

So high-risk an approach is uncommon in European goalies. "They're *blockers,*" Lewis says. "We have athletes. Tim's out there one-handing stops, he's jumping up across, reaching the player, and reaching over and grabbing the ball. Around the rest of the world, they're just . . . goalies. Ours really aren't. Brad and Kasey are two examples of the same thing, and it's no secret why at some point we should see a whole stable of American keepers all over. We offer more."

Such a conceit can be self-serving, but I can't find many Europeans to disagree. In the best of times, the claim of American exceptionalism in politics or culture engenders cries of "Hypocrite!" backed by references to slavery and My Lai. In the spring of '04, it sparks red-faced rage. As the occupation of Iraq slogs on and terrorists continue apace and the torture scandal at Abu Ghraib prison surfaces, the U.S. keeps proving itself as capable as any nation of blundering and reprehensible acts. But in sports, the idea of American exceptionalism has become almost an article of faith in Europe. Armstrong's dominance is only the most obvious example, and those ignoring the unproven swirl of Lance drug rumors often fall back on the Texan's single-minded drive, his American need to be No. 1, as the X-factor. The fact that a Frenchman hasn't won the Tour since 1985 only sharpens the point: *Why is it we can't win our own event, the sporting highlight of every French summer, and this American can't lose?*

Now, too, the European tennis season has hit its stride, and French fans and media are focusing on the so far disappointing Amelie Mauresmo with the annual question: *Why can't a French player win the French Open?* In England, fans are turning yet again to Tim Henman and asking: *Why can't an English player win Wimbledon?* It has been twenty-one years since Yannick Noah won in Paris, twenty-seven since Virginia Wade won at the All England Club (and, even more embarrassing, nearly seventy years since the last English man, Fred Perry, won Wimbledon in 1936). American players, meanwhile, not only win on clay and grass with regularity, but unlike their continental peers thrive whenever they play their home Grand Slam; American men and women win or contest the U.S. Open championship nearly every year. Why?

The French and Brits obviously concentrate on the losing, the choking, the mighty pressure brought to bear on their best by media and fans, but it's that difference that intrigues me. When I begin asking questions, I expect the obvious answers: the talent pool created by U.S. population of 300 million, the wealth that allows for more leisure time and sports, the success-breeds-success history of American tennis. But small as it is, Australia has what may be an even more distinguished tennis history and an equally sports-mad culture, yet they, too, keep gagging on expectations; it has been twenty-six years since an Australian has won the Australian Open. "I hated going back to Australia," says Pat Cash, who lost two straight finals in Melbourne.

I don't hear such talk from Americans. Part of the reason is structural. Tennis is so far down in the pecking order of U.S. sports that it rarely monopolizes the conversation; the U.S. Open, remember, coincides with the start of the NFL season. "Different mentality: They don't feel the pressure; they feel they play at home and that's it," says Henri Leconte, who lost the French final in 1988. "It's not the same atmosphere as Paris, it's not the same mentality, it's not the same pressure from the media. Because America is huge, they have less pressure. You win the U.S. Open: Yeah, it's great for a second. In Europe, if you have a big name in tennis, you can be second most famous sportsman in the country." An American player, then, feels no weight but the personal; there would never be a headline in New York like the yearly London moan: HENMAN HOLDS TORCH OF NATION'S HOPES, because the American public would never invest so much emotional capital in a second-rate player. Americans have the freedom of power. But that carries a unique pressure, too; unlike everyone else, Americans must continally prove themselves the most powerful of all.

"People in the U.S. don't give a shit about you if you're ranked sixth in the world," says American Paul Annacone, Henman's coach and a former top ten player, one day in Paris. "There, you go big or you go home."

"The States has a totally different mind-set," says John Lloyd, who has seen both sides as a perennial also-ran at Wimbledon, a former husband to American great Chris Evert, a Brit living in California. Lloyd has plenty of theories regarding English ineptitude, ranging from "crappy" public facilities to Wimbledon's posh image to the upper-class accents of tennis announcers to the ass-covering world of British coaching. But when it comes to American success, he zeroes in. "In England, the parenting is not geared to winning," he says. "Around junior tournaments in England, the attitude is much more about putting on a 'good show.' It's okay if you don't win. But in the States if you finish No. 2, you're a waste of space. It's a very hungry country. You've got to be a fighter to get through the door there."

When I run this jumble of thoughts by Philippe Bouin, the philosophical, jazzophile dean of French tennis writers for *L'Equipe*, he isn't a bit surprised. In fact, he responds like someone who has been chewing on the question for too long. Bouin instantly brings up Sebastian Grosjean, a French player who has been ranked as high as No. 4 in the world and can beat just about anyone on the men's circuit. "Grosjean is afraid to be a hero," Bouin says. "Like many French people and players, he has problems with saying, *I want that*, and I'll do just *that*—to have that tunnel vision. At school we don't take one subject, we don't focus, we don't like to stand out. None of the students wants to speak because you're afraid someone will make fun of you. Players want to be stars, but not heros. Mauresmo wants it, but she doesn't want it. She's clever, sensible, she almost knows what she wants. But I think she's afraid of success. She's afraid to be the No. 1.

"You Americans have the right attitude for sport—any sport. You're not afraid to say, 'I want to win.' In your mind, you're already the best. You don't have any complexes. The Australians, the English, the French are always asking, 'Am I good enough?' There's no other country like America, which has to be the best." Bouin pauses and then shrugs, presenting, with his glasses and disheveled hair and slack expression, a pretty good picture of Gallic resignation. "Even in war," he says.

On May 3, I fly into Belgrade. At first blush, the assignment can't be simpler: Three 7-footers on the local basketball power, Partizan Belgrade, are making noise about playing in the NBA. But, then, I haven't been to this city before.

Imagine running your hand over someone else's open wound, a gash that can't or won't heal. You see the reckless damage, but have no sense of the pain; that's what it feels like to visit Belgrade today. Riding over the Gazela Bridge and onto the main drag of Kneza Milosa, you pass the bombed-out husks of the Interior Ministry, the Security Ministry, the Army, the Prime Minister's office. Traffic whizzes by—people rushing to work, school, normal life—but a glance left or right reveals the mile into downtown as an urban battlefield made surreal by the absence of war, the missing sounds of siren and bomb. Massive sheets of blackened concrete, held up in midfall by skeletons of metal mesh, hang in silence. The skin of nearby buildings bear the pockmarks of flying stone and steel. Thousands of offices sit empty, windows shattered, yellowed curtains flapping in the afternoon sun. At the top of the Interior Ministry, near the slicing rupture caused by something dropped from the sky, a small tree grows. It is the only sign of life. "Same as the first day of bombing," says Vlada, the driver. "Nothing working."

It has been five years. As it happens, my visit coincides with the anniversary of the sixty-nine-day campaign of NATO airstrikes that brought Serbian president Slobodan Milosevic to heel, halted atrocities against ethnic Albanians, and started Milosevic down the road toward the first war crimes trial of a European leader in over fifty years. Though supported by all Western Europe and an international community sickened by the Serbs decade-long practice of "ethnic cleansing," the 1999 bombing of the country once known as Yugoslavia was labeled an American initiative; coverage universally described it as a "U.S.–led" coalition, and the results sparked the usual buffet of praise and blame. Milosevic and his attendant butchery would not have been stopped without American will or might. But the innocent bombing victims at the Chinese Embassy, the national TV network, the Dragisa Misovic Hospital, along the rails and fields of Kosovo, wouldn't be dead either. The campaign sparked still-virulent regional outrage and anti-American protests in Athens, Beijing, Sydney, and Moscow. Belgrade, I now see, is the one place in Europe today where views of the U.S. haven't been filtered through a TV lens or gauzy memories of World War II, where emotions aren't sparked by some diplomatic bank shot out of Baghdad or the Gaza Strip. Moral superiority? The arrogance of power? Bill Clinton sounded a lot like Wilson, too, in his day. In Belgrade, the American footprint is clear and fresh.

Indeed, it's as if no one wants to move past that moment, never mind forget. Little has been done since the bombings to repair the most prominent damage. Money is short, of course—Serbia-Montenegro's unemployment rate hovers anywhere from 25 to 40 percent—but it's not without resources. Yet when I arrive there's only one major construction project, and you can best tell a society's values by what it sets in stone. While its downtown sits ravaged, while its government tries to craft a progressive image amid lethal assault from rogue paramilitary figures and organized crime, Belgrade builds its playpen along the highway: a gleaming, 20,000-seat basketball arena.

It's hard to take seriously a place with such skewed priorities, but the logic is almost understandable. The Serb image at the turn of the century resembles Germany's in 1945—genocidal brutes threatening to thrust the continent into another war—with one exception. Somehow, even while exploding across the 1990s into pieces that became Bosnia & Herzogovina, Croatia, Macedonia, Slovenia, Serbia-Montenegro, the former Yugoslavia has managed to remain one of the world's great greenhouses for basketball talent. Stranger still, though the capital's regional clout has diminished with each breakaway, Belgrade's reputation as the epicenter of Balkan hoops has grown. In 2002, Serbia-Montenegro won its second straight World Championship, and at a time when NBA cities thirst for just one decent big man, the Serb capital boasts five: Red Star's 7-foot-5 Slavko Vranjes, an already-proven bust with the New York Knicks, Partizan's trio of Nenad Kristic, Kosta Perovic, and Predrag Samardziski and—perhaps the most valuable jewel of all—Reflex's Nemanja Alexandrov.

In one sense, no city provides a more nurturing environment. Belgrade draws on one of the tallest populations in the world. When he arrived from his hometown of Skopje, Macedonia, in the summer of 2001, the fifteen-year-old Samardziski noticed that he fit in for the first time in his life. The cabbies stood 6-foot-5, the shopgirls at least 6-feet.

"I'm walking and nobody's looking at me," Samardziski says. "I'm saying to myself, 'Hey, come on people, look at *me*! I'm tall!' "

He's not exaggerating. During my first lunch there, I see Charlotte Bobcats center Predrag Drobnjak duck in and cross the patio to his table. None of the natives look twice. Only two Americans, decked out across the room in crisp haircuts and suits, glance up from their plates. One, new in town, grins and starts to make a joke. His host cuts him off. "Welcome to basketball country," he says.

More than that, I soon realize. This is the new frontier. In January of 2003, U.S. Secretary of Defense Donald Rumsfeld outraged his ostensible allies when he derided opposition to the Iraq War by saying, "You're thinking of Europe as Germany and France. I don't. I think that's old Europe . . . The center of gravity is shifting to the east." But his flippancy hid a serious point. I come just days after widespread celebrations in honor of the May 1 accession of ten formerly Communist states into the European Union. The papers are full of stories about the expansion of the euro, the poor-relations status of the new members, the EU's seemingly unstoppable future as a counterweight to U.S. economic might. But seeing it all unfold from Belgrade, it's hard to see the newest map of "New" Europe as anything but another sign of Serb isolation. With the new EU nations of Slovenia and Hungary sealing its northern border, Croatia in the fold as an EU candidate and Macedonia applied and waiting, with Montenegro gunning for independence and EU candidacy, with EU candidates Romania and Bulgaria sitting on its eastern flank with admission due in 2007, Serbia resembles an Old West mining pocket still waiting for the pastor and the law to arrive.

The rise to power of reformist, antimob, pro-West prime minister Zoran Djinjic in January of 2001—in Serbia's first free election in fifty years—seemed to signal progress, but in March of 2003 Djinjic was assassinated in a hail of gunfire in a street behind his office. The day I arrive, local media buzzes with the latest dirty wrinkle: Twenty-four hours before, the suspected mastermind of the conspiracy, former para-military leader and Milosevic supporter Milorad Lukovic, abruptly gave himself up to police, sparking rumors about a secret deal and ties between the mob and the Serb government. My stay vibrates with the unsettling tremors of a society fragmented to the core, day-to-day signs of the Wild, Wild East. One morning I wake up in the Belgrade Intercontinental and notice the grass out front flattened by a line of tiretracks. I follow them to a car accordioned into a concrete wall; a man fueled by drink or fear has jumped the sidewalk and crashed. Women in short skirts and heels patrol the lobby, the same floor where, in 2000, the infamous warlord Arkan was gunned down. As Bob Martin, the photographer, and I stand talking one evening, a barely dressed, midtwenties pro beelines from 100 feet away, slowly slinks right between us, eyes focused on something far away. We step back, suddenly mute, and watch as she moves across the room.

But I'm here for another kind of free-for-all, centered on Belgrade's one legitimate worldwide commodity. Basketball. "That's where the most talent is," says agent Bill Duffy, whose company represents Perovic and fourteen others from the Serb–Yugoslav orbit. "Yugoslavia per capita is No. 1 for the production of quality basketball players. Their development programs are the best, and most are in Belgrade. Go to twenty different youth centers there and you see it: They train. They identify prospects at eight years old. Everybody can shoot. It's ridiculous." And there's no end in sight. "There's a couple of fifteen-year-olds on our radar," Duffy says. "That's all I'll say about that."

They're on everyone's radar. The influx of NBA scouts and agents into Belgrade has become so commonplace, so distracting, that Sasha Danilovic, Partizan's general manager, bans them from Partizan workouts. But they're still coming; the NBA needs players. "We went through the American kids at an alarming rate," says one NBA general manager. "The talent pool has shrunk, and we've gone overseas." Indeed, something has gone wrong since the league touched off the game's global expansion by sending its Dream Team to the 1992 Olympics. As hoped, the world game has improved. The NBA has become a hodgepodge of nationalities. But the quality of American basketball has deteriorated. The combination of dunk highlights and high school players skipping college has created a class of flamboyant NBA stars with little regard for fundamentals, passing, or defense, and even less respect for the game's traditionally venerated coaches.

"New-Jack players," Michael Jordan calls them, and he does so with a sneer.

For the moment, Eastern European players haven't been infected. Partizan's practices average five hours a day, with the stress on fundamentals. Players do as they're told. "In Belgrade, they play on Serbian terms," says Mark Warkentien, a longtime NBA player personnel expert. "It's a job, and one they're lucky to have. They're fighting for their spots. Anything they get, they have to earn. Nothing is given. Over here in the U.S., it's an entitlement thing. With AAU teams and all the summer league stuff, the kids play on their terms."

This is strange, like hearing an echo from the opposite direction. Listening to NBA executives rhapsodize about Eastern European youngsters is like hearing the French and English talk about the Americans. As U.S. athletes flow East to make noise in "Old Europe" mainstays like soccer and skiing and cycling, an even stronger countercurrent rushes the other way. You can make the argument that, with no European antecedents, basketball is the most American game of all, but the NBA has gotten too rich, too popular for its own good. It needs a transfusion of new blood, with the hope that it can revitalize the old in the most American of ways: with immigrant energy and desperation. Serbia, to use John Lloyd's term, is the epitome of a "very hungry country." But there's something else. As Warkentien puts it, "You've got to give those guys extra credit for what they've gone through. They have a toughness that can't be taught."

When the NATO bombs began to fall in 1999, Nenad Kristic was sixteen and living in his Serbian hometown of Kraljevo. "I was nervous," says the soon-to-be New Jersey Nets forward. "We spend nights in the basement. It was scary the first time, but you get used to it." Until the age of six, crew-cut center Kosta Perovic lived with his Serbian family in the town of Osijek, Croatia. When fighting broke out between Serbs and Croats in 1991, his family fled their home and possessions with just two suitcases. The family settled in Belgrade, and his father left for nine months to fight. "He was in the front line," Perovic says. "I was so worried. That part of life was very difficult."

But, he adds, "maybe none of this would have start if I had stayed in Croatia. I think it's good."

That hunger isn't restricted to players. Agents compete savagely in America, but their pursuit has achieved a veneer of respectability, thanks to fictional portrayals like *Jerry Maguire* and de facto NBA power brokers like Jordan's agent, David Falk. In Belgrade, though, the game is bareknuckled and raw. Agents use any method to elbow out the competition in hopes of signing the next star, openly try to poach them if they lose out. If you're not hearing rumors from one agent about payoffs to families, teams, or journalists, you're hearing derisive comments about any players not in the fold. The Belgrade shark pool smells elemental, like a mix of cigar smoke and testosterone; you feel as if you've wandered onto the set of *Sweet Smell of Success*. When I contact Alex Raskovic, the 50-ish director of SFX's Belgrade office, to talk about his client, Kristic, Raskovic insists on taking me to dinner. He picks me up in his gleaming SUV with his stylish wife up front and another woman in the back. We drive to one of the best restaurants in Belgrade, Raskovic filling the air with constant chatter, and after we sit he dials up Kristic and summons him to the restaurant. A man approaches the table, selling magazines. Raskovic buys a *Playboy* and, while his wife and the other woman stare straight ahead, thumbs through the issue. Then he orders me a steak.

Kristic hasn't always been with SFX. As the last of the old guard out of Eastern Europe, the twenty-one-year-old center had followed an obsolete map on his way West, and it hurt him. Partizan president Vlade Divac blazed the trail when he joined the Lakers in 1989, and since then eight other Partizan players—the most of any club in Europe—have made it to the NBA. For a time, this proved mutually beneficial: NBA teams paid hefty buyouts that helped fund Partizan's development system, and in return got seasoned, fundamentally sound players. Divac was nearly twenty-two when he hit America, Danilovic was twenty-five. Both men had won championships for Partizan before bolting, and Kristic tried to follow their lead. At the advice of agent Marc Fleisher, he entered the 2002 NBA draft, got selected by the Nets with the twenty-fourth pick, and planned to wait a year and join the Nets for the 2003–04 season. That plan fizzled when he broke a bone in his foot, missing six months before returning to Partizan midway through the 2003–04 season, where by all accounts he's emerging as a stronger, more accomplished player.

"It's better for me that I'm older," says Kristic. He has come in grinning, seemingly happy to be roused out late at night to meet a strange American. Thinning hair all shaggy, he looks like a goofy teenager woken from a deep nap. "I'm not like kid, seeing it like a wonderland."

Still, the landscape changed on him in midjump. When Detroit spent its precious, No. 2 overall pick on eighteen-year-old, 7-foot Serb Darko Milicic in the 2003 draft, with no expectation of his flowering for at least two years, it sent the signal: The NBA wants them young, and it wants them now. Kristic instantly knew that he and Fleisher had miscalculated. Had he waited to declare himself for, say, the 2004 draft, he probably would've been taken in the top five. "If I was [drafted] higher, it's $2 or $3 million more," Kristic says, smile fading. "That's very important."

After about an hour and few small bites, he stands up, shakes hands, and goes home to sleep, the wisest and saddest of Belgrade big men. I try to finish my steak, and for the first time realize that I'm the only one eating. "It's okay," Raskovic the agent says. "I wasn't hungry." His wife and the strange woman look impeccably bored, but Raskovic doesn't seem to care.

By the time they drop me at the hotel, gorged on too rich food and Slavic world-weariness, I'm feeling a bit dizzy. I need some kind of corrective and, luckily, I get one. At nineteen and eighteen, respectively, Kosta Perovic and Peja Samardziski stand to make far more money than Kristic, and their days are already consumed by choosing between the old path and the new. Both teenagers are considered unpolished, but their height has lifted them, they are sure, to possible first-round status. It doesn't matter that Perovic has been playing top-level ball with Partizan for only a season, and Samardziski has yet to play at all with the senior team; like a late-arriving fad, the same rush for high school talent that swept the NBA in the mid-'90s has hit the Balkans. As one NBA executive tells me, I've nearly missed the story. What makes Belgrade intriguing isn't the fact that the city seems to have cornered the market in 7-footers. "What we're seeing is the Westernization of the European game," he says. "Before they came over as men. Now we're taking boys, just like we did in the U.S. And there will be victims."

Within thirty seconds of meeting Peja Samardziski the next day, I feel like I'm looking at one. He bubbles with the uncontained enthusiasm of a five-year-old, "crazy excited" as his father, Boban, puts it. At the age of five, he took a key and scratched "Peja NBA" into the grain of his bedpost. A few years ago, when he heard a scout would be attending one of his games, Peja couldn't sleep for two days. Now, just a few days hence, he'll board a plane for his first trip to New York. His agent has set up workouts with a few NBA clubs, and the thought of it has Peja all but levitating. His hope, his need, is so uncool that it's mesmerizing. It has been a long time since I've seen the American Dream shine so brightly, so innocently, in someone's eyes. "I'll be like Macauley Culkin: Home Alone in New York!" Peja shouts.

He watches NBA games—"Last night, Miami–New Orleans!"—to steal moves. He studies mock drafts on the Internet. He hears his name being bandied 8,000 miles away. "They are talking about me a lot," Peja says. "When I started playing basketball, my dream was America, and when I hear they were talking about me, I was so thrilled. I feel so close, but I know there I must work much harder than I used to do. Because I know how basketball is played in America. There are some foreigners

coming here from the States and I can see how they play. It's just a little
different playing—but not much."

Sitting in the emptying stands at Pionir Hall, Peja says all the right
things: how he's going to New York only to see how far he needs to go,
how he gets no pressure from his family, how it would be better to stay
at Partizan for another two or three years. But he's so sure that he's
bound for the NBA, so sure it's only a matter of time. And his father is
sure, too—"Not just because I'm his father, but I know him so well,"
Boban says. "He *feels* this game. He feels basketball, and he plays in the
American way"—that it's infectious, even a bit frightening. When I'm
done speaking to them, I feel like I've imbibed a powerful narcotic. It's
only after a few minutes, when we've said good-bye and the buzz wears
off, that I begin to find it heartbreaking.

Because I know more than they do. I've spoken to his general man-
ager, I've spoken to NBA executives. I've heard how Samardziski is con-
sidered the least talented of the Partizan bunch, a classic
back-to-the-basket project. He's 7-feet tall, and as the NBA adage goes,
You can't teach height. But Samardziski may well be a stiff. Raskovic, the
SFX agent, makes a point of dismissing Peja from the moment we meet:
At the restaurant, on the phone: "Forget him," he tells me. "My guy,
Alexandrov, is the one you should be writing about."

By the time I go to Raskovic's office on May 6, I know he's right.
Every NBA talent hound I've spoken to acknowledges Nemanja
Alexandrov, the seventeen-year-old 7-footer for Reflex, as Belgrade's
greatest prize. Unlike Partizan's big three, he can play small forward or
big guard. Already, he has demonstrated so much athleticism and
grace—Kevin Garnett's name, by way of comparison, keeps coming
up—that many project him as a future No. 1 pick. "The apple in a
bucket of oranges," says one NBA GM of the crop of Belgrade big men.
"He's the guy."

Raskovic knew I'd be coming by. He makes a point of interrupting
his conversation with a man hunched across the table. I try to be polite
and back out, but Raskovic insists on introducing me.

"This is Perovic's father," he says. "He's an old friend." Perovic, as everyone in the room knows, is represented by his rival, agent Bill Duffy. Raskovic smiles, as if he can see my mind working out what I've stumbled upon—and likes it. A few hours later, when we're driving over to Alexandrov's house, I pointedly ask Raskovic for the first name of Perovic's father, his old friend. Raskovic studies something interesting out the window. "I don't know," he says.

We drive over to the home of his phenom, Alexandrov. Sitting in the living room with his parents and Raskovic, the boy indeed carries himself like a different breed. Unlike the Partizan players, he sees no benefit in staying with his team one day longer than necessary. Asked if anything can keep him in Belgrade next season, Alexandrov says, "For now? No."

His parents, Aleksander and Svetlana, live in a towering, four-story house, bewildered by the chaos building around their son. "We used to have a family life in a family house," his father says. "We were thinking for him and his older brother they were going to work with us in the real estate business, having them live next door."

"Everything is going around so fast," says his mother. "He's just a kid."

She goes to the kitchen, and comes back with a slice of some very sweet pie. "The most important thing is for him to be a good player ... " she begins.

"And not to freak out," says his father. "Not to see himself as more important. To stay normal, average person. Not to be hit by the glory. He has to carry the glory in the right way."

But hearing all this, Nemanja doesn't seem the least concerned. He shows off the battered hoop where he learned to play in the courtyard. He leads the way into his bedroom, and explains the different team photos on the wall in his bedroom, including the one that, like the torch-passing photo of a teenage Bill Clinton shaking hands with JFK, shows an eleven-year-old Alexandrov meeting Vlade Divac at basketball camp. So fast? For Nemanja, it can't come fast enough. Asked if he's worried that what happened to Detroit center Darko Milicic—a year spent sitting on the bench—could happen to him, he says, "I think about it, but I think I will be different. Different position: I don't know. Maybe." He shrugs.

Nemanja leaves the bedroom and sits back down where his parents are. He has a diamond stud in his left ear, a new iPod in his room. Now that his deal with Reebok has been settled, he's decked out in a fresh set of gray velour sweats, the logo stitched over his heart. "Look at him," says Raskovic with a puzzled grin. It's the first time I've seen the agent even slightly at a loss, as if he's come face-to-face for once with a phenomenon—Slavic ambition wrapped in a hip-hop aesthetic—beyond his ability to absorb, much less articulate. He kicks at Alexandrov's shoe. "He's wearing this—excuse me—street stuff, black." I can't tell if this is criticism or praise.

It doesn't matter. Everyone is wondering whether Alexandrov will be in Belgrade in 2005, but they're missing the point. The song of America is in the air. The kid is already gone.

Ten

Never, never, never believe any war will be smooth or easy, or that anyone who embarks on the strange voyage can measure the tides and hurricanes he will encounter. The statesman who yields to war fever must realize that once the signal is given, he is no longer the master of policy but the slave of unforeseeable and uncontrollable events.

Winston Churchill

In the hills, the French nights unfold with a lovely sameness. Our kitchen explodes in a dinnertime frenzy that, contrary to all parental notions of presleep calming, winds the kids into a leaping pack of hyenas; our too loud, too harsh English ("Dammit, do as I *say*!") spills out of the shutters, bounds over the graveled roads and vine-covered walls, and lands, surely, plop onto the civilized tables of our neighbors. From them, of course, we never hear a word. The nearby houses remain hushed, and the wind brings only murmurs, an occasional clink of crockery from somewhere unknown. The sky goes gray with streaks of peach, darkens to purple, bleeds into black. The scars on the rock faces we've named fade; the hills become looming shadows. One by one, lights in Greasque, in St. Savournin, in Cadolive and Mimet disappear, and the darkness is broken only by the squawk of dogs and crickets, a plane descending into Marseille. This has gone on for nine months. Then, on May 19, Olympique de Marseille plays Valencia in the UEFA Cup final, and the hills start to speak.

This is a surprise. The UEFA Cup is Europe's secondary soccer championship, a sop for those not good enough for the Champions League, and OM was knocked out of that the November night I saw them at Stade Velodrome. Winning the UEFA Cup certifies nothing so much as second-rateness; you are king of the mediocre, the best lesser light of the year, like a college basketball team crowned champion of the NIT. Why, I wonder, does anyone care? But then, I'm still digesting the European sports mentality. The Chicago Cubs haven't won a World Series in almost a century, and until they do their fans will feel as if they've won nothing. But European soccer dispenses baubles to seemingly everyone. English weekends are loaded with championships come spring; even after its shockingly poor 2003–04 campaign, Man U still manages to pick up some "hardware" by winning the once-vital FA Cup. OM is nowhere near the crooked heights it climbed in the early '90s, but contesting the UEFA Cup final means progress, and in so stratified a culture, I suppose, the merest upward movement is cause for celebration.

Indeed, since the night I saw them, the fortunes of Real Madrid and Olympique de Marseille have oddly reversed. It's as if Zidane somehow jinxed himself by going, despite misgivings, against his own people. Real's *Galacticos* have fallen with an even more colossal bang than Man U; its addiction to high-profile strikers and big-name signings for the sake of ticket sales has proven disastrous. Beckham is the convenient symbol: Just last weekend, Real lost an unthinkable fourth straight to sink to third in the Spanish *Liga*, and the Brit star, dreamy locks exchanged now for a shaved dome, got thrown out of Real's final games for cursing an official. He looks awful. His game has gone flabby. Drained from a tabloid holiday over his supposed infidelties, not to mention a wife determined to slurp up any stray celebrity to drop from his cup, Beckham resembles nothing these days so much as a convict on the run. He has always been a sweet man, a kind of innocent, but criticism follows him now from Brighton to Barcelona. When a club like Real Madrid loses, everyone goes to jail.

Marseille, meanwhile, fired its coach in midseason, replaced him with a longtime assistant and began to play with conviction. Its luck changed as a late-blooming striker, Didier Drogba, began collecting goals like a Ronaldo. Now it's the UEFA Cup final, and once again the Bouches-du-Rhone region finds itself depending on an African import; Drogba's rough-and-tumble game had been carved out in the Ivory Coast. I sit to watch the game on TV and remember the words of a local publisher named Francois over dinner just two weeks before.

"The liberals at dinner parties will never say this, but we actually support the U.S. in Iraq for the worst reason: Because we don't like Arabs. They're not like us," he said. "Yes, the Bush administration has done badly, acted clumsily and arrogantly at the same time, but we know Saddam was a bad guy. He had to go. And, really, we don't like them ..."

So is the dark-skinned Drogba French? Is the immigrant Drogba Marseille? The game kicks off, and I begin to hear grunts, whoops, and yelling. At first I think it comes from the TV, but then Valencia scores just before halftime and I go to the terrace and voices rise out of the trees, the darkness, dismay, and yearning igniting the countryside. When Valencia scores again to effectively seal matters twelve minutes into the second half, I'm ready; I sprint outside and listen to the "Agggghh!!!s" hopping from house to house, the stray *Allez!* rising in the universal tone of someone about to punch a wall. And I remember: *Marseille has only one thing: Olympique de Marseille and Olympique de Marseille.*

Four days later, Fran and the kids take me to the Marseille train station. An eleven-hour ride to Paris isn't my choice: Every high-speed train, every flight out of Marseille is booked, and I have to get there for the 2004 French Open. Everyone hugs me and I kiss each child, but Fran and I are years past a *Casablanca* good-bye. The kids alternate between chasing each other around the station, begging for a snack, or looking at me like a traitor. I am the man who comes and goes. Fran kisses me and tells me to call, but beneath that is the silent accusation: Off you go again.

I have no defense. The work may be hard, but by traveling I still get to eat in peace, indulge in adult conversations, think. Even today, I'm the lucky one: What should be monotonous torment turns out to be the opposite. I step on the train, into a first-class cabin. The French national railroad is your basic commuter line, and no sane Frenchman would book it for a Sunday marathon, so my car sits half empty, rolling slow by the sparkling sea and farmland, slower still through vertiginous mountain passes. It's like happening upon one of those travel channels when nothing else is on; once you give in, there's something hypnotic about seeing life reduced to a series of gorgeous scenes framed in glass. We chug through towns made insignificant by the TGV and highways, lives obscured by man's endless need for speed. The sun gleams under a perfect sky. I place the iPod buds in my ears, open one of my five newspapers. Fran would never forgive me if she knew. I can do little but stare and read, and remember.

No amount of writing, no amount of reading, no journalism school, no professor—and certainly not the most generous reservoir of energy and desire—can make up for what amounts to the writer's moment of truth. This moment is particularly important for the writer of nonfiction, slave as we are to the tyranny of fact, quotes, numbers, and the verifiable biographies of the endlessly chronicled. Anyone who dedicates themselves to fiction understands at once that he conjures up a world and must think like God. Such a notion contravenes every instinct of the journalist; indeed, the mere voicing of such a thing in an American newsroom would prompt derisive howls. But without that explosion of ego, the writer is doomed to a life of frustrating mediocrity, years of stringing together paragraphs of juicy quotes and unprecedented information with no hope of making it stand together and sing. I know this. I know because for years I was awful. Then my moment came.

Understand: I am under no illusion. I have won awards, been anthologized, published a book that received sterling reviews. I have been told by readers that my stories brought them to tears; I have been treated by bosses as if I were as vital as presses and ink. But no one knows my limitations better than I, and the fact is that I am a good writer at best. This is no complaint. I came so close to a life of mediocrity, so close to being plagued forever by the torture of recognizing superb writing without being able to produce anything approaching it myself, that I will gladly take good. A few years after I had dug in at the *Miami Herald*, a newly minted writer for a small paper in Connecticut, fevered by ambition and a near cultish obsession with sportswriting, went out of his way to say he admired my work. But he was puzzled. "I went to the Library of Congress and looked up all your stuff from Sacramento," he said, and then paused. His mouth set into a line and then twisted, as if trying to contain a truth politeness urged him not to voice. But he couldn't help himself. "You weren't very good," he blurted finally.

He didn't have to tell me. My bosses there gave me so much time and space and opportunity that it stuns me still, considering my output. I got one intriguing assignment after another: Larry Bird in Indiana, Doug Flutie in Boston, former gang-banger Kevin Mitchell at home in San Diego, basketball coach Don Nelson as he scouted Mitch Richmond in Kansas, the '87 earthquake in L.A., the Bash Brothers in Oakland. I tried, Lord knows; I worked seventeen-hour days, read everything, ginned up my copy with song lyrics and knowing asides and gimmick leads, Letterman posings and silly puns, tried on voice after fradulent voice. Nothing worked. Soon I was twenty-seven, and *the goddamn thing just wouldn't come.*

Then, in July 1989, I covered a truly forgettable fight: Mike Tyson against Carl "The Truth" Williams in Atlantic City. Those few days beforehand, the whole smorgasbord of loony-toon sports was laid out for me— Don King screaming *Arigato!* to Japanese journalists; Tyson at his genuine, ferocious peak; The Truth nattering on about his "genetic schematic," all of it taking place in the seedy confines of America's ugliest resort town. But I didn't really see what I was immersed in until I picked up a *New York Post* and read a column by Pete Hamill. Hamill is one of the deans of the New York school of New Journalism, and when I tried to tell him years later what he did for me, he had no idea what I was talking about. But then, the great ones don't think it so much as breathe it; being God is almost second nature. On that day, Hamill caught a moment the rest of the world ignored: Carl Williams sitting with his entourage in a hotel coffee shop, eating lunch a few days before the fight. Hamill watched him.

He wrote down every detail, every bit of conversation he could catch. He caught the revealing light of the coffee shop and laid it between the words you read, the words about a second-rater hurtling toward his greatest chance and greatest sorrow, toward a certain destruction that, indeed, would take all of 93 seconds. Hamill captured the fear behind the bragging, one man's titanic struggle not to flinch. By reading it, you felt the truth without being told: Here's a man at a circus. Soon the smiling faces will fade. Soon, he'll be alone with a new kind of hurt.

When I looked up from the page, I could barely breathe. I looked around. Everyone in the place kept eating: Mouths chewing french fries, a face hunched over a spoon dripping soup. My leg pumped up and down like a piston.

The audacity: Hamill interviewed no one, quoted nobody, cited no inside knowledge, made no grand claims. No journalism school would teach such a thing. Usually, a reporter—this reporter—would have sat down with "The Truth" and recorded his half-baked thoughts, trying to catch a revealing word, and then rustled up quotes from his friends and trainer to convey some semblance of "fairness." Hamill just watched. He listened. He took in every detail, that mundane moment made profound because of the money and attention and public violence to come. He took the universal act of a man eating lunch and made it as specific as a single cube of ice. He inserted his ice pick, poked and twisted it 'til it had lodged dead-center, held that one instant up to the light. Hamill didn't try to impress with clever wordplay. The story wasn't about him. The story was Carl Williams, but one reading would tell you that Williams, his entourage, the scene, the fight, Tyson, New Jersey—all of it—was working for Hamill. It was *his* story. Everyone worked, fought, spoke, and ate for his piece and the insights on the human condition he wanted you, the reader, to pick up without even knowing. Start to finish, Hamill decided that he *knew*, and because of his confidence the reader was convinced, too.

Now I couldn't wait to get to the fight. I couldn't wait to start typing. As Memphis George put it: You ain't no good if you don't steal. So from Hamill I stole tone. I stole authority. Most important, I stole

Hamill's attitude like a thief handed a bankcard and pin number. Now *I* knew. Now I was in charge. Now the action, the athletes, the quotes and notes—all of that was working for me. I took the leap; I decided that I understood Tyson and his entourage. I wrote a follow-up piece full of cheap psychology and astounding errors: a flip dismissal of opinions by people who knew better than I, a laughable line about Tyson swearing off drink. While everyone else was predicting his demise, I predicted a long era of Tysonian dominance. I filed it thinking I had transformed sports journalism. I felt like I'd mined gold.

Six months later, James "Buster" Douglas knocked Tyson out. If I'd had any illusions about the impact of the piece then or later, they were lost after Douglas's big night in Tokyo; nobody bothered to chide me for my callowness. I never heard a word about it, good or bad.

For a first effort, though, it wasn't horrible. Instead of straight reporting, a jazzed-up Associated Press recitation, I established a voice and went for broke. I had read something in Tyson I was sure no one else had seen—never mind that plenty had—and that something hit me like a well-aimed stone. Everything went toward proving the ultimate point: Tyson was a child desperate for limits, a bully begging to be stopped. For the first time, I used sports to probe a man's character, and by writing it I had learned something. I was sure I was a bit wiser. The dirty secret of journalism is that the best writing has almost nothing to do with objectivity; Hamill taught me that. The reporter must be fair, talk to everyone, notice everything. But then the writer must take over, decide his point and marshal the material. It's a gamble, because Keats was right: "Beauty is truth, truth beauty—That is all/Ye know on earth and all ye need to know." When a writer nails his subject, it wields power no matter what the words. When he doesn't, no amount of beautiful language can save him. My Tyson piece is near worthless, because 98 percent of it is wrong. I really got only one thing right.

Thirteen years after Atlantic City, after Tyson had threatened to eat his children and crush his skull, Lennox Lewis humiliated Tyson for eight rounds in crusty old Memphis. It was June of 2002, and Lewis bullied the bully, bloodying his face before knocking him out. Iron Mike's strange mystique died for good then, and the aftermath confirmed the one true thing I had seen years before. Cornered by cameras in the ring, Tyson stood next to Lewis looking reduced, broken, oddly shy. "There's no way I could ever beat him," he said of Lewis. "He's just too big and strong." Then, as Lewis answered a question, Tyson did something even more shocking than chomping an ear. So tenderly, he reached up and wiped blood off Lewis's face. Watching at home, I leapt to my feet and hovered close to the TV. There it was at last: Mike Tyson in love.

I've always relished sparring with the French writers when we meet in London or New York or Paris, wry little debates about American intentions and French pretensions, American bumbling and American greatness, French weakness and French pride. They have Latin America or the Shah of Iran in their holsters, of course, and cornered on some point, I'm not shy about reaching for the biggest clubs—how we had saved France's bacon in World Wars I and II, how we had taken on the Panama Canal because the French couldn't finish the job, and, hey, nice work on that "impregnable" Maginot Line! Effective!—winking at my lack of subtlety but wielding it nonetheless. Droll, *non*?

It was a fun game in the fat and quiet Clinton era, but I know things will be more complicated this time. Being an American abroad under the best of circumstances exposes nerves never stimulated at home; you feel your country more intensely, care more about how it's viewed, whipsaw endlessly between patriotic pride and defensiveness. Now all that has been stretched to the extreme. The sixtieth anniversary of D-Day will fall on the French Open's final Sunday, and the quaint blending of American sacrifice and French gratitude will unfold in the context of an American plague year. A month ago, the scandal at Abu Ghraib prison broke and blackened the Bush administration's suspect action in Iraq; American soldiers had tortured Iraqi prisoners, it turns out, hooding and hooking them up to faux electrodes, stripping them of clothing, forcing them into humiliating sexual positions. Men were forced to lie on men, to simulate oral and anal sex, their skin bleached yellow by camera flash. The photos ran around the world. A female American soldier stood pointing at one victim's penis, cigarette cocked and thumb raised, wearing a smile as wide as Texas.

The next morning, I take the Metro out to Roland Garros. Almost too soon, I bump into my favorite antagonist, Cecile Soler of *Le Figaro*. We sit for lunch. As usual, she is more gracious, allowing me to broach the subject, and she then sits quietly when it becomes clear she's made a mistake. When I start talking, I can't muster any of the lightness that usually frames our skirmishes. Instead, a dam breaks; all the words spinning in my head for the last month come in a rush. I spin out my theory, a half-baked stew of op-ed opinions, too much coffee, and a view of the United States formed by a youthful obsession with 1940s postage stamps, that . . . *Abu Ghraib is the latest and most damning manifestation of "ends justify the means" cultural rot that overran the U.S. in the go-go '80s, laced with reborn Reagan patriotism-lite, and now it has filtered down to the institution that, in its pioneering of race relations, its quiet example as the nation's ultimate meritocracy, had, despite excesses like My Lai, proven itself time and again as an example of the best of what America has to offer . . .*

People stop by our table to say hello. I halt, midword, take a bite. They go away, I finish the word and hurtle on. I have a vague sense that I should back off, slow down somehow, but my brakes have failed. Now I'm careening downhill.

. . . *60th anniversary of D-Day, right? Well, the U.S. won the peace in Europe after World War II* (Jesus, I can see her thinking, are we going *there* again?)—*because the American foot soldier didn't rape and pillage his way across the continent in a victory spree, because the Marshall Plan* (Christ!) *offered an open hand and not a clenched fist, because the animating core of American action, no matter how corrupt or misguided, shoved the balance to the plus side of the ledger and gave the U.S. the world's benefit of the doubt . . .*

Cecile looks down at her plate. My food is getting cold, but I can't stop. I know that voice, of course. I had heard it every day of my boyhood, the voice of Parris Island and the G.I. Bill, the voice of history as I know it. Now I'm getting louder. This isn't a chat. It's a harangue.

. . . We could always console ourselves that we were different, better, because we weren't just about power and force and money, we were the example the world could follow. Yes, this opens us up to the charge of hypocrisy, but wouldn't it be a tragedy if there wasn't one human entity pushing fitfully, clumsily, but pushing us all toward an unreachable ideal? Of course! But now, the message sent by Abu Ghraib is: No. We're fighting a criminal band that plays by no rules, so we must suspend the rules that made us unique. Torture? Sure. Bullying? Smile for the cameras. This is a war of ideas, we keep being told, but now the idea we're sending is simple: View us by what we do, not by the principles we're supposed to be about. We are just like everyone else now . . .

I take a sip of water. The air hovering over Roland Garros is thick, humid, filled with the muffled announcement of tennis scores. The matches are well under way. My voice has gotten husky suddenly, I feel my eyes stinging. My father was in the military, I say. He would've been sickened by Abu Ghraib.

Cecile, I suddenly realize, hasn't said a word. She stands up to go, for the first time looking at me with something approaching worry. But she has matches to see. I stay behind at the table. The sweat trickles down my back. After a while, when no one is looking, I stand up to go watch tennis, too.

It is, as always, a strange Open. The French is the most unpredictable Slam, its crushed-brick surface—*La Terre Battue*—the slowest on tour, its roll of champions filled with one-hit wonders from Spain or South America who rarely make a dent elsewhere. It's also the sport's most stylish and strategic event, and though Chris Evert, Jim Courier, and Jennifer Capriati have won here, it's the Slam that Americans find most difficult. The greatest U.S. player, Pete Sampras, famously never won the French. American players don't grow up playing on clay, but Philippe Bouin of *L'Equipe*, of course, has a more intriguing theory: "It's the most foreign Slam, the one that feels most like foreign soil. This is the only Slam with a foreign language, where they don't speak English, and they don't know how to cope with it. Americans like it best when they can impose their American way, and when they can't they get . . . *afraid*."

For me, such an alienating atmosphere produces the opposite effect. In the dislocating confines of Roland Garros, I usually feel oddly at home. But this past year has made me jumpy; living in France has forced my contrariness into a corner. I've been reading about all the France-baiting back in the States: Everyone knows what nation "cheese-eating surrender monkeys" refers to, and Republicans have spent the spring and summer of '04 getting cheap laughs out of John Kerry's ability to speak French. Senator Trent Lott called the Democratic presidential nominee "a French-speaking socialist," Commerce secretary Don Evans mused that Kerry "looked French," and House Majority leader Tom DeLay opened speeches by saying good afternoon, then adding, "Or as John Kerry might say, *'Bonjour,'* " to raucous applause. France is, more than ever, cultural and political enemy No. 1 for Americans, and the feeling is mutual; a recent French poll has given Bush a negative rating of 85 percent. I hurry over to the bull ring court just in time to hear 47-year-old Martina Navratilova, an American citizen who defected from Czechoslovakia, during her first-round loss yelling, "God Bless America!" after an error. A French crowd that has cheered her every move and utterance sits silent for that one.

Yet as the tournament churns on day after day, the most jarring sign of American displacement, the sight that sparks for me dozens of daily "we're-not-in-Kansas-anymore, Toto" moments, is written in English. Just off Roland Garros's main square with its dashing statues of France's original tennis greats—Borotra, Brugnon, Lecoste, and Cochet—tucked in among benign shops selling rackets and sandwiches and shirts, sits the storefront office of "Al Jazeera Sports Network." The news wing of the Qatar-based network, of course, has become a controversial nuisance in the U.S. adventures in Afghanistan and Iraq, broadcasting messages from Osama bin Laden and showcasing far bloodier footage of American acts than its counterparts in New York. I step in with a few questions, and the men in charge of Al Jazeera Sports insist that they have no interest in politics, even admit that their coverage from Paris might stretch Muslim cultural boundaries. If Serena Williams wears pink hot pants, highlights go on the air. "Not a big problem," says network spokesman Ivan Blum. "But we don't do beach volleyball women. That's too much."

Blum goes on to say that Al Jazeera Sports scrambles like any other network to report the result of top-ranked American stars, and focuses on Arab tennis successes like the fabulously gifted men from Morocco. But there's one line it will not cross. Even though Morocco's Hicham Arazi has made a deeply symbolic move here by playing doubles in Paris with Israel's Harel Levy, Al Jazeera has no plans to run a feature on the two; they will not, in fact, even report the news of their first-round loss. "Anything with Israel we don't show," senior producer Faris Zaki says during a break. Why make enemies out of their viewers? "They won't like it," he says. "It's painful . . . Everyone will be against us."

The best policy, then, is to treat Israeli players the way many in the Arab world would like to treat Israel: as if it didn't exist. "Americans in sport are very distinguished; we can't ignore them," Zaki says. "But with Israel we can turn a blind eye. As if nothing happened."

Whatever the reason, the 2004 French quickly shapes up as an American disaster. On Day 1, just a few hours after my lunch with Cecile, Andre Agassi suffers the worst loss of his career to a French qualifier named Jerome Haehnel, a homeboy upset that has even the hometown conflicted. At thirty-four, Agassi has become beloved by the French crowds: In 1999, he began the last, best stage of his career by winning in Paris and beginning his romance with future wife Steffi Graf. With his postvictory bows and kisses, his ability to construct nonanswers out of a whirl of words, he carries himself with a flair many on the continent find attractive. The fact that Agassi calls the '99 French the most memorable win of his career doesn't hurt; the French secretly love it when an American deems them important. But now it looks as though Agassi has come to the end of things. "Who's kidding who? We don't have that many matches left," says Agassi's trainer and close friend Gil Reyes outside the locker room after. "We're down the homestretch. All I ask is that we don't limp through the finish line."

His putative replacement, Andy Roddick, at the moment world No. 1, isn't making friends in the meantime. In the afternoon, after arguing with

Nikos Polias, Greek marathon runner, Panathinaiko Stadium, December 2003
(Photo courtesy of Bob Martin/*Sports Illustrated*)

Gaddafi Stadium, Lahore, March 2004 (Photo courtesy of Bob Martin/*Sports Illustrated*)

Guard, Gaddafi Stadium, Lahore, March 2004
(Photo courtesy of Bob Martin/*Sports Illustrated*)

Batmaker, Multan, March 2004 (Photo courtesy of Bob Martin/*Sports Illustrated*)

Shoaib Akhtar bowling a bouncer to Sachin Tendulkar, Multan, March 2004
(Photo courtesy of Bob Martin/*Sports Illustrated*)

Street cricket, Multan, March 2004 (Photo courtesy of Bob Martin/*Sports Illustrated*)

Tim Howard, American goalkeeper, Manchester, February 2004
(Photo courtesy of Bob Martin/*Sports Illustrated*)

Nemanja Alexandrov, basketball player, Belgrade, May 2004
(Photo courtesy of Bob Martin/*Sports Illustrated*)

Christos Tzekos and Kostas Kenteris, Athens, December 2003
(Photo courtesy of Bob Martin/*Sports Illustrated*)

Adam Nelson, American shotputter, Olympia, August 2004
(Photo courtesy of Bob Martin/*Sports Illustrated*)

Malgorzata Sobieraj, Polish archer, Athens, August 2004
(Photo courtesy of Bob Martin/ *Sports Illustrated*)

Kite flying at Mont Sainte-Victoire, December 2003 (Photo courtesy of Justin Gillis)

Addie, Jack and Charlie, Greasque, December 2004 (Photo courtesy of Fran Brennan)

the chair umpire in his win over compatriot Todd Martin, Roddick is booed as he walks off the court. Two days later, Roddick sums up the great American failure when, after snapping during a third-set contretemps at the chair umpire, "I am smart enough to know when I start my fucking motion. It's not rocket science," he loses to 125th-ranked Frenchman Olivier Mutis. Roddick is the last of ten Americans beaten in Paris—five of whom have gone down at the hands of Frenchmen—and, for the first time in the Open era at any Grand Slam event, no American advances to the third round. Mutis has beaten two of them himself. When asked in his press conference about the damage he's done to Franco-American relations, he puts on a mock-sad face and says, in English, "Sorry." Then, in French, he smirks and adds, "I said it was a good draw to play the Americans—and I was right."

That Mutis takes pleasure in beating back the Yanks is no shock, I guess, considering Roddick's stature and the love-hate relationship between the two cultures. In 2003, the crowd at Roland Garros booed Serena Williams so savagely for a legitimate protest that she wept. It's not just the desire to see an upset that prompts it: With her dominance then, her spectacular muscles literally dwarfing all her peers, Serena was a picture of American might—and who in Paris didn't like seeing the cocky American humbled by diminutive Belgian Justine Henin-Hardenne? This year, though, the atmosphere is more charged; all Europe has bottled up emotions seeking release. I scan an essay in the June 5–6 *International Herald Tribune* by Josef Joffe, editor of Germany's *Die Zeit,* that's impressive as much for its honesty as its insight.

"On the 60th anniversary of D-Day, Europe is awash in a tsunami of anti-Americanism that is light-years removed from a rationally argued critique of U.S. behavior in Iraq," Joffe writes, and after touching on Bushist behavior and the natural antipathy the weak harbor for the strong, he cuts to the core with a laser directed at Germany, Europe, but France most of all. "Rational reasons cannot explain the sheer contempt and loathing of America. Maybe Freud can help. He would probably mumble: 'Go back to D-Day and recall that we hate those most who helped us most.' We will never forgive the Americans for saving us so often from our own worst failures.

"America is a constant reminder of Europe's catastrophes; hence the irresistible urge to even the score by stripping Uncle Sam of the last vestiges of moral worth. Unwilling or unable to use power, post–cold war Europe must still turn to the United States when the Balkans flare up and bad guys like Slobodan Milosevic need chastening. And then there is Temptress America, a culture that radiates outward and pulls inward. Europe eats, listens, dances and dresses American, and if the lure of low culture weren't enough, there is the glamour of U.S. universities that makes the worst anti-American diatribe usually end with: 'Can you help get my daughter into Harvard?' "

I have seen this myself. Cecile Soler, for all her critiques, rates American men superior to the French and considers any year a waste if it doesn't include some time in Miami. Philippe and Jocelyne, bewildered by American politics, can't wait for their visit along the East Coast next year. Born in Canada, raised in Florida, but holder of a French passport because of her French mother, Mary Pierce has run a strange course with the French public. With her background and fractured accent few consider her French in anything but name, and they embraced her at arm's length when she won the 2000 French Open crown. She is respected here, nothing more. Unlike Mauresmo, Pierce's name never appears in lists of favorite French athletes. But she has seen life from both sides, and her assessment of gut-level regard is crude but on target. "Americans don't like the French; they think they're rude and arrogant," Pierce tells me. "And the French don't like Americans because they think they're loud."

The nice thing about national cliches is that they can be applied to anyone. The French complain about American arrogance, too, and they're more than capable of shouting. My first Tuesday at the Open, I return to my Left Bank hotel and turn on the TV to see a panel discussion program devoted to immigration. Everyone on the panel, curiously enough, is white. A leftist member of the European Parliament, Daniel Cohn-Bendit, sits red-faced and roaring at Marine Le Pen, the grinning blond daughter of Jean-Marie, in a back-and-forth that might well have been lifted from CNN's *Crossfire*.

"Zinedine Zidane is French!" Cohn-Bendit says.

"Non!" Marine says, the smile gone from her face.

"Zinedine Zidane is French!"

"Non!"

"Zinedine Zidane is French!"

"Oo-la-la . . ." Marine says, tossing her hair.

The fortnight unrolls, as expected, amid a daily barrage of newspaper stories, documentaries, tributes to the American troops from long ago— historical navel-gazing both banal and stirring. The French compare their gratitude then with attitudes now, relations then and relations now, Bush to FDR, the ignorance of a new generation to the work of the old. Everyone notes how it will likely be the last big anniversary to draw a large group of veterans; they're dying off daily. At Roland Garros, writers and TV produc- ers cast about for a convenient symbol of Franco-American amity or con- flict, a reason to wave a flag or hold a moment of silence, *something* for D-Day weekend. But once the American women also go bust at Roland Garros, the search for an emotionally resonant result leads only to Mau- resmo, the tour's hottest player on clay. Despite an elegant and powerful game, because, perhaps, of her too-inquisitive, too-balanced mind, the twenty-four-year-old Frenchwoman has never gotten past the quarterfinals at her home Grand Slam, and employs a psychologist to help deal with the pressure. Now she's hoping that her policy of not reading newspapers, not chatting with strangers during the Open, can somehow change her luck.

Now, after rolling into the quarterfinals again, Mauresmo says she's ready. But, she tells me, she could never be as loose as, say, the 2003 U.S. Open champ Roddick because "we're not raised the same way. Ameri- cans in New York don't handle the pressure the same way we do as French in Paris. We have different culture and different ways of handling things. I see what Roddick was doing, he was very open. But I like the idea of being focused on what I have to do." She smiles ruefully, as if knowing that this year's result, like all the rest, is inevitable.

"Maybe," she says, "next year I will do it like him."

Two days later, Fran takes the TGV up from Aix. It's one of her few chances at freedom: We've been in France nine months, and her dream of day trips to cool villages, overnights to Rome or London or Paris, has dissolved into a long slog of holding down the fort; she's the prisoner of Greasque. Now a babysitter has come through, and she is free for twenty-four hours. She arrives at Roland Garros, bag in hand, and I've got tickets. Tonight there will be dinner, and tomorrow a stroll at the overpriced art shops around the hotel. But this is the prize; it has been years since we've seen a tennis match together. We rush to our seats, twenty rows up, dead center: Perfect.

Mauresmo walks out over the red clay to play Elena Dementieva, and the thousands watching try a delicate dance: to embrace—but not crush—her with their collective hope. We're not nearly as invested. A great match would be nice, but it's in the breaks of the action that Fran and I rediscover our old rhythm: Scoffing at the half-baked comments of the spectators around us, pointing out faces in the crowd, laughing at the dozens of human gestures, expressions, foibles on display. We watch people and talk about them. We giggle at our snarky commentary. I tell about my chat with Mauresmo, and how much I'd like her to win. This might be her best chance. So we pull for Amelie together.

She can barely swing the racket. Dementieva crushes Mauresmo, France's last gasp, 6–4, 6–3, but long before it ends the scene becomes both pathetic and boring. It's astonishing how quickly one's sympathy drains away: Mauresmo has repaid our hope and support with not even a hint of struggle, so now we just want her to go. As she wanders in puzzled silence on the red clay, picking at her racket strings, we amuse ourselves by concentrating on the two old, great French players urging her on. At one end of the stands, Yannick Noah glowers with his hand over his face. On the other end, Henri Leconte keeps standing and sitting as the last points unwind, standing and sitting, slashing his hands about, face red and twisted as he yells at the sad woman down on the dirt.

Mauresmo doesn't look their way. She packs her rackets, hoists her duffel bag and walks off to polite applause, burdened still with the question of the day, year, age: Why must France so often lose?

Summer

Eleven

This is the period of life in which such moments of which
I have spoken are likely to come. What moments? Why,
the moments of boredom, of weariness, of dissatisfaction.
Rash moments. I mean moments when the still young are
inclined to commit rash actions, such as getting married
or else throwing up a job for no reason.
    This is not a marriage story. It wasn't so bad as that
with me.

Joseph Conrad, "The Shadow-Line"

The fan never understands. The fan always asks, "Really: What's he like?
Good guy? *Nice*?" He sees his hero enduring, overcoming, waving a flag,
happy, winning; he wants him to be kind, too. The fan doesn't want to
hear what I have to say: No. Your hero is not nice. The hero is never nice.
Each of the great athletes or coaches I've covered—Dean Smith, Magic
Johnson, Larry Bird, Sampras, Bill Walsh, Tony LaRussa, Joe Montana and
Jerry Rice, Barry Sanders, Shaquille O'Neal, Agassi, Tiger Woods   bears
at heart a cruelty that, unlike those of us who are taught to conceal it
from an early age, is rewarded each time it's revealed. You can't be a superstar without this cruelty, because high competition demands it: Boiled
down, you are beating another man, revealing his weakness before millions. Jordan is the era's exemplar; the fiercest of practice players, he
famously punched one Bulls teammate in the mouth, and derided
those who didn't meet his standards of toughness as "faggots." This

shouldn't shock. Winning is not just excelling; it's also a process of deny-
ing someone else, sometimes savagely, and no one can be great without
loving what they do. The best athletes are hot to the touch and cold at
heart, unburdened of the politesse that keeps civilization running. Nice
makes them losers. Professionally, sometimes even personally, nice only
leaves them dead.

Some greats, though, learn the virtue of disguise. Magic's cruelty hid
behind a smile made more beautiful by the fact that it was genuine, and
this was no contradiction; prisons are full of polite killers. As his fame
exploded, Jordan tried to match his on-court intensity with a well-tailored
suavity and an articulateness he never quite mastered. He rarely bad-
mouthed opponents, no matter how evident his distaste, and his
postgame remarks had about as much color as a bank statement. It's as if
Jordan was somehow trying to distance himself from himself, rise above
the passion he had so relished just minutes before, and the effect was
chilling. By the end of his career, his face was everywhere but his personality had been erased. Twenty years of celebrity, and he couldn't have
been more unknown.

Perhaps that distance was necessary. In April of 1992, I was writing
columns for the *Miami Herald* when Jordan came in with the Bulls to play
the Miami Heat. His fame had become madness by then; people parking
outside his house to photograph him playing with his kids, *Saturday Night
Live* getting its highest ratings ever when he hosted. In a few months, he
would go to the Olympics in Barcelona as the megawatt member of the
legendary Dream Team, its undeniable Elvis. The argument kept getting
made without rebuttal: With No. 23 jerseys being spotted in China, the
Middle East, deep Africa, Jordan had become the most famous man in the
history of the planet. This night, he had gone out to get a pregame man-
icure, and a crowd streamed behind him as he crossed the street. A TV
crew interviewed the manicurist. She said he had big hands.

I came upon Jordan telling this story in the cramped visitors locker
room at Miami's old downtown arena. This was during the forty-five-
minute period before the game when NBA locker rooms are open to the

media, and at the tail-end of an era that league executives look back on as a halcyonic sliver of bliss. In the years before his father was gunned down and Jordan left to play minor-league baseball and revelations of his gambling losses made him refer to the media with a derisive "you guys," Jordan would sit before his locker for the full forty-five, answer all questions, fill the notebooks of columnists in need of early copy and TV stations in need of early tape. His example set the tone for the entire league, and when Jordan soured so did the rest of the boys who wanted to be like Mike. Go to an NBA locker room before a game today in search of a star, and you half-expect tumbleweeds to scuttle over your feet.

"It becomes a big spectacle whenever I make a move," he was saying when I joined the half-dozen reporters circling around his chair. A man held a microphone to his lips. All of it was being videotaped; the cameraman broke the most basic rule of journalistic self-respect by interrupting to ask Jordan to sign his lens. Jordan waited for someone to call the man off, then shrugged and scribbled, saying, "You guys are something." He has always been smart enough to know that he didn't "deserve" his renown. When a parent would enthuse that he wanted his boy to be like him, Jordan would cringe.

"I didn't plan this," he would tell them. "I stumbled upon it."

It had been a couple years since we'd spoken. Within seconds it was clear that Jordan's early joy—the kick of fame—was gone. He spent most of his days surrounded by people he couldn't understand. "It's amazing what a name on a piece of paper, a name on a lens, can do for so many people," he said. "I never once, in my whole life, had the urge to ask for an autograph. When I saw Sidney Poitier from a distance, it wasn't like I had to run up and say, 'How you doin'? My name is Michael Jordan.' I'd look at him. I admired him. But I would keep on. That was just me."

He spoke of how he could trust almost none of the smiling faces, the agents, the media, the businessmen who filled his time off court. His friends were held by a common thread. The mortician, the insurance salesman, the supermarket supervisor, the lawyer: All of them came from his hometown or college, all of them were people he knew before 1983—the year he emerged as a college sensation. "They don't treat me differently," he said. "They're the reality of my life."

One by one, the other reporters drifted off, and suddenly it was just us, alone. I had always thought Jordan's eagerness to talk in the past was just so much idle patter, or at worst the celebrity trying to show off how he hasn't changed. But then I asked him to confirm a story, my favorite because it's so innocent in its arrogance, so fun. During the off-season between his freshman and sophomore years, Jordan had been crossing campus in street clothes, heading back to his apartment, when he came upon a group of fratboys playing pick-up ball. "Michael, play with us!" they yelled, and when he demurred because he couldn't risk getting hurt, one guy sang out, "Come on, Mike, I want to tell my grandkids I played ball with Michael Jordan" and threw the ball at his feet. At that, Jordan set down his bookbag and threw up a jumper that dropped through the net like a stone. Then he picked up his bag and said, over his shoulder, "Tell 'em that."

By the time I finished repeating this tale, everything about Jordan had changed. He had spent the previous half hour answering questions about the playoffs, being a role model, but now he sat back. A smile broke across his face. He began talking almost to himself, falling into the closest approximation of the word *reverie* that I'd ever seen. "That was about a half-court shot," he said slowly. "About a half-court shot . . . That was pretty funny . . ." His voice had lost all its professional edge, all that authority Jordan had picked up without even knowing it. Then he went quiet. I asked if it was hard to remember such a thing.

"Those are times I *try* to remember," he said. "It's not tough remembering those days, especially with what I deal with all the time now. It's not tough."

So I sat down next to him, and we went back. We started talking about those days, the people we knew. The Barcelona Olympics were coming in a few months: I speculated that it would be a long time before he could have that kind of life again. "I know," he said, blowing out the words in a whisper. "I've progressed to the point where you have to monitor everything that you do. I go to get my nails done, and people sit out there forty-five minutes . . . an hour . . ."

I mentioned one guy we knew, Scott . . . *something*, and for a few moments we both sat there hemming and gasping—"Man! What is it?"—trying to remember his last name. Once, in the summer after Jordan's freshman year, when I was tending bar and emptying garbage cans, Scott took me over to Granville Towers and we engaged in an absurd, shouted conversation in the parking lot with Jordan dangling out his apartment window. "The one who dressed up as a girl?" Jordan said, and he started to laugh.

And then Jordan put his hand on my arm and squeezed in the effort to remember, and he left it there, squeezing, squeezing, as we spoke, as if it were much too important a fact to let go. The locker room was closing. He had a game to play. But he needed to get back there.

"Scott . . . Scott . . . Remember? The guys who were homecoming queens?" Jordan said, his words picking up pace. "Those guys went to high school with me. One guy was Steve Latham, and the other . . . I can't remember his name . . . *Kendall! Scott Kendall!*"

Now we both were laughing, with the effort and the remembering and the way we had reeled in the memory. Sure: Scott Kendall wearing a dress.

"That was the best time of my life, in college," Jordan said. "I was able to do whatever I wanted, yet I was still enjoying the success of playing basketball for a big Division I school and a very promising career. The best time of my life . . ." He stopped and stared for a moment. "And I skipped out on my last year."

Now I knew. We weren't friends, not at all, but all those years when Jordan would feed me gossip or insider knowledge or just a heartfelt quote, he wasn't being generous. The money and fame had twisted his life into something unrecognizable, and though he was anything but tortured—fame fit him like an immaculate suit—Jordan needed to see faces like mine. He had known me then. I was a whiff of home.

So in a sense, I figure I'm prepared for Lance Armstrong. A five-time winner of the Tour de France now gunning for six, a survivor of testicular cancer, an American cocky enough to take on all of Europe needed a meanness, that get-the-fuck-out-of-my-way fire, to make it this far. But off the bike, he has also become a corporate creature, the heir to Jordan's crossover endorsement throne, and I go off to meet him sure that he, like Tiger Woods, has learned how to hold off the world's relentless eyes with a dull duality, a blandness designed to scare no man waving a dollar.

Quickly, I realize I'm wrong. Armstrong begins speaking about his teammates on the U.S. Postal squad, and how, the rest of the cycling year, he tries to switch roles and ride as a helper for them, and it becomes clear that he likes to manipulate. He likes to work the levers of self-interest. He likes, almost as much, to show how cold he can be. "I'm first in line to help out," Armstrong says. "Tyler Hamilton was on our team and won this race in 2000, and I worked eight days to help him win the race. For me it's absolutely no problem, especially for someone on the team. Because if you do a favor for somebody like that? Four weeks later, he's going to kill himself for you."

He's sitting on a bed. I've flown down from Paris, leaving the French Open on its final Friday and landing in Geneva and driving a few hours back over the border to the French mountain town of Megeve. In a few days, Armstrong will begin his final tune-up for the 2004 Tour with a prestigious little race known as the Dauphine Libere. I've come to talk to him for the magazine because what he's about to try is unprecedented, because Lance Armstrong may well be the most important American athlete of the new century, but at first what strikes me is his consideration. He had been driving, too, this day, across Switzerland after a holiday with his girlfriend, the singer Sheryl Crow. He called me time after time as delays pushed him far past our appointment. Indeed, Armstrong has made himself agreeable, flexible, even stripped himself naked for me; when I knocked on his door, he answered it dripping, having just emerged from the shower. His body is whippet-thin, of course, stringy and burned down to inhuman functionality by the sport's demands, and the absence of excess flesh makes his knobby head proportionally huge, eyes animal alert. Cycling's core irony is physical: Its supreme practitioners glow with the hollow beauty of stained-glass saints, yet too often appear beneath headlines about syringes and dumped pills. The nasty juxtaposition smacks too much of junkie aesthetics—the sacrifice of love, money, anything for one good fix.

A pair of racing shoes, a banana, an apple lay scattered on a table. It's near dinnertime, June in the mountains. The light in the room dims as night falls. Armstrong doesn't speak like a legend; better, he doesn't speak like someone protecting his own legend. What he has to say comes unfiltered, as if he has become immune to small worries over "perception." The fight against cancer made him more compassionate, friends tell me, more willing to write a letter to an ill stranger, but it also stripped him of the need for false comfort. Somewhere he had learned: No one saves a life only because it's the right thing to do. Given a less than 50 percent chance of surviving, with the cancer spreading to his lungs and brain, Armstrong found the clearest way to bend people to his will. He took his athlete's remorselessness and turned it outward, reading the selfishness in all those around him, using it to create selflessness. Wracked by chemotherapy, fatigue, despair, he still had the presence of mind to measure every face in the room.

"I tried to endear myself to these people," he says. "I tried to make this personal for them: nurses, doctors, X-ray techs. I didn't care. I was in there, thinking, 'I know you don't want to sit down on the side of my bed and tell some stories, but . . . have a seat and tell me some stories. Because I want you to *invest* here. When I go I want you to be upset. I want you to *want* me to make it.' I did everything I could to just be their friend. Perhaps that's what I do here."

His celebrity has grown well beyond standard issue, beyond, even, the lifelong fascination accorded mere Hall of Famers. Cancer patients everywhere use Armstrong's example as reason for hope, and on this day he wears on his wrist one of the new yellow rubber bracelets bearing the words, *LiveStrong,* that soon millions—including John Kerry on the campaign trail—will be wearing. Who, by now, doesn't want a piece of the Lance mojo? His name graces two best-selling books. With a 2-to-1 margin over second-place finisher Muhammad Ali, he has been voted the greatest role model of the last fifty years in a recent *Sports Illustrated* poll; he makes $16 million a year. His popularity, of course, is based on Armstrong's personal narrative but has little to do with him personally. His survival is the star. The cancer cut through hype. It has taken fans down past the shallow depths of celebrity, past the knowing wiseass patter of sports anchor America and into the bone-deep realm of character. What Armstrong has done is more important than what he's like, and indeed, if he has softened some, become a bit more polished and accommodating, no one describes him as intrinsically different. If anything, his back-from-the-dead success has only buttressed his self-importance. Who's going to argue with him? Isn't he alive, and better than before?

Later, I'll talk to Armstrong's most loyal colleagues, and it's amazing how many will use the word *arrogant* or *obnoxious* to describe their first impression. Jogi Muller's first meeting with Armstrong came during a race more than a decade ago, when he heard a twangy voice behind him demanding he move out of the way. "He came in as a great talent, but he was a Texan brat," says Muller, the media coordinator for Armstrong's team. "But he learned it's a European deal. And he's improved."

Armstrong keeps his friends and teammates close, but can be ruthless when he thinks they cross him. It is one of his regrets, Armstrong says, that when his close friend Kevin Livingston bolted in 2001 to race for another team Armstrong froze him out, as he casually puts it, "ice cold." This is not an isolated case. Christian Vande Velde left Postal in 2003 after five years, and he went respecting Armstrong as a leader. But injuries limited Van de Velde's contributions, and as they declined so did Armstrong's support. When asked if his illness changed Armstrong, Van de Velde says, "Lance is Lance. He's definitely the same more or less. He's definitely a very good businessman. Sometimes he doesn't let friendship come between him and business."

Spanish climber Roberto Heras also left Postal in 2003, and Armstrong can't be more dismissive. "Roberto's a good guy," Armstrong says. "But he never fit in with the team. When we're in the bus, the locker room, snapping towels and cranking up ZZ Top and laughing? He's not a part of that. Roberto didn't use this team to improve himself—didn't use our knowledge, didn't use our experience, didn't really care. Roberto's a good pro, but he could be a lot more professional."

It should be said that Vande Velde's assessment comes across less as criticism than description of a natural event, like a flash flood: It is what it is. He doesn't argue his diminishing usefulness to Postal, and when contacted Heras declines to respond to Armstrong's withering words because, in essence, he doesn't disagree. Just because Armstrong can be cold or harsh, it seems, doesn't mean he's wrong. Top athletes game out the pluses and minuses of ambition—the sacrifices made, the armor needed—as meticulously, if not as consciously, as any politician; somewhere along the way Vande Velde and Heras found themselves unwilling to lose a certain sensitivity, and God only knows how many Tour stages that cost them. More than any fan, they understand what it takes to win six Tours, and sweetness has nothing to do with it. Lance is Lance, they figure, and he wouldn't be what *Lance Armstrong* has come to mean without a scathingly critical eye, a superhuman focus. Armstrong knows he has paid the price in lost friends, lost time with his three kids, a broken marriage. But at thirty-two, he's also aware that he made the choice. He could have been like right-hand man George Hincapie, a man talented enough to win Tour stages and lead a team, who has instead carried Armstrong's water for each of his wins.

"We're not very similar," Armstrong says of Hincapie. "I've never heard him say a bad thing about another person ever; there's a lot of assholes in this world, and he's never crossed that line. I don't have the power or the magic to do that."

Such a manner may be *de rigeur* in locker rooms across America, but it's almost designed to irritate a French sensibility that likes its judgments softened with a civilized kiss on the cheek. Armstrong's lack of subtlety automatically leaves him out of the subgroup of Americans the French adore. He's not stylish or seemingly deep like Ali or Agassi or Clinton. But when he began his comeback in 1998, Armstrong's culture clash went deeper than etiquette. Unlike the U.S., a place with no cycling tradition and an audience conditioned since *Brian's Song* to celebrate any sports-beats-cancer story, France didn't accord his tale the same unblinking belief. For French media and fans, cycling is covered as exhaustively as the NFL in America, and constant drug revelations in the late 1990s had made the sport seem as much movable pharmacy as moveable feast. Armstrong admitted to using the banned blood-doping substance erythropoietin (EPO)—(legally, because he was off-tour at that time)—during cancer treatment in 1996 and '97. However, large segments of the European press and public can't believe that a man whose body had been so ravaged could come back stronger than ever—stronger, even, than a world-class field of cyclists who continue to use performance-enhancing drugs—without doping himself.

"We struggled—the French and I—for years to try to understand each other," Armstrong says. "I always loved the event, but it was me just trying to understand the event's place in their history, and them struggling with this guy coming along, acting very American, bringing a pretty unbelievable story on the heels of a lot of bad stories in cycling. So I had four years of real friction . . ."

In 1999 and 2000, French federal investigators probed Armstrong's team, and found, eventually, no reason to charge him. Spectators beside the road would yell, "Do-pe! Do-pe!" at Armstrong as he passed. Then, in March of 2003, "the war starts," he says. "For me, there's the war, there's Bush, and there's the fact that I'm from Texas and he's from Texas, the fact that I serve on his cancer panel, the fact that we could be viewed as friends, there's a lot of things where they could say, 'You're a bad guy.' The French don't support the war and the next thing you know: We hate them and they hate us. Sixty days before the Tour, I'm thinking, *These people are never going to let me finish.* Because the roads are open. If there's ten French guys who don't want you to win the Tour, you don't win. If there's one, you don't win. I'm thinking, 'I'm doomed.' "

Never mind that Armstrong opposed the war. "There's a lot of bad guys out there running small bad countries," he says. "Why not go and get them?" By June of 2003, the scenario was almost too rich to be believed: France's greatest sporting event, one that winds over country roads and torturous mountain passes and down the Champs-Élysée in annual invocation of Gallic soul, would be dominated by an American, and a high-strung, shoot-from-the-hip Texan at that. The problem with such a formulation, though, was that it assumed that all involved would revert to type. And as soon as the 2003 Tour began, no one did. Suffering from a stomach ailment and burdened by his divorce, Armstrong was anything but his usual unstoppable self. He avoided one crash by cutting through a cornfield, crashed when his handlebar got tangled with a spectator's purse, went into the penultimate day sure he would lose and ended up winning by just 61 seconds. For the first time, Armstrong had looked vulnerable. And the French crowds—contrary as always—embraced him as never before. "All the jeers and taunts from earlier years had totally gone away," Armstrong says. "The French fans were completely supportive."

That is about to change. A week later, I drive up from home to catch Armstrong's assault on Mont Ventoux—a wind-whipped peak in central France that, in its rock-strewn extremity and lack of vegetation, looks even under a blast of June sunshine like a black-and-white transmission from Mars. I race up in my rental car through insanely picturesque towns like Suze la Russe and Vaison La Romaine, past the occasional FN poster and the shirtless grandpa pedaling slow up its twisty miles, breaking through at last to see something resembling an Arctic outpost under siege. Hundreds of cars and campers line the road, thousands of fans tuck in along the few straightaways and the dozens of hairpin turns. The annual crash and clamor of race day has swamped the few permanent facilities—a TV antenna, an observatory, a few shops—into irrelevance. From Ventoux you can see the far-off outlines of Mont Blanc, Sisteron, a nuclear power plant, all of southern France laid out in pointing distance. A helicopter flies *up* to land near my lunch table. It makes a perverted kind of sense that Armstrong calls Ventoux his favorite stage in all of racing; the place is bony, hard, untouchable.

With all his victories in France, Armstrong has never beaten the mountain, and now it looks as if he never will. He loses the day's time trial and his shot at winning the Dauphine, though that's the least of his problems. Because everyone is now aware: What Armstrong calls a "National Lampoon book on Lance and drugs" is about to hit. When his post-Ventoux press conference opens in the village of Saint-Paul-Trois-Chateaux, all evidence of his recent detente with the French has disappeared. The unmoving air in the room swims with murmurs about Armstrong's loss, the latest rumor, drugs and—meatiest of all—his possible hypocrisy.

The morning papers are reporting that, the year before, Armstrong had written an e-mail alerting cycling authorities to the rising use of artificial hemoglobin by riders, and implied that his aim was to implicate the Spanish cyclists who had pressed him during his win in the 2003 Dauphine. Never mind that he never mentioned the Spanish. The fact is, Armstrong has never been content, like most cyclists, to merely deny doping use and hope the questions fade. He has been a loud advocate of antidoping measures but, in Europe anyway, his crusading assertions that he rides free of performance-enhancing drugs has always inspired much eye-rolling. Despite the fact that Armstrong has been repeatedly investigated—and declared clean—by French law enforcement and the sport's governing bodies, when you hear "Saint Lance" in French press boxes, it's always said with a sneer. So now the French antennae, ever primed for proof of American rhetoric at odds with American deeds, is quivering: Is he a snitch? A cheater? Both?

"The last five years, there has been some difficult relations with the French public," one French journalist asks. "Will you try to approach a bit more to the French public? Or you don't care?"

"What kind of a difficult relationship are we talking about?" Armstrong shoots back. "Today how many people were standing on the side of Mt. Ventoux? 100,000? Maybe? How many times did I hear something negative? Three individuals? Do you have a calculator?" He pauses, staring, long enough to let the man squirm. "It's not very many people. I'm very appreciative of the support, and I try my best to be as friendly as I can, I try to speak the language when I can. Let's not create a problem that's not there."

A few more questions, and then another French journalist turns the conversation to doping. He asks about Armstrong's e-mail, first reported in *Le Monde*. Armstrong asks if anyone from *Le Monde* is in the room. No answer.

"Surprise, surprise," he says. "Because they're *soooo* interested in cycling . . . I guess." Armstrong says how he's "fighting for cycling" by writing such missives, but "never—and I repeat never—were the Spanish ever implicated. And for a journalist to write in an article that I had a tough time in the Dauphine Libere and the e-mail came after the Dauphine because there were five Spanish riders in the first ten? That is complete nonsense. It's not correct, it's not fair, and it's not ethical—and I find it terribly ironic that they're not here to listen to the clarification."

The press conference limps to a close, and Armstrong walks out into the night. A cameraman, walking backward in front of him, films Armstrong under a spotlight as he signs autographs, shakes hands, passes the monument to war dead. He sees me, and grins. "Do you think I set the record straight on that?" he says. It isn't a question.

He knows he's asking for trouble. Not because "I attack them," as he says, but because soon the book will be front-page news and he can use some French friends. Armstrong isn't interested. He has little use for the French media—"These guys are sneaky, bad," he says. "A lot of them." And, besides, it feels good to lash out after a bad day.

"I love it," Armstrong says. "But it would've been better if he was there. Like the guy who asked the stupid question about the French people hating me? That was good; it was *there*. I had to take him on." He's wired in a way I didn't see the week before, energized by the tussle. We move into a small room off the lobby of his hotel. Armstrong sits at a table, runs a hand over hair trimmed to the length of a squirrel pelt. He has three weeks left before the Tour, and the day's events have convinced him to intensify his training. Armstrong doesn't like the taste of losing on Ventoux, and he doesn't like the French media questioning his motives. But he loves having both experiences for fuel: *You think I'm done?*

"I'm hungry," he says. "I'm hungrier than I was last year."

I try to get tricky now. I want to see what he has left. I tell Armstrong that, with five Tours in his pocket already, he doesn't really need to win a sixth. He's made his mark. His world won't end if he loses this year's tour . . .

He cuts me off. "I don't want to think that," Armstrong says. "If I do a great ride today? Iban Mayo beat the record by a minute: Say I beat it by two minutes and beat him by a minute? *Christ.* I'm sitting here, I'm probably having a fucking big old glass of wine at dinner, doing stuff I shouldn't be doing, thinking, 'I'm there!' Whereas now I'm in my room banging my head on the wall thinking: 'Aggh!' That's perfect. To me, that's what makes a champion."

The following week, *L'Express* magazine runs excerpts from *L.A. Confidential: The Secrets of Lance Armstrong*, a book by longtime *London Sunday Times* cycling reporter David Walsh and freelancer Pierre Ballester. In a searing assault on Armstrong's integrity, his former masseuse from 1999, a thirty-three-year-old Irishwoman named Emma O'Reilly, implies that Armstrong used EPO before his first-ever Tour win. She also alleges that he asked her for makeup to cover bruises on his arms caused by injections, gave her a bag of empty syringes to dispose of, and sent her to the U.S. Postal team's headquarters in Spain to pick two dozen unspecified pills for him. The book also regurgitates still-simmering questions about Armstrong's relationship with Michele Ferrari, an Italian doctor on trial since 2001 for prescribing and supplying riders with illegal drugs. Ferrari, who once equated taking EPO with a large dose of orange juice, is an acknowledged training expert whom Armstrong has worked with since 1999 and continues to consult with and defend because he hasn't been convicted. The timing can't be worse. Just a day later, Armstrong flies to Washington, D.C., for the press conference announcing his team's new sponsor for 2005–07, the Discovery Channel.

Driving back to his training home in Girona, Spain, one night later, Armstrong calls from his cell phone. He labels the charges "absolutely, positively false." I ask if he has in the past or is using performance-enhancing drugs, and Armstrong says, "For the millionth time: I don't do that. The team doesn't do that. Look at the record, look at the amount of controls, look at my activities within the sport—engaging with the governing bodies, engaging with the organizations to increase and to promote and to encourage the fight against doping. It's out there. Look at the two-year, French federal investigation. They looked everywhere: Blood, urine, hair, personal contacts, phone records, you name it—and . . . zero. *Zero*. It's pretty compelling."

He mentions a story in the *International Herald Tribune* from the day before, in which Walsh is quoted as saying that his book provides "all circumstantial evidence" and "we don't actually prove anything." Armstrong laughs. "I mean, what the heck is that?" he says. "That's got to be one of the dumbest statements known to man if you're about to get your ass sued left, right, and center."

I can't define his mood at first. Armstrong sounds neither scared nor defensive. He doesn't even sound all that angry. "We're going after her," he says of O'Reilly. She has no proof, he says, and she will have to prove what she says is true. The torrent of words forces me to scribble faster. Armstrong has hit his pace: "I've been attacked every day for five years and I could keep going, but I've had enough. Now we're going after all of them. How would you like it? If they did it once, you wouldn't go after 'em; you'd say, 'Alright, whatever dude' . . . "

Then I realize. Armstrong sounds like he did after the press conference in Saint-Paul-Trois-Chateaux, right after sparring with reporters. I can almost see his face: Lit up by the dashboard glow, teeth gleaming. "But they've been doing this five, six years? We're bringing it, man. It's *on*."

A long court battle? Nasty depositions? The risk of staining his reputation forever?

He sounds delighted.

Twelve

Retreat Hell! We just got here.

Attributed to several World War I Marine Corps officers,
Battle of Belleau Wood, France, June 1918

On a rainy Saturday in June, the day before we leave for Wimbledon, I take Jack to the police station in our town. The latest bank statement shows $1,600 charged in Belgrade long after I left that country; somebody at the Intercontinental stole my card number. I fill out a police report, and as the officer and I navigate around my choppy French, a burly man walks in with a boy. I'm having problems with my wife, he explains, we're divorcing and fighting in front of our son and . . . well, what should we do? The boy looks around the office, impressed. The French officer lifts an eyebrow, tosses out some kind, useless words and states the obvious: This isn't a matter for the police. The father inclines his head. The two walk out, and once the door clicks the officer stops scribbling. He looks at me from under his eyebrows, smiling almost shyly, as if I'd witnessed something embarrassing about his own family.

"It's a big problem here in France," he says. I nod knowingly. A few minutes later, a clamor of beeping car horns spill in from the street outside, and I've been around long enough to know it isn't about a soccer game. "Marriage?" I ask.

"That's the tradition," the officer says of the customary automotive salute to a just-ended wedding. "And often it ends up like that man and his boy."

The printer begins spitting out forms. I ask about guns in France, and the officer says they are strictly licensed, mostly available to the hunters we hear nightly, those echoes cutting through the hills at dusk. But, no, not just anyone can get a gun. "That's a big problem in the States, eh?" he says. "I see it on the news all the time."

I give him this, agree it's a problem; now we're even. Jack, though, keeps staring at the pistol on his hip. The officer's face softens. He slides the gun out of its holster and holds it out. Jack reaches, but then the officer remembers and pulls it back. He grins, drops the clip, looks down the chamber. He hands the gun again over the desk, and I remember the first one I ever held, a thick BB pistol the weight and heft of a .45 that my dad kept in the basement.

Jack takes the black thing in both hands, breathless, dazed by the honor. "It's heavy," he says.

In the spring of 1994, I noticed for the first time that my father was becoming Nixon. I wasn't surprised, in one way, because I had always expected some such transformation. But I figured it would happen dramatically: One day, I was sure, all the thoughts I suspected he'd kept spinning in the back of his mind would come pouring out pure acid, the words flowing in a torrent of raspy nostalgic fury at, who else? New York Jews and crazy blacks and weak-assed liberals and their stalking, venomous press and worse—worst of all!—those abortion-happy, ball-slitting, soul-killing women who in muddle-headed response to Gloria Steinem and Hugh Hefner have gone and gutted the last, best hope of a world gone to hell.

It had to come out, didn't it? My dad was full of a fire he could barely contain, but he had spent a lifetime fronting it with an urbane jauntiness. He *never* spoke that way; he would have condemned anyone who did. No, he was brilliant, and his harangues came couched in disclaimer:

"We need good liberals, *of course* women should be paid as much as men, I don't care about Nixon! Nixon could be a real ass! But you see . . . For twenty years they tried to *get* him, and when Watergate came they *got* him, and in doing so they crossed the line no one had ever crossed: They *got* the presidency too . . ."

On and on it went, while my brothers and I sat mystified, the man unrolling endless spiels that gathered in a rush toward some thundering, incontrovertible point. He'd end by bellowing at no one in particular, lasagna cold on his plate, face burning: "The flag isn't a piece of cloth . . . It's a symbol . . . Do you know we never lost a battle in Vietnam? Did you know *that?*" Then he'd clomp out of the room, heels pounding the floorboards as he marched up and down the house trying to wind himself down. To me, in my self-righteous college know-it-all days, it seemed a short leap from such fury to planning the next Nuremburg rally. Time would bring it out, I was sure. Time and circumstance.

But I was all wrong. My father's Nixonian phase didn't unfold like the paranoid flower I'd expected. It was all physical. I never realized until later that my father had always had the accoutrements: Brown hair combed back, cheeks tending to jowly, and this tender awkwardness, a disconcerting, jerky inability to maintain physical contact that left all those in his presence so happy to leave the room. My little brother, after his first twelve-step girlfriend, became fixated on the fact that a hug from my father consisted of him sort of grabbing you around the top half of your head with one arm while batting, like a spastic flipper, the other about your neck and shoulders and shouting, "Hey-ya! Hey!" But the fact is, he never hit any of us. We never knew that the man had fooled the Marine Corps recruiter, doctor and drill sergeant—and the rest of his world forever—by overcompensating for a crippled left hand with bluster. To us young kids, before his work fell apart, he was only mesmerizing, magnificent: He'd swim out past the break while we splashed along the Jersey Shore, then swim parallel for what seemed miles; he'd get on water skis and scream, "Yee-HAAAA!" He lined us up like small soldiers and commanded, "Walk-a-proud, Joe!" and we'd strut about giggling as he sang about the shores of Tripoli. His ear-splitting manner of finishing off a phone call: "Right YOU are!" before crashing down the receiver always sent us howling. Every conversation, no matter how innocuous, began as a shout, rolled to a mild scream and ended with doors slamming around the house as those involved scrambled to find refuge. He wasn't cuddly, but he sure made everything hop.

The last years, though, had been bruising: There was one final stab at success, a marketing partnership with two other men, but my dad's talent for filling the air with impressive words had been undermined by all those years in the cellar. He had implied a string of prospects that didn't exist, and the partnership dissolved amid a stew of resentment and threatened lawsuits. My mother, once close to leaving him, resigned herself to living her last years with a man she once loved, once admired, and adopted a tenuous tolerance. She kept that hidden, mostly, but there came moments when the loyalty cracked. *Look,* her rolling eyes and sighs would say then, *I'm suffering with this man, but what else is to be done?*

Oddly, we all treated his failure as if it didn't exist. Dad was downstairs. Dad was working on something, though God knows what it might be, and no one dared say, "Hey, shouldn't the man go off to work sometime?" My father could have been a writer. He had the personality, at least: At once commanding attention and sealing himself off, demanding and deflecting, he lived the way I would someday work. The writer, of course, wants attention but only on his terms: A byline! A book! Any self-revelation is strictly controlled; the story and style obstruct the teller as much as they reveal him. *Pay no attention to the man behind the curtain . . .* His contradictions drove us all a bit mad, but the illusion was captivating. Each day a line, each month a page, all these words and a man somewhere among them. We were his readers and we couldn't stop.

And the cancer crept through his insides, slow growing, yes, but grinding him up like nothing else—the failed business, the belligerent sons, the untamable dog—could. After forty years, all that Semper Fi training had drained fully from my father's backbone. He stooped, just slightly, just enough for me to notice for the first time when, on April

27, 1994, Roy Nixon, singing "Shenandoah," at his brother's funeral became the newest Nixon mask to parade before the American public. This time the features were twisted in pain, tears coursing down the cheek, unchecked and salty over the rim of his gaping mouth. Richard Nixon was dead and his brother Roy sang, and watching on TV I saw Richard's face in his face and then, leaning forward off the couch, I saw my father there too.

I had turned on the funeral like everyone else, because Nixon was the central dark figure of our time, but as the gorgeous California service—simple and sun-dappled and so totally out of character for the man being buried—unfolded on CSPAN I found myself mesmerized. It wasn't because of death, and after a while it wasn't even because of my dad. It was because, suddenly, I knew I was watching one of those rare moments when the tumult and fear and triumph of an age—all the cold memories percolating again in an instant—gather at one spot. When I first saw the scene: The white clapboard house in Yorba Linda, the filling stands and, most astonishing, the camera scan of all those worn faces, I made a mistake and thought it was *my* age, my time, that I was watching. Here they came, shuffling slow to their chairs, dancing still to Nixon's music (he had arranged everything, even down to the soft playing of "The Battle Hymn of the Republic" and "My Country, 'Tis of Thee," and some Aaron Copland), here came Bill Clinton and George Bush and Gerald Ford, here came purse-lipped Jimmy Carter and Ronald Reagan, wearing an expression of eternal puzzlement, and even Eisenhower (not Ike but one of his sons, blessed though with that same midcentury face). But most of these I had only absorbed as a kid, less as men than natural phenomena like light and shadow. It wasn't until I saw Roy Nixon that I understood it was my dad's era unfolding, falling now into the past. Later that night, when they replayed it and Fran slept, I went back downstairs and watched again. I sat in the dark in Miami and saw them walk in the California sunlight, all the faces.

Three months later, I got a letter from my father, along with a copy of a "Presidential Sports Award." He had been setting up a target in the basement and firing BBs at it from his pistol, the same pistol we'd seen all our lives, black and sleek and always heavier than you'd expect. We'd sneak it out and pop BBs against the walls; years later, the slightest broom sweep would kick up a few metal balls, tarnished now, and send them rolling under a filing cabinet.

"Dear Scott—Thought you might be interested in the enclosed Xerox copies of award I just received for evening activity over three months. It's part of my personal rebuilding program and a satisfying symbol of pressing on and achieving despite my temporary incapacity of bad back, hypertension, prostate problem, hemorrhoidal and radiation effects and classified 'totally disabled' by the VA. What a litany of woe! However, I *feel* good despite all glitches and though bloody I ain't bowed—just slowed and somewhat immobilized and looking forward to seeing and getting together with you and Fran (to whom, my best regards) at sometime soon, hopefully. Love, Dad."

Next to his name, he drew the usual mustached cartoon of himself, this time waving a small American flag.

The big kicks hit all at once. I went to Australia in January of 1996, where Fran met me, pregnant with Jack. We had a couple days, then the call came that her father had died. We drove, flew, taxied back to Connecticut forty hours in time to make the burial. Someone slapped a shamrock on the coffin; the gravediggers lost grip halfway down the hole and one end dropped with a bang. Snow swirled in the gray air, and Fran went into labor 10½ weeks early. She lay in bed that weekend, and by Tuesday had settled enough for us to fly home to Miami. A month later Jack came prematurely, and we learned after that her grandmother died nearly the moment the water broke. Six weeks later, my dad went into the hospital. The prostate cancer had spread, fueled by testosterone; we all had a laugh at that. Of course it was.

I went back to Stamford for ten days. My father had shaved off the mustache that he'd hid behind for twenty-five years, had lost twenty pounds. He looked younger until the moments when pain seized his gut, his balls, his ass, then he'd gasp and shut his eyes. The hospital was better at night, quiet, dim, run by whispering nurses on soft soles. The machines blipped, but it didn't sound like a threat then, and you sat in a timeless limbo, cut off from the world, smelling an air too medicinal, too clean. You don't really mind the time passing then; you root for it to keep going—another hour, another day of waiting and watching a life reduced to the confines of one room.

One night, my father was able to get out of bed. We had only had two other personal talks in my life, really, the first on a Saturday in spring when I was sixteen and he drove me to work. "The company may own your ass," he declared. "But you own your soul." I wasn't sure what he was talking about then; I said, "Yep, I got it," and slammed the door.

The second came when my mother and he came close to splitting. It was an autumn afternoon, before he got sick. We sat in the smallest room in his house, and stripped down of the pride he had clad himself in for as long as I'd known him, my father asked what he should do. I don't know if I wanted them to stay together, but I resented being pulled to the core of my family's trouble. So I did something mean that day: Instead of appealing to love or religion or family, I noticed the James Montgomery Flagg recruiting poster hung on the wall and summoned up the Marine. "What are you *doing*?" I said. I asked the old corporal how he could let himself be beaten. I asked if it was smart, when he had all these projects that I had never seen the worth of, that I knew would never get done, to lose his few assets—his wife, his house, the time and space they gave him—by giving up and going away. *Be smart*, I said to one of the smartest men I knew. *Compromise*, I said to the man who had taught me to never compromise myself. *Lose the battle and win the war.* Something was wrong about it, but I couldn't stop myself. I knew that he would just end up in the basement again, clipping things out of newspapers, banging shut his file drawers. I knew, too, that this was about as cynical a way there was to keep a marriage alive. But when I left that room, he didn't seem quite so defeated. I felt unclean, but didn't care. Just so long as I wasn't my father's father anymore.

So my mother and father stayed together, and I guess they had some good moments. During my time at the hospital, my mother came in once and tried to convince him to accede to another operation. My dad didn't want to hear. He lay on his back with his eyes closed, his mouth twisted, and said, "Marilyn, stop it. Stop it." I don't know if he was speaking of her words or the pain. *"Please,"* he said, *"stop it."* In a way, only she could.

"There's something in her hands," he told me. "No matter how bad it hurts, when your mother puts a hand on my back it's gone." After a few days, Fran flew up with our firstborn, and my father reached out from the bed and stroked his grandson's head and said, "We love you Jack, we love you Jack, we love you Jack" with my mother standing there, too, so he had to mean the two of them bound, united, *something . . .*

A few nights later, he got out of bed and we had the third of our talks. He sat under a bright flourescent bulb, looking crumpled. He stared at the floor a while, and when he looked up from the metal chair by the bed, it was all gone—pride, fight, weakness, hope. He looked at me from under his still-thick eyebrows, a Great Depression kid, son of a drunk and a war hero, sixty-six years old. All the history was gone, too, the bantering, the trivia challenges. I didn't think of Nixon at all then, thank God, just a great man who never knew greatness. "I'm really up against it this time, aren't I?" my father said. His voice shook a little. He sat under harsh light. I couldn't think of one clever thing to say.

It was a few months later, in October of that year, that I went to see Ted Williams at his house in Florida. At that point, resentment over his son bubbled only within the confines of Ted's world—among friends and former employees who felt John Henry had frozen them out—and in the fraud-rampant galaxy of sports memorabilia. For five years, John Henry had made it his mission to expose forgeries of his dad's signature, barging into stores and fingering tainted merchandise. One dealer, a John Henry ally, called him "one of the most disliked people I know." Rumors circulated from bad to worse: John Henry had the old man signing mercilessly, padding his inventory for the profitable moment when Ted died; John Henry, even with Ted too sick to sign at all, was flooding the market with items emblazoned with a suspect signature. Ted, after spending an hour signing photographs in his kitchen, denied it all.

"He doesn't make me sign any more than I feel like signing," Ted said. "I just decide: Boom! And that's it. John Henry's been a helluva guy and a helluva son. He's smart, and he's honest, and of course he thinks, 'Jee-sus, Ted Williams is really something.' "

Still, there had been a time when any of Ted's pals could go to Ted with a project, a favor to ask, a call to make. No more. "Every project has to go through John Henry," said one friend of Ted's. "Every time you make a move, John Henry says, 'How much?' " His greed was laughably transparent, but John Henry also changed Ted's diet, cut out fats and alcohol, yanked him out of bed when he cursed and didn't want to exercise. John Henry took showers with Ted to make sure he didn't fall, clipped his toenails. He kept Ted alive. "I could not have done it without John Henry," Ted said to me. "Could not."

Who could say how much of John Henry's devotion had to do with his father's worth as a meal ticket? When, six years later, the news got out that Ted's body and decapitated head had been frozen at minus-320 degrees in an Arizona lab, I couldn't dismiss the thought that icing Ted Williams's DNA was just another memorabilia grab, writ large and bizarre. But I also knew that Ted was capable of agreeing to just about anything his son cooked up. Because for all his scheming, John Henry gave off an overwhelming need for his dad's approval; it rose off him like thick cologne. It may have been the one thing he was completely honest about. "This is everything," he said of the previous five years with his dad. "I didn't have anything else."

When I heard about John Henry after Ted's death, still trying to play baseball by suiting up with independent league and minor league teams, then risking ridicule by coaxing a tryout from the Red Sox, I wasn't surprised. John Henry had been doing that all his life. Despite all evidence that he had little talent for—or real interest in—the game itself, he kept returning to baseball. People always told him how much he looked like his dad; with the right break, he seemed to believe, maybe he could *be* Ted Williams. Talk about a Ted Williams movie had circulated for years. John Henry wanted the lead role.

"I know I could do the swing," he said of perhaps the most-finely honed weapon in baseball history. "Easy." John Henry never understood that the perfectionist passion that sent Ted into blind rages and bats against walls and fishing rods to the bottom of the sea, that sent him into the streets of Boston muttering, "Teddy Fucking Ballgame, the best fuck-ing hitter in the major fucking leagues," was the key difference between father and son, between his father and everyone else.

He never stopped trying. John Henry had played for his college team, and bolted school to play semipro ball in California. "Dad wanted me to be the first Williams to graduate college and now I'm leaving college and he doesn't think I'm ever going to come back," John Henry told me. "I remember the day I left: It was Christmastime and I told him and he couldn't believe it. But he dropped me off at the airport knowing I was going to California and he looked at me, and he just said, 'Well. Good luck.' It was weird: He was always trying to guide me away from baseball. And if you go back into his career you'll see it wasn't all fun and games; it was hard work, and a lot of aggravation dealing with the press and he probably knew there'd be a lot of that coming down on me. But he said, 'Don't fuckin' give up.' The last words out of his mouth. It was kind of cool. Like he was semi-behind me."

Maybe he was working me then. John Henry didn't know it, of course, but I was ripe for such sentiment: a father and son reconnecting, family strains, illness. I was a sucker, too, for anyone with ties to the American Century. By the time I came to see Ted, I could listen to codgers all day. My father was scheduled to leave the hospital the day he died in May. Williams was a Marine. And once Ted started talking at his kitchen table, telling tales, going on about Herbert Hoover, campaigning with the elder George Bush, the 1991 Iraq War, the 1996 Massachusetts senatorial campaign between Kerry and William Weld, after he started ranging across the era he'd lived and helped define, when he started challenging me with questions, I couldn't help but humor him. It was all too familiar.

"You read about all the different personalities over the last fifty years," Ted said. "The greatest American in my lifetime; who do you think it is? YOU won't be able to get it."

I found myself smiling. It had to be military. "Vinegar Joe Stilwell," I said.

Ted stuck out his jaw. "Negative," he said.

"Patton."

"Negative."

"Powell."

"Negative."

"Eisenhower."

"Negative. This is the greatest military man in our lives, in the history of the United States. You ought to know it there; I'm not going to give you anymore. I'm going to say GOOD-BYE."

When I said Douglas MacArthur, Ted didn't say bother to say yes. "Can you imagine what he did in Japan?" Williams said. "He handled it stiff, he handled it diplomatically. His knowledge of the monetary system, the religious situation of Hirohito, how to handle the Japanese." He began to shout. "Every place he went, he was No. 1. Ehhh . . . EVERY place he went! And there was so much jealousy over him: from the military, from the politicos, from even within his own ranks in the Army. They knew he was so far ahead of his class."

No, Williams said, he never met the general. But he did get a signed picture: "To Ted Williams, With best wishes, Douglas MacArthur." So we carried on like that awhile, me feeling the old juices flowing, not understanding then that this was the last time I'd ever fall into that familiar conversational rhythm. It had happened so easily, so naturally, that I guess I shouldn't have been stunned by what he said next. Williams was famously conservative. Once, when President John Kennedy phoned him at his baseball camp from nearby Hyannis Port, Ted bellowed, "Tell him I'm a Nixon fan!" and refused to talk. His views hadn't changed.

"You want to know the man who impressed me the most, the man in my life that struck me heavier, with more gleam around his whole body?" Ted demanded. "I said, 'Boy, what a man.' It was Richard Nixon. I met Nixon in the late fifties, early sixties, and I was absolutely overwhelmed by him. He was just so genuine. Ahhhh, Jesus Christ."

The plan for Wimbledon is a nice family trip. We'll eat breakfast together, I'll commute in and out to the tournament for two weeks, Fran and the kids will be near friends; I'll have time to see them at night. That's the plan, anyway, except the commute from Hampstead to Centre Court runs seventy-five minutes each way. That's the plan, but rain savages the first week, limiting story options and forcing a wait until 9:00 P.M. for matches to be officially canceled. I've always covered Grand Slams exhaustively, ten-hour days the norm, but the weather traps me even longer and drives the kids mad with inactivity. The family sees a photo of the Williams sisters shopping on the front page of *The Sun* and wonder why I couldn't escape, too. I should sense trouble when I bet Jack on the Andy Roddick–Taylor Dent match, and he says, "If I win, you have to take a day off work."

Done, I say grandly. Sunday is the traditional off-day: We'll play, we'll have fun.

That falls apart, too, of course. The rain keeps falling, Wimbledon forced to play on the first Sunday for only the third time in history. On the walk to the train after, a torrential storm drops like a waterfall; I'm soaked through within minutes. The next morning I wake with a fever.

The rest of the tournament plays out against a backdrop of low-grade anger and guilt, and when I return home to France the air is still thick with it. The fact is, Fran has forever been dismayed by my manic exactitude when it comes to work, my fear of being fired, of slacking off, of not doing the job. I *always* have to make the extra six phone calls, talk to someone who might say something intriguing, bolt from dinner when the phone rings. I have to transcribe every interview to make sure

I get it right, up 'til 3:00 A.M., read everything, then get sick when the adrenaline drains off. For twenty years, I've worked as if someone held a knife to my ribs. Wimbledon is the latest example. That first night back, we lay on our backs in bed and start shouting.

"We're getting just the shell of you," Fran says and she's right and I know it . . . but circumstance holds the ultimate trump card. Because hasn't it all worked? Haven't we made it, two struggling kids from Stamford? Aren't we here in the South of France, living the dream?

"But what's it worth," she says, "if we don't see you, if you never enjoy it? Why does it always have to be so intense?" And hearing that I feel strange, as if my body has gone dead and I've been reduced to just one pounding heart and a string of words rising out of the covers, a flash of comprehension total and true. My voice keeps breaking as I try to get it out of me.

"Look," I say. "This is the only thing I know. No one taught me how. My dad failed, my brothers barely left home, there was no idea how to channel everyone's vague ambitions into something real. I stumbled on it. I made it up. I don't know any different. No one showed me how to navigate, how to work hard—not out in the real world—so I just hit the gas and gave it everything and it happened. I kept getting offers. I know it's hurting the family, but how can I say it's the wrong way to be? I can't do something else; I write, I report, I watch games, and those skills don't translate into many other jobs. And you know what? The worst possible thing happened: It *worked*. We did it. We own a home. We're in France. Most people would do anything for a chance like this . . ."

The next morning, Fran wakes and we lay there for a bit and she says, "Well, that felt good, didn't it?"

And she's right: Months of tension have dissolved in the sleeping. But part of me feels hollowed out, sad, because here I've gotten as far away as I could imagine, 6,000 miles and a quarter century removed, and it's all with me still. I've gone further than I deserved, reached a perfect venue for reinvention; no one knows my father, my family. Even my country is hidden behind of jungle of caricature and embarrassing news.

Who could ever find me? Who cares? Yet I've failed in the only goal that mattered once. I haven't gotten away; I can't unload that weight. I carry the old house in my bones, the attic in my brain, the hallway where I slept and the kitchen below in my throat, the cellar where the old corporal sat and tore out clippings and filed his life away down in my gut forever. I can't escape it, and I realize now the part that shocks me most. I probably don't want to.

Thirteen

Midway through July, Peter and Virginia Carry stop by for lunch. They're en route back to their perfect home and village, and though our place has gained no more sense of being lived-in, though the fact of this has Fran cleaning and cutting and cooking in the hope that such frenzy might overwhelm the air of half-assed temporariness that inhabits the place, I'm not concerned. I like Peter very much and know he likes me, because he has already gone to my most vulnerable place and pronounced it good. He likes my work. I know this because before retiring Peter was executive editor of *Sports Illustrated*, and he wielded the most powerful tool available to provoke, inspire, and manage a stable of writers: the compliment.

As a breed, writers are pathetic creatures. Lazy praise or criticism is easily ignored, but give us someone who understands what we're trying to do, who sees why we placed that description *there* or that quote *there*; give us a boss who knows it's not just about meeting deadline and word count, and we'll live and die on their insights, kicking like a belly-scratched dog at one good word. Three days after one of my stories ran, the mail would often bring a note from Peter, composed on a beat-up manual typewriter, full of kind phrases that would make you want to run through a brick wall, notebook in hand. It was only when he retired that I found out that I wasn't alone in saving each missive; every writer at *SI* had their personal cache of Peter Notes. The best, though, came just a few days after my dad died. This one was handwritten, three pages long, full of empathy and thoughts about his own father's passing. "You'll find that, although you may find relief that his terrible suffering is done, your sense of loss, loneliness is just settling in," it read. "All I can say is: Try to overwhelm your sadness and frustration with what sweet memories you have; take pride in the man you've become, someone . . . of whom your father could be so proud, and ultimately recognize your sadness as a fine and necessary expression of love." We had never really spoken much before that. *Sports Illustrated* is a massive business in a massive conglomerate. Peter made it human.

But I also know we'll be okay this afternoon because we have a TV. We're now into the meat of the '04 Tour de France, and Lance Armstrong already has the race between his jaws, and Virginia Carry can't really concentrate on anything else. She loves Lance. I like this, because it's not often that someone with her perspective has such an unqualified response. The Carrys despise Bush. The Carrys see life in worldly shades of gray. The Carrys speak fluent French, live here for long stretches in a Francophile's paradise, and in this year's race Armstrong has been shadowed by doubt. Early on, French TV crews allegedly tried to break into his hotel room to search for drugs. Thousands of American fans screamed support, but during the claustrophobic time trial up Alpe D'Huez Armstrong found himself booed and cursed and spat upon. Fans painted obscene anti-Lance messages on the pavement, all across the country, sprayed him with beer and water.

I'm not sure he'd want it any other way; Armstrong's continuing refusal to distance himself from his "conditioning consultant"—alleged steroid supplier Dr. Michele Ferrari—betrays a near-pathological contrariness. For me and the French, the association allows for only two conclusions, neither good: Armstrong is criminal at worst, stupid at best, and loyalty is no defense. He has jettisoned people much closer to him than Ferrari, and his inability to see that Ferrari's ongoing role damages him—and, most important, undermines his every utterance against doping—only baits more speculation. If his cancer battle made him larger than life, if his unquestionable cycling achievements make him a sporting legend, the same qualities that inflate Armstrong's stature also leave it full of holes. As this race grinds on, he's become both bigger and more suspect than ever, and has no one to blame but himself.

But Armstrong's American devotees care little for such distinctions, boiling their devotion to three unassailables—Lance survived, Lance tests clean, Lance wins—and there's something enviable, winning even, in their ability to sidestep the fog of logical rumor.

Fran serves up a tart out on the terrace, and we sit, just like the rest of the country, for a civilized two-hour lunch. Even the kids settle down. The Carrys talk about leaving by midafternoon to beat traffic, but the TV is on and U.S. Postal has formed this perfect flying wedge to protect Armstrong, a riveting portrait of arrogance in action. Peter dozes off on our stained IKEA couch, a small victory for our hospitality; he couldn't snooze, I figure, if he didn't feel at home. Virginia pulls up just inches away from the screen, yelping, cheering, leaning in as if to somehow transmit a bit of her support through the TV.

"Is it okay," she asks, "if we stay until the end? It's Lance, you know . . . I've just got to see Lance."

Late in July, my younger brother Eric is getting married in a state park called Starved Rock outside Chicago. It's my only trip back to the States since we've come to Europe, and I make it alone, landing at O'Hare and picking up a *Tribune* and knowing for the first time that I had made the right decision. The *Trib* has literally shrunk since I'd seen it last, its broadsheet pages reduced by a few inches in a frightened industry's latest cost-cutting trend. Though the paper is better than I remembered, the story of the day concerns a chunk of falling concrete at Wrigley Field, and I feel no pull, no regret, at missing out on writing it. The final weekend of the Tour de France looms, but Armstrong has already locked up a race that now feels very far away.

As a piece of racing, his performance has been masterful. Armstrong has summoned one dramatic rush to the finish line after another. He has worked the peloton like a maestro, making it play only the song he wants to hear, won five individual stages, dominated the climbs, seized the individual time trial up Alpe D'Huez with all the ferocity he lacked when I saw him on Ventoux. It has been a rolling portrait of pitiless greatness. In a race marked by the odd timidity of rivals Mayo and Heras, Jan Ullrich and Tyler Hamilton, Armstrong is on his way to collecting perhaps his easiest title.

I drink beers that night with an old Chicago friend and gird myself for reentry, and the next morning eat a massive breakfast and buy shorts at The Gap and family supplies at CVS, wandering the wide suburban sidewalks and vast parking lots, shocked by the sheer bulk of trundling humanity. I've never noticed the massive calves and guts of Americans before; in our year out, somehow, people have gotten huge. When, a month later, I see the stencil about fat Americans in Athens, I will think instantly of this morning, of buying and eating in a setting so efficient, so calm, so narcotically fresh and cool, that it seems unreal. I don't want to leave.

But I drive the two hours through midday traffic that soon empties into a broad and vacant highway, to a minimall where my rented tux waits in a plastic bag, through the ravaged town of Utica hit just months before by the random spin of a tornado. I roll over a bridge and into Starved Rock, late. The Friday rehearsal has already started, but my mother and little brother hug me and my older brothers elbow me and my sister grins, and I stand among the other groomsmen I don't know, faces more important to Eric now than I've been for years, an alien among earthlings. It's not only that I've come so far, of course; it has been years since I've spent any time with the family alone. They've read my stories, but my traveling has melded into a string of unfamiliar names. I have no tales of swimsuit models and no insider knowledge on the Yankees or Giants or Red Sox, so that wears off quickly and soon the old dynamic kicks in. I'm just the fourth of five again, verbal, combative, the wiseass more than happy to stir up trouble. My mother backs Bush, and the rest of the family tends Republican, and as the house liberal I find myself asking a lot of rhetorical questions about Iraq that make no impact. People nod and head off for another bratwurst; a pleasing darkness settles slow over the party. Drinks slosh in plastic cups. A band begins to play.

We're saved by that, I guess. The bride-to-be sings and Eric sings and they sing together because they're singers. The band plays old songs that we knew as kids together, listening to Cousin Brucie on WABC-AM out of New York, and after a few drinks we sing too out in the crowd. I say some dopey things and Todd and Sue laugh and my mother grins uneasily—God knows what I'll say or do next—but happy to hear us. We know what only parents know, she and I: Nothing in life sounds better than the sound of your kids laughing together. So I put on this fake redneck accent and make Steve giggle, and Todd and I smile and agree on sports and politics, closer than we've ever been, too alike for comfort, really, considering that at one point my lone ambition was to beat him bloody. But that's gone. We're in our forties now and people we knew have started to die, and if apologies are never uttered, the smell of mercy hangs between the words, replacing memories I had nurtured once like black flowers. That angry thrill of sharing the same blood never fades, though, and Steve is the easiest, as always. I order drink after drink and do everything possible to keep him near.

Late Saturday afternoon threatens rain. We gather in a clearing outside the hotel. A softspoken little man named Pastor Chuck introduces himself as "a certified family counselor for the last five years" and chortles at jokes only he can hear. The bride's seven-year-old son serves as ringbearer. At some point, Pastor Chuck mentions our father being dead and my knees give and I feel my brothers sag, and I look up at the gray sky. Two hawks bank overhead, and I lose track of the ceremony watching them trace arc after arc. Then comes the I-dos and the kiss and, as rehearsed, the wedding party of about twenty follows the bride and groom out of the clearing, everybody self-conscious and walking slow until the bride's son breaks away sobbing. His mother begins to trot after him, train in hand, and Eric half runs beside her and the wedding party, lacking all instruction in such an event, begins trotting too, all of us in a pack under the trees chasing a boy who, if he ever looks back, will see two dozen adults in formal wear copying his zigzagging course across the grass.

My brothers and sister and I have bought the couple a bed as a gift, and at the reception after, we sit and try to compose something for the card. We're on the cusp of solving the trickiest line when our mother walks up and asks to know what we're doing. Todd snaps at her and she back at him, and the next thing we hear she's gone; it takes a delegation to convince her to come back. The bride and groom don't notice this, though, and toasts are given and cake eaten, and since I'm living in France I get introduced to the bride's grandmother and grandfather. She was born in Verdun and loves to dance. Jim had been in the U.S. Air Force serving there and has now begun a rough decline. There has been a recent operation, toes cut off, gathering weakness. Everyone clucks sympathy, but for this night, anyway, it seems misplaced. Jim, armed with slickbacked hair and a jaunty mustache, rolls about in an electric cart cracking jokes, giving kids rides in his lap, barreling into clusters with a "Coming through!"—all but daring anyone to ask if he's happy. After maneuvering in and bumping my seat, he informs my mother and I that he's just had a nosebleed and sails off cackling.

Too much triumph over adversity makes me nervous after a while, and I'm in the midst of transitioning from sympathy to irritation when the dancing begins. Eric dances with the bride, Eric dances with Mom, the bride dances with her dad and after those set pieces the crowd thins. I'm picking at my cake, alone and liking it, when I look up to see Jim wheeling out to the middle of the dance floor. The bride takes his hand and wiggles a little as he sits there smiling and broken, and at this point, usually, that's it, nod to the handicapped guy done with. But then Jim places his hands on the armrests and pushes himself upright, and she takes his weight and he totters and I hold my breath because something disastrous seems certain.

But now he's surrounded, his wife and two daughters and grandaughter circling around him and holding the man up on his stumpy black shoes, and Jim bends his legs and the music pumps and, yes, he dances at his granddaughter's wedding. The sparse crowd cheers. For a minute or two, the cart sits empty next to the gyrating family circle, chrome shining beneath the spotlights. The circle turns, holding the ailing man up, and a shiver runs up my back. I'm beginning to see it.

Nothing in my life—love, wife, family, career, the world to explore—would have come without them: parents, brothers, sister. Without a family to flee, without a hometown to hate, without the shame of mediocrity, without the tools they gave me without even knowing, I wouldn't have had the necessary fuel; I would've gone nowhere fast. That shudder I feel is the shattering of my most precious myth: I've gotten nothing on my own. The brother rolling in nightmares, blurting "No . . . NO . . . NOOOO" like someone buried alive; the brother passing out in a nightly cloud; the sister who looked on while her boyfriend buried a fist in my wiseass gut. I'm not here without that, nothing without them. We are family. We fed off each other in a terrible way once, but I sinned worse than any. I erased all the good, the laughing, that had been in that house, too, and willed an entire world, my family, into an oblivion they didn't deserve. I see Steve coming to whisper a joke in my ear, and I know. I owe them more than I can ever repay.

Jim drops like a sack of stones into the electric cart, gasping and drained. Damn, I whisper to no one. *Damn.*

■ ■ ■

When I get back to France, the papers are full of Armstrong. He won this tour, his sixth, by six minutes and nineteen seconds, but it might as well have been an hour. Reaction ranges from awe to the now-familiar distaste, and Armstrong, true to form, did himself no favors at the end. The tour's acknowledged *patron*, he wielded his authority like a king, taking so much joy in his mastery that he couldn't see when it made him seem small.

During the eighteenth stage, on July 24, Italian Filippo Simeoni moved up to join a pack of six riders vying for the day's win. None were a threat to Armstrong's lead, but it didn't matter. Armstrong doesn't like Simeoni. A sanctioned doper himself, Simeoni had been one of the few riders to testify against Ferrari, saying that Armstrong's consultant had shown him how to take EPO without getting caught. In July of 2003, Armstrong called him "a liar" in *Le Monde*. Simeoni confirmed that he planned to sue Armstrong for defamation early in this Tour, and now, on Armstrong's watch, he made his move to win a stage. Never mind that Simeoni's testimony actually could help clean up the sport. Armstrong chased Simeoni down and joined the lead pack, telling them he wouldn't back off—giving them the honor of contesting for the stage—unless Simeoni dropped out. Armstrong then escorted him back, humiliation complete, unaware or uncaring that he, not Walsh or Ballester or Simeoni, had just spotlighted his relationship with Ferrari in a way that court reports or mere quotes could not. Cycling's biggest star had used cycling's biggest stage to call attention to cycling's worst conflict: his own.

Armstrong didn't see it that way, of course. "Simeoni is not a rider that the peloton wants to see in the front group," he said after. "All he wants to do is destroy cycling, to destroy the sport that pays him."

To Europeans, anyway, the Simeoni incident sealed Armstrong's reputation as a bully. When Ferrari is found guilty three months later of sporting fraud and acting illegally as a pharmacist and handed a twelve-month suspended sentence, Simeoni's words from that day will echo back. "Armstrong demonstrated to the entire world what type of person he is," Simeoni said. "I suffered an injustice from him while everyone was watching."

Armstrong will respond to Ferrari's conviction the next day, October 1, with a statement that, while asserting that Ferrari "never suggested, prescribed or provided me with any performance-enhancing drugs," will also sever his "professional relationship" with the Italian doctor. Simeoni won't be mentioned.

By then, I will have ridden hundreds of miles more on my bike, knowing the rumors, knowing about the book, knowing all about Ferrari and EPO. I'll have bulled up the Chain de l'Etoile to Mimet, hustled across to La Diote and Greasque and back home again, knowing all that and still unable to help myself. I will always think then of Armstrong—not Mayo, not Ullrich, not Simeoni—and push until my thighs burn. I will think of Armstrong, and find myself going harder still. American cycling legend Greg LeMond is right: Armstrong is either the greatest hero or the biggest fraud in sports, but until his Shoeless Joe moment arrives—and even if it does—his appeal burrows deeper than journalistic values, speculation, even rock-solid fact. I'm like Virginia Carry, like so many: I want Lance to win. The disease he beat runs in both sides of the family. Precancerous cells have been scraped from my skin. I go fast, then faster, and think of the champion, because in the end I have no choice. I'm pretty sure what color my bullet will be.

Fourteen

I jam my foot on the gas, wrench the wheel, just miss two men stepping off a curb. The light is red, but I have no time for law and order. Cars pour into the intersection around me. Someone beeps; pedestrians glare. My face is a mask of blank arrogance. Isn't the road mine? Aren't I a Greek cab driver? I roll through as if by birthright. I must get to Omonia Square—the flat, faceless, traffic-hell plaza squatting at the heart of Athens's daily life—to have any hope of getting to Olympia today, and I'm happy to take down anyone in my way. For effect—not to mention courage—I greet each obstacle with an angry spew of Greek words, though my vocabulary is limited to the polite ordering of a meat sandwich. "*Paracalo*," I shout. "*Enta'ksi . . . souvlaki!*"

I didn't start out this way. No, when I first crept onto Syngrou Avenue, I was the typical tourist adrift in a boxy rented Hyundai, timid and apologetic. Cars passed me like bullet trains. I gripped a map in one hand, and instantly got lost. But then I noticed something odd: Weary people kept waving me down. Not me, exactly, but the canary-yellow car I drove, the taxi they thought I was. Here it is, midday in July, with exactly one month remaining before the opening of the most troubled, criticized, suspect Olympic Games in history. Workers are feverishly planting trees, shrouding ugly buildings, in the hope of presenting a more civilized face to the world. Yesterday, the first of the week's two blackouts short-circuited traffic lights and paralyzed the city. I have to get out, fast, and meekness will get me nowhere. Just around Hadrian's Arch, panic gets shoved aside by angry desperation. You want a cab? "*Enta'ksi,*" I growl—which means "okay" but sounds like "taxi." I nearly lay out three motorbikes while whipping into the left lane.

Later, I learn my transformation is all too normal. "At first, like in the U.S., you try to follow the rules," says Marianna Koliopoulos, who emigrated to the U.S. with her husband in 1972 but returns to Greece each summer. "But after a while you drive like a Greek; you don't look at the road, you don't really stop at stop signs. It's a little crazy."

Actually, I'm starting to enjoy myself. I nearly collide with a stalled van—sending pads, pencils, fruit, and water hurtling against the dash—then swerve in front of someone not nearly as quick or clever as me. I consider sparking up a cigarette, whipping out my cell phone, picking up a fare and charging double. Once you embrace it, there's no sport like driving in Athens. Construction has eaten the city alive, turning the typical paralysis into what national track-and-field coach Odysseus Papatoulis call "this madness" of diverted lanes, jackhammered streets, and, now, a cleanup destined to continue well after the Opening Ceremonies. When Greece's soccer team returned to Athens on July 5, after winning the 2004 European championship, the celebration at Panathiniako Stadium was nearly derailed when the team bus got stuck in traffic. Still, chaos triggers its own kind of rush: Within a half hour, I bull into Omonia's mad whirlpool of cars and heave right, hurled by centrifugal force onto the route to the national road. "*Para-calo!*" I shout.

I'm heading to Olympia for good reason. After 1,612 years, the place matters again. Olympia will be the site of the Olympic shot-put competition, and no decision by organizers could be more inspired. In a turn-back-the-clock event for the ages, the Olympics will return to its birthplace and, with the glaring exception of twenty-eight television cameras circling the field, take sport back to the basics. Tickets will be free. The scoreboard will be hand-operated. Winners will receive wreaths woven out of local olive branches, getting their modern world medals two days later in Athens. The intent is clear. As repository of the Olympic ideal, as physical proof of why an overwhelmed Greece is hosting these games, tiny Olympia will serve as reminder of the simplicity and amateurism that supposedly animate the Olympics. For one day, fifteen thousand spectators will swarm in, and one of the planet's great museums will come alive. I'm going now to find out how they intend to pull it off.

But mostly, I have to get away from the city. I need a story—this time, a story without fear. Like the rest of the world, I'm tired of hearing about Athens's construction delays, the $12 billion price tag, the terrorism threat that has pushed security costs six times higher than any in Olympic history. I've had enough of the usual Greek wallow into paranoia. Though 85 percent of the nation supports the return of the games, it's not uncommon to hear someone suggest that Greece's Euro 2004 soccer championship was somehow fixed to juice Olympic ticket sales, or to hear Greek officials wax romantic and fearful in the same breath. "I feel great, but I take care," says Rita Papadoupoulos, manager of the Ancient Olympia venue. "All the people are afraid to go to the Metro station: I tell to my children, 'Don't go there; I'm afraid of that. Be careful.'"

Just this morning, in the minutes before I left for Olympia, I opened an official Athens 2004 magazine to an interview with newly elected prime minister Kostas Karamanlis.

"We are," said Karamanlis in the perfect blend of Greek fatalism and cockiness, "doomed to succeed."

Indeed, so many nightmares have been table-topped for the Athens Olympics that the most likely disaster seems quaint: Just a month before Opening Ceremonies, only 1.8 million of the 5.3 million tickets available have been sold. Small crowds seem inevitable. I want to take solace in the words of Mayor Dora Bakoyannis, who told the crowd at the soccer reception, "We have received a lot of unfair criticism. But now, just like in the European Cup, we can prove to the world that when united and determined, the Greeks can achieve anything." But it's not easy.

So I race to Olympia, looking for relief, hope, a blast of fresh air on a spin around the coast. Once you hit the Peloponnesus, the road narrows to two lanes. To pass, you swallow hard, straddle the center line, and force cars in both directions to move out of your way. I abandon all hope of safety, lock in at 80 mph, and follow the parade of maniacs shooting for Patras, Pyrgos, and Olympia, ripe for metaphor and feeling lighter by the mile. The four-hour jaunt begins to seem more and more appropriate. Getting the Olympics back to Greece, to Olympia, has been an unprecedented task, full of wild twists and white-knuckle moments, and it's easy to accept the shot-put's day in paradise as a momentary cure for Olympic ills. Too easy, in fact. As I get closer and keep chewing on it, the conceit begins to feel phony, forced, a silly acceptance of sports played out at Potemkin Park. The summer has been full of revelations about the BALCO drug lab, and the resulting parade of disgraced American track stars, but that's not the worst of it. Unlike most people, I've seen the Greek runners up close, too.

On one of my first trips to Athens the previous November, I caught up with the country's greatest hero. Four years earlier, at the 2000 Olympics in Sydney, sprinter Kostas Kenteris pulled off the biggest shock of the games when he blazed to a win in the 200-meter final, cracking a forty-year American monopoly and becoming the first male Greek runner since 1896 to win an Olympic gold medal. A ship, a jet, a stadium were named after him. I went to the national training center at Agios Kosmas, watched Kenteris lope around the track in the chill, spoke to him two days later. Few athletes had been better positioned by timing and fate to channel his nation's hopes and history; Kenteris's race, even, was the original event of those ancient Olympics. No one seemed to embody better the ability of Greeks to compete on the world stage. But even then, Kenteris was looking at the Olympic homecoming with a measure of dread.

"What I fear most is the last moment," Kenteris said. "I just pray that I'm going to be fine up to that last moment. I want to be safe, I want to be in good shape. There's a fine line between success and failure, and I want to be sure that I don't cross it."

He isn't the only one walking a wire. At that time, no one had felt the full impact of revelations leaking out of the BALCO lab in Northern California, but the widespread use of performance-enhancing drugs and designer steroids like THG had made drug busts a common occurence. Athens had been chosen as the 2004 host city as a corrective to the rampant commercialism of the '96 Atlanta games, and the organizing committee had billed 2004 as a return to Olympics "on a human scale," an Olympics as it was founded in 776 B.C. and revived in Athens in 1896. The coupling of a corrupt present with the noble past—holding the shot put at Olympia, using antique Panathinaiko Stadium for the archery competition, running the marathon on the original route from Marathon to Athens—gives the Athens games unparalled resonance. But it also has raised the emotional stakes to an unbearable level. All the usual rhetoric about "the Olympic ideal" carries a weight in Greece that it didn't in Sydney or Salt Lake City; the setting demands consideration of what the Olympics were supposed to be. The modern games at Olympia? I press down on the gas, and remember what Greek marathoner Nikos Polias told me last winter. *God forbid if a shot-putter comes up dirty. God forbid if he or she is Greek.*

That, Polias said, "would be very bad for everybody."

Yet, few in Greece seem concerned. Focused on its rise as a European track power, with European champions Mirela Manjani in the women's javelin and Katerina Vongoli in the discus, 100-meter Sydney silver medalist Katerina Thanou and Kenteris all on track to blossom in time for

Athens, the Greeks have spent the four years after Sydney all but courting suspicion. One reason is that the top Greeks rarely compete—or submit to testing—at any but the major championships. The other is that, despite feeling overly scrutinized, they haven't gone out of their way to toe the line of the International Association of Athletics Federation (IAAF). In November of 2002, the IAAF issued a humiliating public warning to the Greek Track and Field Federation (SEGAS) after an alarming number of their athletes—nine out of the world's fourteen no-shows for the '02 season—couldn't be found for out-of-competition drug testing.

In April of 2003, SEGAS was embarrassed when coach Christos Tzekos misinformed the federation about the whereabouts of his pupils Kenteris and Thanou. Testers looking for them in Crete came up empty, and SEGAS had no idea the three had abruptly flown to Qatar.

"Because something happened in Qatar, we went there for a few days, there was bad communication between people, there's this huge thing," Tzekos told me. "It's nothing. Why you make something that's nothing? There is no reason."

Tzekos is a polarizing figure in Greek track, credited with overhauling his runners' training methods and mentality but suspect because of his secrecy, slick suits, and decidedly un-Greek way of comporting himself. In February of 1997, he got into a shoving match with an official in Dortmund, Germany, who insisted on taking three of his runners, including Thanou, for a random drug test; the three runners left the stadium untested. Both the IAAF and the Greek track federation banned Tzekos from coaching for two years. "He's like American: a crazy man," said one SEGAS official. Indeed, when I spoke with him, the thirty-year-old Tzekos credited his time spent selling nutritional supplements in the Chicago suburbs in the early 1980s as the transforming experience of his life.

"I follow my philosophy," he said. "If somebody wants to join me, join me. If somebody doesn't, doesn't. But I will do what I have to do, and then we will see who is right." He finished with a laugh and a flourish: "I'm not hiding from anybody. I'm here!"

By the time I make it to Olympia, then, I'm in no mood to embrace some halcyonic ideal. I park outside the village, walk down a deserted road, and over a elegant little bridge. The only sound comes from the soft wind, a clamor of cicadas. People step past the columns and tumbled stone, stroll under a pocked stone arch and into the stadium. Considering all the expectation piled upon the name alone, Olympia is stunningly bland: A 190-meter-long patch of dirt broken on each end by a line of marble, surrounded on all sides by banks of scrubby grass and high pines. On one side stands the ruins of a stone altar, on the other the remnants of a grandstand. Yet no one seems disappointed; one by one, every visitor plants a foot on the starting line. They pose for friends, and sometimes a voice yells, *Go!* I watch as a father chases his teenage son for a few yards, then tumbles laughing into the dust.

Still, compared with the mess and carping of Athens, Olympia does feel special. More than a third of the local population of 1,800 have signed up to help out at the shot-put event, and there's no missing the *It's a Wonderful Life* flavor of the place, its unabashed pride. Sensing one of their own, no doubt, three local cabbies take me in hand to talk history, show off photos of their days as torchbearers, and give detailed directions. The people are so generous, so proud, in fact, that I grow almost protective of them. I begin to worry: What happens when someone tests positive? What happens when the real overwhelms the ideal? Then I wander out of the stadium and notice a line of sixteen pedestals, and read the nearby plaque: *On those pedestals sixteen statues of Zeus once stood, paid for by the fines imposed on cheating athletes, whose names were inscribed below as warning to all who pass.* Hypocrisy? Olympia, Athens, Greece can survive that, can survive anything, because the Greeks have known longer than anyone that nothing is pure.

That's when I realize that the 2004 Olympics could be nowhere else but Greece. No place better captures the mood of the day; no place better represents the low expectations, the fear of the unknown, and the hope that, somehow, everything will turn out right. There has never been a civic dash quite like Athens's frantic finish, and damned if I haven't gotten my metaphor after all. We're all driving to Olympia in the summer of 2004—the doping and the clean, the cheaters and cheated, the hacks and riders alike—all scared and swearing and braking for nothing. The uncertainty is maddening. Threats and corruption fill the air. It's impossible to feel sure about anything.

At dusk, I climb back into my canary-yellow car, and decide to take a shortcut back to Athens through the mountains. Stupid move. The road winds like a coiled snake. Nearly every curve holds a small metal box on spindly metal legs that I first mistake for mailboxes; then I stop at one and peer inside. It's a small homemade chapel, filled with candles unlit for ages, faded pictures, ragged paper. Mile after twisty mile I've been passing them and I'll keep on passing them for an hour more, memorials to the cocky drivers who've crashed and died up here.

The hills grow pitch-black. Once in a while I'll blow through a sudden, harshly lit village, attached to the surrounding rock like a barnacle. In between there are no streetlights, no other cars, but I've gone too far to turn back. The sky breaks out in a spectacular rash of stars. I grip the wheel, and open my eyes wide. There's nothing uplifting about waiting for a crash, an explosion, for some stranger to make a reckless move. But you never feel more alive.

On the evening of August 17, with the Athens games four days old and already a stew of absurdity and triumph, I make the twenty-minute walk from my hotel to Panathinaiko Stadium. I'd passed the horseshoe-shaped marble edifice squatting in the city center many times in my previous visits, but have never been inside. I have to take a shot: Built in 1896 for the modern revival of the games, Panathinaiko is where the shepherd Spirodon Louis finished his legendary marathon win that year, escorted by royalty and a crowd overcome by joy, setting the standard for every Greek athlete since. I expect to be turned away. The morning's archery competition ended hours before, and the stands and field stand empty; really, I have no good reason for being here. Still, I have an Olympic credential around my neck, and no one blinks when I walk through a gate, down a flight of stairs, and into the sloping tunnel that, for 108 years, has taken champion and loser alike to the field. Fungus and water streak the walls, and as the tunnel elbows left, one side of the concrete wall and ceiling give way to an enormous bulge of white-streaked rock. Whoever designed the tunnel had decided—with a humility no modern contractor would possess—to work around it, and as I stroke the surface my mouth gapes.

A workman approaches. I try to catch his eye, maybe even share the wonder with him. Head down, he coughs up an alarming ball of phlegm, sends it flying, and passes without a word.

I wander onto the field. A white security blimp hums overhead. I climb up into the stands, to the top of Panathinaiko, to the farthest corner I can find, and sit down. Over the trees, the sun has sunk to the topmost edge of the Parthenon, its fading light burning in a kaleidoscope of reds and roses and orange through the polluted air, softening the marble seats to the softest shade of peach. After a few minutes, a security guard hurries up, eyes my credential, and smiles. A light breeze competes with the sound of traffic, all of it whooshing through the pines ringing the stadium rim.

This is the day Kenteris and Thanou checked out of the hospital. Before Greece's Olympics had even begun, its two heroes had become a national embarrassment. The previous Thursday, on the eve of the Opening Ceremonies, Kenteris and Thanou checked into the Olympic Village and learned they would be subject to a mandatory drug test. The two made their way to Tzekos's home, where, cell phones and all, they were somehow unable to be reached by the Greek and Olympic officials wondering about their whereabouts. Rushing back to the Village together on a motorcycle, the two claimed to have been involved in some kind of road accident. Though witnesses were scarce to nonexistent, and all injuries invisible to the naked eye, the two entered an Athens hospital for the next four days. Rumors flew. The Opening Ceremonies came and went. Despite Athens being applauded for its gorgeous venues, its efficient transport, and its exhaustive security, the comically corrupt spectres of Kenteris, Thanou, and Tzekos have haunted the days since.

A hearing of the International Olympic Committee has been set for the following day, but everyone's patience has collapsed. Even Greece's president has called the imbroglio a "disgrace." Each day, the Greek newspapers have blistered the three with questions and condemnations—and one decidedly local twist. Despite the fact that Kenteris and Thanou had a history of ducking drug tests, despite the fact that they had missed a test in Tel Aviv in late July and another one in Chicago just days before the games began, despite the news that both sprinters had been named in a damning e-mail exchange between BALCO owner Victor Conte and a different Greek coach, Greek officials and media have spiced their outrage with a theory too time-honored to ignore: Somehow, the Americans are to blame.

The morning after the "crash," Athens's mainstream newspapers stated flatly—and without any sourcing—that the U.S. Olympic team, led by chief executive Jim Scherr, had threatened on August 11 to pull the U.S. team out of the games unless the IOC tested the two Greek sprinters. To see such illogic in action is breathtaking: U.S. officials, it seems, would happily risk worldwide ridicule and endless lawsuits, destroy the gold-medal quest of Michael Phelps, and the dreams of 537 others, if only to sabotage Greece's already-suspect heroes. When I reach him, Scherr calls the claim "utterly ridiculous" and, though the U.S. has a long history of finger-pointing, denies that anyone from the USOC contacted the IOC or the World Anti-Doping Agency about the Greek sprinters. "We have our own problems with drug testing," Scherr says. "We have done nothing in any way instructing or pressuring the IOC or WADA to pressure them in that regard."

A statement like that, I know, won't convince anyone in Athens. Until recently, most Greeks thought their elections were dictated by the CIA, and it isn't hard to find people who insist that the agency pulled the levers for the now-defunct terror group November 17. Polls of Greek citizens regularly put opposition to American foreign policy at about 95 percent, meaning that nearly every smiling Greek harbors suspicion about American motives. Although Greek volunteers can't be any more hospitable,

U.S. team officials, coaches, athletes, and fans have been served a steady diet of sometimes justified, sometimes absurd criticism. If they aren't reading about how the Bush Administration has broken the Olympic truce with the much-hated Iraq war, they're pounded as doping criminals or upbraided for their arrogance. As for the American way of life, the Greeks vote regularly with spray paint. "Fuck the USA" reads the graffiti across the street from the U.S. embassy in Athens. "Fat Happy Americans" reads the message stenciled on walls all over the city, punctuated by the chilling symbol of a torture victim from Abu Ghraib prison. No American team has ever opened a games amid this much contempt.

And the U.S.O.C. isn't in any position to cry foul. More than two dozen American athletes (not to mention two Americans who were to have played for the Greek Olympic baseball team) had either flunked drug tests or had been implicated in drug scandals in the year before Athens. For its perceived hypocrisy on that issue and reasons ranging beyond any stadium, the U.S. has replaced the Soviet Union and East Germany as the sporting empire the world most loves to hate. American athletes prepared for Athens under unprecedented pressure from politicians and team officials to behave themselves: no untoward flag-waving, no provocative celebrations. Former U.S. Olympians Janet Evans and Bob Beamon crisscrossed the U.S. in July and August, showing video examples of how not to act: swimmer Amy Van Dyken spitting in her opponent's lane in 1996, the 4x100 relay team's oblivious preening after winning the gold in Sydney.

"In this environment we have to mind ourselves," Evans said when I called her in Athens. "The main thing we said is, 'Be yourself. But if you do what Amy Van Dyken did, the repercussions will be tenfold. You will look like the Ugly American.' Everyone's watching us."

With all that in mind, the Opening Ceremonies turned out to be a smorgasboard of double standards. "Walking to the stadium," said U.S. canoe team member Brett Heyl after, "we didn't know whether there would be boos or applause." The non-American fans responded with polite clapping and a distinct smattering of catcalls that, considering the a la carte nature of anti-Americanism in the world today, came as no surprise. The same person deriding a Starbucks on the Champs-Élysée will more likely than not profess admiration for American openness or innovation or education. And if the Greeks present Europe's most knee-jerk case, they're also quick to say how much they love American music and people. Besides, the U.S. team didn't give them much to work with. In fact, the athletes who acted most "American" in Friday night's parade marched under different flags, but no one hissed when the Haitian team came out windmilling their arms and cupping hands to their ears. Everyone found it charming when one Italian broke free to kiss the lens of a TV camera.

The Americans, though, did mostly as they were told, reducing their usual exuberance to tight smiles and furious waves, looking stiff and nervous. Afterward, U.S. officials declared themselves pleased, but it was a bit sad to see, too, because the freewheeling nature of American athletes has always been as envied a quality as the country's wealth and power. There was a lightness in Mary Lou Retton that you didn't see in Nadia Comaneci, a glee in Jackie Joyner-Kersee you don't see in Maria Mutola, a looseness in Sugar Ray Leonard you didn't see in Teófilo Stevenson. Now? "It's a different world," Evans said. "There are things we didn't have to deal with years ago. On top of the competing, there's a different pressure on them."

Night is falling around Panathinaiko now, its floodlights holding off the dark. A line of flagpoles ring the top of the stadium like lace on a sleeve, and I walk along trying to see how many I can recognize: Brazil, Turkey, Argentina, Canada. Many bleed color combinations I don't recognize, but I know somewhere in the world those colors hold a mad importance, have asked men to die and suffer and rejoice and starve, to live with tyrants and colonists and freedom, too. Left of a light stanchion, the American flag flaps dully, flanked on one side by Japan and the other by Mexico, then Israel a few steps away. I've spent the weekend thinking and writing about anti-Americanism, so I'm ripe for the thought: As ideals, America and the Olympics find themselves, in this time and place, under siege. Both have made themselves vulnerable to charges of hypocrisy, to attacks for their "gigantism," cultural imperialism, aggression, commercialism, greed. Abu Ghraib has shredded the idea of the United States as a moral force worldwide, and the deceptions that led to Iraq will echo across decades. Mistakes must be rectified, guilt punished. But the equation, in the end, is simple, the fact of America undeniable. The world would be far worse off if it didn't exist.

Same with the Olympic Games. Over the previous decade, the IOC has emerged as the only peaceable force with the clout to impel Athens to a once unthinkable state of structural efficiency, giving the nation a gift that will give and keep on giving for the next fifty years. The city has indeed been granted its second chance now, and a mere sporting event has provided it. Yes, amateurism is dead and doping is rampant. Sure, the Olympics have drifted far from the mission envisioned in 1896. And, of course, the rings themselves have become symbols for all kinds of physical and financial corruption. But year after year, nations line up begging for a chance to host the games. The route from there to flame lighting is always ugly, but come the Opening Ceremonies the Olympic Games hold the transformative power of war or natural disaster. There is nothing else in postmodern life remotely like it. Somehow, a massive human entity has been invented that chews money, breathes hype, bleeds sanctimony, and inadvertently encourages the young to damage their bodies forever. Yet on balance, it has emerged as a force for good. It doesn't destroy. It builds. In the long run, like America, the whole thing is something of a miracle.

A sliver of moon, dyed orange, hangs over the Acropolis. I walk down the stadium steps that, in Boston or New York, would've have been destroyed decades ago. The place is so useless: no luxury boxes, no seat backs, no valet parking, a track and a patch of grass surrounded by the memory of a million butts and faces and voices, by the passion of the dead and the hope of the living. Cicadas clatter in the trees. I walk past the classical busts, past the two targets and the archery scoreboard, past the ATHENS 2004 logo laid out in white on the infield. I leave, cross the street into the National Garden, and stumble into a plaza where, when I look down, I notice dozens of words etched into the stone in languages ranging from hieroglyphics to Hebrew: *Philosophia,* says one. Then: *The Memory, Refletio, La Meditación, Idea, Memoria.* I wander there squinting until I realized I have a headache. More than anything, I suddenly realize, I want something to eat.

By the next morning, all lofty perspective is gone. Now that fears about security and venue construction have turned out to be unfounded, Athens has become one of the great battlegrounds between drug cheats and those determined to catch them. On this, the same day that the original shot put will be contested in Olympia, Kenteris and Thanou end their Olympic careers. The climax comes at the IOC press conference, when communications director Giselle Davies steps up with the drug-fighter's version of a big-game hunter placing a boot on the carcass. With IOC legal advisor Francois Carrard making sure everyone takes note— "*There's* your dramatic gesture," he says—Davies holds up the now-useless Olympic credentials of Kenteris, Thanou, and Tzekos for all to see. She may as well be holding up three scalps. *Click,* go the camera shutters. *Click, click.*

It's a powerful image. Encased in plastic, embossed with the mystifying symbols and numbers and letters summing up—to some computerized superbrain—the life and work of everyone rushing about an Olympic games, the credential is one of those items, like air and food, taken for granted until taken away. Lose it, and access stops; suddenly you can go nowhere and do nothing. In Olympic terms, you're dead. For everyone involved, Kenteris and Thanou have taken on the role of symbols: To see their useless photos now is to see the anticipation that all Greece felt about the Athens Games just the week before. The two of them, winners of gold and silver in Sydney, are grinning so sweetly in their photos because this was to be their games, their city, their time. Now the credentials dangle from Davies's hand. A week after it began, a day after Kenteris vowed to fight "to the last drop of my blood," both had trooped into the day's IOC meeting and given up their credentials in what Davies terms "unequivocal surrender."

The image on Tzekos's credential reflects something else, too; of the three, only his is dark and glowering, the one resembling a mug shot. No one's reputation has been poisoned more. After all, neither Kenteris and Thanou have ever actually tested positive for performance-enhancing drugs, so there will be some "comeback" bid launched down the road. But the coach is done. He made few friends in the Greek track federation with his secretive ways, and after his hearing Kenteris announced "the end of my cooperation with Christos Tzekos."

Many writers succumb to the urge to label all this a modern Greek tragedy, but the fact is, the Kenteris-Thanou affair was farce from start to finish. Sprinter Ben Johnson had at least gotten a taste of glory. He set the world record in the 100 meters and then got busted at the Seoul Games; he knew greatness, no matter how tainted, knew what it felt like before watching it slip away. But Kenteris and Thanou never rose high enough here to make their fall tragic. Now, instead of embodying Olympic values, the values Greece gave the world, they have become vessels for the paranoia and conspiracy mongering that marks Greece at its worst. "They were wrong," one Greek cabdriver tells me afterward. "But I heard on the radio. The Americans did something . . ."

At first, the day seems to be salvaged by the idyllic event being played out in Olympia, and those who make the four-hour trip come back raving about the place's simplicity, about the honor of competing, watching, reporting at such a hallowed site. But the competition there also cements a good news–bad news tone for the entire Athens games, elation and disappointment walking hand in hand. As if decreed by gods no one believes in anymore, the Athens Olympics has taken on the strangest rhythm: It's all compelling, but hardly clean. In the end, a record twenty-eight athletes will flunk drug tests or no-show their test or refuse to present a sample in Athens, speckling each day with corruption. Olympia? Four days after the shot put, the gold-medal winning woman, Russian Irina Korzhanenko, will test positive for the steroid Stanozolol.

The same day, the little Greek weightlifter who had earlier won his country's first medal will get stripped of it, too, crying and declaring that someone had spiked his orange juice.

I keep looking for that one moment that justifies one's love for the Olympics, and I can't find it. Or maybe it's just that the faces that embody the best of Athens—Michael Phelps, the U.S. softball team, Hicham El Guerrouj grinning and Paula Radcliffe weeping—keep getting thrown out of focus by the constant jostle of bad news: the Danish sailor who accidentally kills a tourist with his car and keeps competing, the Olympic guard who accidentally kills himself playing Russian roulette, the Greek judo champion who, after leaping from her balcony before the Games began, dies in the hospital. Every four years, millions of people turn to the Olympics like Anthony Quinn in *Lawrence of Arabia*, looking for "something honorable." But in Athens, every good moment is matched by something petty or stupid or self-destructive, by tragedies played in a minor key. And I'm like everyone else. I'd be happy with just one clean day.

Midway through the games, I begin work on a story about a triple-jumper from Sudan. It's interesting because she's not from Sudan, because she lives in London, because her husband is serving a fifteen-year prison sentence for smuggling and dealing heroin. But it's my kind of story because the woman, Yamile Aldama, is only the most bizarre example of nation hopping—the increasingly common practice of athletes and countries paying their way to Olympic credibility by exchanging sporting talent for instant citizenship and raw cash. It's my kind of story because I love the intersection of sports and national pride, and this practice undermines the flag-waving appeal that has, for more than a century, made the Olympic Games important.

"What is this going to do to the games? If the IOC loses nationalism, maybe it loses its spectator appeal," Kevin Wamsley, director of the Center for Olympic Studies in Ontario, tells me over the phone. "They'll have to get a handle on it to protect their own interests. Maybe they come down on the national Olympic committees and say, 'This isn't acceptable. You're destroying the product.' "

It's my kind of story, too, because Aldama is Cuban, a cog in that country's formidable sports machine who competed for Cuba in the 2000 Olympics in Sydney. My bosses know I'm game for anything that originates in Havana. But what they don't know is that it's my kind of story, most of all, because it's Cuban but not political. Aldama left the country legally, so although it's Cuban it has nothing to do with defection. Nobody has a chance of getting hurt.

There's an element of journalism I like to call, "The Get." The Get is not to be confused with a scoop, not in the narrow sense of breaking a story before the competition, although it always involves gathering valuable information. The Get is the moment that every journalist who makes the extra phone call, chases after a source, doubles back for one more quote is living for. It's the instant in the interview when your subject decides to give up—through word or deed—what he wouldn't tell or show anyone before, the unlocking of a revelatory instance, a twisted family dynamic, the tracing of a hidden line of corruption or iron will. Sometimes you feel it coming, signaled by an exhalation, the lighting of a cigarette; sometimes it hits like a sudden brick to the head. But there's no mistaking that it's the jewel that turns your jumble of confusing facts into a *story*. The Get makes everything clear. In the writing, it's where all the words lead. It's the organizing tip of a funnel through which that chaotic swirl of information gathers and gains unifying force, the thing that makes a reader tear up or say, "Holy Shit!" The Get raises chills, because you can't quite believe it while it's happening. One friend, writing a profile on the dissipated life of NFL linebacker Ted Hendricks, watched him get so drunk he pissed his pants. Another, writing about Bill Clinton's cheating at golf, played a round with the president in which he obliviously broke rule after rule. I once wrote a piece on Chicago Bulls superstar Scottie Pippen, the father of three illegitimate children: The Get is when I spoke to his beautiful new wife, and she insisted he had only two.

In 1990s Miami, when hundreds of Cuban Olympic athletes risked future and family by jumping to the U.S., one Get proved untouchable. In Cuba, all athletes understandably refused to denounce the Castro government or admit to thinking about leaving; once they were safely in the States, though, they admitted their bitterness and—if their families were safe—hatred of the regime. I started going to Cuba in 1991, and never once, to me or anyone else, did a Cuban athlete in Cuba openly criticize Castro, much less admit to mulling the ultimate question. Defection was a subject like sex and death—endlessly pondered, rarely discussed— only more so. No American journalist pressed the issue, not if they had a soul, but we all were waiting. The ultimate Get was a Cuban star in Cuba willing to state the truth. And at the end of 1998, for a book I was writing, I got it.

Hector Vinent was one of Cuba's greatest boxers, a light welterweight who had won Olympic gold medals in 1992 and 1996. With black-bearded photographer Victor Baldizon, that December I chased Vinent in an abused auto across the island and back again before meeting him at El Morro Castle on Havana Bay. Vinent was living on the street. He had no way to support his children. He had been banned from boxing because the regime was sure he wanted to defect. And now, he told this American reporter, yes, it was all true. He planned to win back his spot on the Cuban team, and on its first trip overseas defect to the United States. He also wanted people in Miami, his former teammates, to send money just in case he had to hire a smuggler's speedboat. Twice, I asked Vinent: Are you sure you want to say this? He shrugged. His fingernails were cracked, his skin dry. He looked as if he were covered in ash.

"What else can they do to me?" he said.

Besides, Vinent knew my book wouldn't be coming out for another year. By the time it was published, he figured, he'd be set up in a cottage in Hialeah.

I went home and wrote. Soon after, I found out that Vinent had been arrested for hitting a Cuban policeman; he would have no chance to make the team now. Should I publish? Everything he had said came free of qualifiers, and part of me believed he'd want the story out now so his friends in Miami would know. My book, *Pitching Around Fidel*, went through editing, galleys, fact-checking, and on the night in early 2000 before hundreds of copies were to go out to reviewers, I happened to e-mail a friend in Cuba and ask, casually, if he'd heard any news about Vinent.

"He's fighting tonight in the final of the national championship," came the reply.

I felt as if the walls around me had collapsed. What to do? Somehow Vinent had slipped out of trouble; now, if he won, he would be back on the national team. But before the Cubans could make their first trip, the book would be published with all of Vinent's harsh criticism and desperate intentions. He would be banned again, probably go to jail—his one chance at freedom gone. I knew instantly: Here it was, my moment of truth. I couldn't believe such a hacked-out cliche could actually come to pass. Where was the audience, the director, the swell of dramatic background music? I looked around at my office: the phone, computer, books, scattered paper. Everything looked the same. By all rules of journalism, publishing his intentions was completely defensible. *Wasn't Vinent on the record? Maybe he didn't care. Who was I to decide whether truth would see the light of day? Besides, if Vinent were banned because of my book, he would become a cause celebre, sales could jump . . .*

I wondered for an hour if I held a man's fate in my hands. Vinent knew nothing of the "rules" of American journalism. There was no way to contact him, and no time to waste. I had to call my editor, right then, or the books would be sent and Vinent's story would go public. Then again, I could just do nothing, walk out of my office, let time chew up all options . . . A book versus a life: My stomach felt as if I had swallowed a stone. I dialed my editor, Dan Halpern, and said the book could not go with the Vinent passage intact. The next day, he hired someone to rip my coup, my precious little Get, out of each copy, replacing it with a note of explanation referring to "the political situation in Cuba." I revised the passage, toning down Vinent's intentions. I consoled myself by insisting I had done the right thing.

A few days later, I got a two-word reply from my e-mail asking for news of Vinent's fight: "He lost." I stared at the screen. Here was my moment of truth, pickled in irony. Vinent didn't even make the team. His plan fizzled before it started; he never would've been able to defect anyway. My great moral stand had been for nothing. If anything, by taking out my Get, I had watered down Vinent's bitterness enough so that his plight didn't get the attention its original power might have attracted. By doing what I thought was the right thing, I may well have done Hector Vinent the worst service possible. Had I been a coward? A self-dramatizing fool? I still have no answer.

But I do know I lost something there, the appetite, perhaps, for a certain kind of meat. After a decade, I had said all I wanted to say about Miami, Cuba, Castro, defectors, freedom. I'd had enough with juggling absolutes, with the city's visceral passions, with waiting for Fidel to die and the next hurricane to hit. I wanted a wall between life and work. I wanted calm. We had children now. I needed a place where disasters didn't alight, settled and safe, dull even. We headed North, to the capital, and our friends tried to warn us. You're going to be bored, they said. Nothing surprising really happens in Washington, D.C.

On the evening of August 26, they hold the men's 200-meter final, the race that has been sold out for a year because Greeks so yearned to see Kenteris run. Some 75,000 people pack the stands of Olympic Stadium, but now Kenteris isn't there, so the event becomes a chance to protest the Olympics, the alarming costs, the years of inconvenience, the drug scandals, perhaps the foolishness of Kenteris and Thanou, but, most of all, the Americans and their big money and misbegotten war. As the introductions begin, the stadium erupts in booing and whistling and the chanting of *"Hel-las!"*—Greece—so loud that hearing a starter's pistol is impossible, and louder still whenever an American runner is introduced.

"Everytime they booed I looked up," said U.S. sprinter Justin Gatlin later. "And the camera was on a U.S.A. guy." American Bernard Williams, who had tested positive for marijuana just two weeks before, who had clowned the most during the U.S. relay team's overcooked celebration in Sydney, cocks an eyebrow and wipes his forehead mockingly. The clamor grows.

Lane 2 stands empty because a runner has no-showed, highlighting Kenteris's absence even more. The crowd chants, "Ken-TER-is! Ken-TER-is!" Twice, the runners line up in the blocks and endure a false start. Namibian veteran Frankie Fredericks, hands clasped prayerfully, begs the crowd to settle down. For four minutes, the howling continues as the runners wait. Finally the stadium quiets. The gun sounds, and twenty seconds later the Americans sweep—Shawn Crawford first, then Williams and Gatlin—and take a small step toward redeeming the U.S. team's reputation by huddling sedately. The crowd sags, applauds politely, and heads for the exits, satisfied at being heard, at that small taste of power. Afterward, Crawford and Gatlin declare compassion for the Greeks' feelings, speak of winning with dignity. Williams, unable to resist himself, boasts: "We swept just like a trashman sweeping up garbage."

The next day, with U.S. Secretary of State Colin Powell due over the weekend to attend the Closing Ceremonies, a protesting crowd of 2,000 roams through downtown Athens en route to the U.S. embassy, spray-painting graffiti, torching trash cans, chanting. Police use tear gas and pepper spray to quell the crowd. A huge banner reading POWELL GO HOME is draped across a prominent hillside, and Powell apparently gets the message. By the next day, his trip has been canceled.

By Sunday, August 29, the Olympics final day, I've resigned myself to leaving Athens saddled with ambivalence—loving the city but dismayed by its all-consuming negativity—sure that it will be the first Olympics I've seen without that one unforgettable *moment,* that "something honorable" that encapusulates everything we come to the Olympics for: sportsmanship, endurance, maybe even innocence. Since the previous winter, I've been hoping for Greek marathoner Nikos Polias to pull a Spiridon Louis in the Olympics final event and run the race of his life. But soon after the marathon begins Sunday afternoon, Polias melts into the pack. I begin thinking about home.

Then something strange happens. Just minutes from a wholly unexpected victory, the marathon leader comes under attack. At the 23rd mile, a man—a defrocked Irish priest—leaps out of the crowd and grabs Brazilian runner Vanderlei de Lima, shoving him off the course and into a line of fans. Here's what we've been waiting for. Here's the danger most feared in Athens, the danger feared in all our lives now: an attack, unprovoked and random and coldly vicious. Athens organizers spent well over $1 billion on security, but now that security has failed. An athlete has been assaulted on the route where the marathon, where sports, began so long ago. In a small way, it brings home today's truth: You can spend all you want, you can demand that authorities blanket the airports and malls with reassuring men in uniform. But, in the end, if some clown is willing to risk himself to do damage, some damage will get done.

Still, this isn't a bomb, a tank of nerve gas going off in a crowd. The pest is quickly subdued, and de Lima quickly works himself free. He still has a 20-second lead. The moment passes from frightening to absurd. A defrocked Irish priest? Wrong religion, wrong country. There doesn't seem to have been a weapon. Watching it replayed, you even laugh a little. It's a relief to laugh. De Lima wasn't a prerace favorite, and he had already begun to fade before the attack, so it's likely that he wouldn't have won. He finishes third, gets himself a bronze medal. That seems right. And if that were the end of it, de Lima would soon fade into memory, just another victim of something he doesn't understand.

But de Lima does something more, something instinctive, thrillingly human. As it was for Spirodon Louis, the final lap of the marathon takes place at Panathinaiko Stadium. Now de Lima comes into the stadium under the harsh spotlights, under the eyes of a world that wants to feel sorry for him. But he doesn't want that. He wants to play. So he grins, and sticks out his arms like wings. He dips one arm and banks, dips the other and banks; he makes like a five-year-old and does a fine imitation of an airplane tacking back and forth across a runway. In the final lap of a race that, certainly, all his friends will soon tell him he has been robbed of, de Lima doesn't look angry. He's . . . enjoying himself.

He is thirty-five years old. How many more Olympics will he have? How many nights breaking into the light of Athens? Later, of course, lawyers will get involved and try to muster pity and protest that Vanderlei de Lima should be awarded the gold medal. Later, too, de Lima will say, "Maybe God put this man in my way to test me, to see what I could do, and to show me how difficult it is to win a medal at the Olympics." But on this day, in the heat of the race, his message can't be clearer: *Let everyone else feel sad. I'm alive. I'm in the Olympics. Attack me? I'll just go harder. Throw me off my rhythm? I'll finish. You can't bring me down. In fact, I think I am going to fly.*

I've been away too long. The 2004 Olympics end just in time; my last morning in Athens I wake after five hours of sleep to a calm and horrifying dream. I'm speaking to my landlord Philippe and he looks up and sees storm clouds looming over my shoulder, streaked black and red and coming like a contagion. He turns and runs back to his house, and I run into mine, filled with strange hallways and furniture, and no one is there. *Fran,* I yell. *FranFranfranfranfranfran* . . . But all that comes back is my own voice, echoing. They're all gone.

The Republican Convention began the day before in New York, and the front page of the *International Herald Tribune* is dominated by a huge picture of a Texas delegate, sporting the requisite cowboy hat and an oversized, "Everything's Bigger in Texas: Bush 2004" button. In the taxi to the airport, I open *Kathimerini* to a two-page interview with renowned Greek composer Mikis Theodorakis, who spouts off bizarre theories about Jewish evil and a surety that an American hand had somehow directed the September 11 attacks. I think of my talk the year before with marathoner Nikos Polias. "America controls everything," Theodorakis said. And who controls America? "There is a group of Jews who surround Bush and control the policy of the U.S.," he said.

The taxi rattles along the straight new highway. I'm tired, suddenly, of Greece and its conspiracies, of Europeans and their hatred of Americans, tired of foreign tongues and great wine and startling views, tired, even, of those who've embraced me and my family and helped create a year we already know is one of our best. I'm sick of the Acropolis, the Eiffel Tower, Big Ben, wall-to-wall soccer, sick of my eagerness and curiosity. For the Olympics, billboards have been placed on the airport road pronouncing the lofty theme of the games: WELCOME HOME, they say, mile after mile. But now it's over, and I stare out the window, and somewhere along the way the tone has shifted on me: Welcome home? Yes, I think, taking myself by surprise. I will.

Fall

Fifteen

Europe. Europe looks like a smile.

Kevin Bacon, *Diner*

In the end, we stay on to bear a sort of witness. I've convinced myself that it makes no sense for Bush to win reelection: Gore had won the popular vote by a half-million votes in 2000; the Democrats had to be more motivated, the Republicans a bit less. No U.S. president has ever presided over so many obvious foreign policy embarrassments, none has been so transparently inept or deceitful. Our house in Washington has been rented by one of the White House legal counsels, and when he asks for a year extension I almost pity the man's self-delusion. Doesn't he understand that, come November, he'll be looking for work? Soon, this short and searing chapter of American life will be over.

The light begins to change, summer brilliance fading into that brittle metallic cool of October. We borrow the Carrys' place up in the Ardeche for a weekend, and are given just one directive: Be careful of the new, wall-to-wall white carpeting. Jack and I have one supreme moment; together, we spend an afternoon leaping out of the tree into the cool river. I also leave the top of Charlie's medicine unscrewed, and he takes it and shakes it, and Fran turns the corner and screams as the pink ooze settles into the carpet. We spend the final day scrubbing and staring at a fist-sized stain that will never come clean.

Bush's approval ratings sink; John Kerry surges through the debates. In one sense, you'd never know that we're in France. The U.S. election dominates European newscasts and papers as if Paris is some precinct in Iowa; analysts debate the impact of Ralph Nader, Florida, voting machines, and Iraq as if it's their nation preparing to go to the polls. Whenever French, Australian, Austrian, German, English people learn I'm American, their first question is as predictable as the sunrise: *What's going to happen?* I travel to Basel, Switzerland, the last week of October to profile tennis great Roger Federer, and find myself doling out hourly reassurance: *Don't worry*, I say. *The American people aren't as blind or stupid as you think.*

No one believes me. After talking about Federer awhile, Heinz Gunthardt, Steffi Graf's former coach, turns to the topic that really intrigues him. I tell him how sure I am of a Kerry victory, and Gunthardt shakes his head. He has friends in America. He has heard too much fear from them to be optimistic. Besides, he says, we're very different cultures. "There's misunderstanding, because we're not as similar as we think we are," he says. "Our standards of living are very similar, but not the way we think, the way we look at the world. When it comes to religious questions, the Americans are so different. I watched a roundtable discussion yesterday on CNN about the separation of church and state. I mean, you couldn't have a roundtable discussion about that in Europe—because there's nothing to discuss."

I think Gunthardt has somehow heard it wrong—isn't the America I came from built on a wall between church and state?—so I don't have much of a response. Instead, I warn him as I've warned Europeans all year. Be careful, I say, about painting all Americans the same; Bush *lost* last time, remember? Gunthardt nods. That apparently rigged result in 2000, he says, is the reason so many Europeans have given Americans a four-year grace period, separating people from policy, embracing them while detesting their government.

"But you know how a lot of Europeans think?" he says. "You elect someone the first time and you have no idea who you elect? Hey: Fine.

But if you elect him twice, that's completely different: Shame on you. Now you know what you have, you're showing your colors. You either want the guy or you don't."

Four years earlier, all through Election Night 2000 and deep into early next morning, Fran and I had sat jammed into a corner of our new living room in D.C. A TV set, a couch, and chair had been shoved together to the only area untouched by construction, and in darkness we bled the old radiators and watched the returns that sent experts into a dizzying blather of predictions. Weeks passed and Bush and Al Gore wrangled over Florida, the state we had left behind, and builders swarmed over the house leaving beer bottles and carelessness in their wake. The heating system died. A conservative Supreme Court overturned its own principles against judicial activism and awarded a conservative the presidency of the United States. Gore conceded graciously because Democrats do nothing if not lose well, and I passed through winter vowing never to move again.

But Washington was hardly the benign tonic I had planned for. The upheaval had stirred something in the family chemistry. A month after we arrived, Jack, four then, was riding in the back of the car when he abruptly shouted how much he missed one of his girlfriends from Miami.

"You really love Gaby, huh?" I said lightly.

"Yeah," he answered. "But not so much. Because when you love someone so much you're going to get hurt."

I nearly veered off the road, twisting to look at him. Jack stared out the window. Finally, I sputtered out the pathetic chestnut, "Well . . . I love Mommy so much."

"Well," he answered, in the irritable tone of an old man stating the obvious, "then you're going to get hurt."

On September 11, 2001, we watched the Twin Towers burn and one side of the Pentagon crumble. The morning was sunsplashed, gorgeous; rumors spread about bombs going off downtown. We raced to school to pull Jack home. We jerked our heads out the window whenever a plane flew over. Every night after that, I would stay up writing until 3:00 A.M., then go into the backyard and listen as fighter jets droned in unending patrol across the black sky. A month later, a series of anthrax spores were sent through the D.C. mail system, killing five people and sickening thirteen others. Our local postal facility shut down, contaminated; each time mail dropped through the door slot we hesitated before touching it. The most normal things—bills, baggage, trucks—assumed an air of menace. I had gotten what I wished for, all right: Washington was nothing like Miami. Daily life became a mix of banality and fear, beside which Miami's lunatic parade seemed positively quaint. The days were peppered with Through-the-Looking Glass moments, odd run-ins with security, absurd conversations that somehow made perfect sense.

In the spring of 2002, I began getting odd messages demanding that I phone Ralph Nader. I'd call back, hear nothing for weeks, then get another frantic dispatch. I'd just about given up when, finally, a woman's voice murmured on my answering machine: "Mr. Price, please call Mr. Nader. He really wants to talk to you about your *book*."

My book? What would Nader, the third-party candidate whose run in 2000 had swung the vote—particularly in Florida—Bush's way, want with my Cuba book? Like the rest of my generation, I had grown up in a world helped shaped by the crusading consumer advocate; cars were safer, corporations more responsible, solely because Nader existed. After 2000, Nader was mostly despised by Democrats, but I didn't care. The hardcover edition of the book had just been remaindered, and the paperback ranked somewhere near 500,000 on Amazon. Nader wanted to talk about my book? There could only be two possibilities—he loved it or hated it—and of course it didn't matter which. An author wants to be read, most of all; an author wants to feel that his work hasn't dropped down a well so deep that even its splash is soundless. It was clear: I had touched Nader. Or enraged him. Maybe he wanted to take up Vinent's cause. Whatever: My book had reached someone important . . .

"Oh! Mr. Price!" his secretary said when I called, sounding relieved beyond measure. "Mr. Nader really needs to talk to you."

A click, an exhale, and then came that voice, stern and husky and not, in the famous Gatsby formulation, sounding anything like money. I had seen Nader countless times on TV denouncing something. I had seen him host *Saturday Night Live*. It could only be him.

"Scott?"

"Yes."

"I bought your book. I bought 2,500 copies of your book. *By mistake*. Do you want to buy some?"

We spoke for half an hour. Nader began by explaining that he bought remaindered books from publishers to give away at rallies and as part of an initiative to improve reading. He wouldn't detail his "mistake," but tossed out a price of $1.00 apiece. I sort of giggled and, ignoring his offer for dignity's sake, started asking questions. I figured he would shut me down, but Nader didn't seem to have anything better to do. After a while, his Nader-ness wore off and the slouching beast of the American left turned out to be funny and endlessly curious, but every few minutes I found myself staring at the receiver and thinking, *Don't you have some true-believer lackey to handle this kind of call?*

But on we went, Ralph and I, babbling away about our home state of Connecticut, and Cuban sports, and how former president Jimmy Carter was, at that moment, in Cuba for an unprecedented visit. "*Jimmy's* down there?" Nader said, and now he was off and saying he hadn't read my book but planned to, and how he'd interviewed Castro in 1959, and how maybe he should go down to Cuba, too. Would I be interested in going along? No, I told him—and this felt like a cool thing to tell Ralph Nader—I had been declared persona non grata by the Cuban government, so that wasn't in the cards. But he had moved on, hit by a sudden realization, a wave of panic.

"The books are coming," he said. "I don't have the space for that. What am I going to do?"

So I told Nader I would try and help him solve his storage dilemma— maybe I'd buy some, maybe I had some people who might be interested. It turns out I knew only one, but I was able to get in a few more calls with him. On the first, we were cruising along in the jokey, good acquaintances way that Nader and I had come to share and I was even thinking about inviting him over for a barbeque when he told me that he had just published a book. I laughed and said, "Hey, when it gets remaindered maybe I'll buy a few copies."

The line went silent. Then, in a tone declaring that, indeed, he might have something better to do, Nader said, "There will be no remainders."

The next time we spoke, all seemed forgiven. Nader said that he was reading my book, and would start giving it out at rallies. Emboldened, I asked if he was going to run for president again in 2004, and he said, "It's too early." Whether that meant too early in the campaign cycle or too early in the morning was never made clear. I told him I would buy 250 copies; why not? Compared with Nader's price, my publisher was ripping me off.

We spoke one more time. In July of 2002, I read that Nader had met with Castro in Havana. I waited a few weeks and then called him, and like every other tourist Nader still had that man-I-was-in-Cuba buzz going. "I brought a bunch of your books down with me," he said. "I brought a copy for Fidel but by the time I met with him I had given it away."

I suppose I should've been dazed by the whole exchange—what could be more surreal than having a man who altered American history trying to sell you your own book at a discount? But in that place and time it didn't seem strange. Washington's normal mood swung on a weekly basis from frivolousness to panic and back again, and it was about to rev to a level unmatched even by September 11. On October 2, a sniper began shooting people all over the D.C. area in a three-week rampage both meticulous and freewheeling; no neighborhood seemed safe. People were shot in parking lots, bus stops, on the way to school, thirteen in all, ten dead, imbuing the most mundane of tasks with this sick jangle of apprehension. Homeland Security had talked for a year about dirty bombs and chemical attacks, but the most effective way to terrorize the nation's capital, it turned out, was to send a pair of riflemen around the Beltway in a customized snipercar. Choppers hovered over our house in Northwest D.C., beaming searchlights down onto the border with

Maryland. Schools went on universal lockdown, with no recess, no out-
door activity. Parades and parties died in the planning. The night the San
Francisco Giants clinched their spot in the 2002 World Series, the
eleventh victim got hit, and we flipped the channels back and forth, from
shooting scene to strike three to shooting again.

Jack's T-ball season became swiss-cheesed by postponements. There
was talk of a four-game jamboree in late October, complete with cop
cars and a shield of parents ringing the field, but in the end too many
decided against setting up their kids as targets. Yet I took him out to that
same field one Friday afternoon and threw soft pitches and watched him
get fired up and grow bored like kids do. What was my point? Stubborn-
ness? Living without fear? Once or twice I looked around at the tree line
and felt exposed and stupid, but then he'd hurl the ball my way and I'd
forget about it. It felt good to be outside. The next night, just before
Game 1 of the World Series began, No. 12 took a bullet in the stomach.

The morning after, a Sunday, joggers huffed along in our D.C.
neighborhood. Some college kids played soccer. Winter was coming, and
we all knew there weren't that many good days left. As it was in San
Francisco after the '89 earthquake, and in Miami after Hurricane
Andrew, the communal horror had a way of rooting us to the city with
a depth that comes normally with the passage of many years. By the time
they caught the snipers on October 24, we had become full-fledged res-
idents of the capital of fear, and my old friend Dan McGrath had called
with the job offer. "We've got to get you out of there," he said. Might I
want to move to Chicago?

I allowed that, yes, I just might.

On April Fool's Day, 2003, Matt Doherty resigned under pressure as
head basketball coach at the University of North Carolina. The instant I
heard, of course, I thought of Jordan and that 1982 National Championship team. Doherty had been the best kind of glue player then, and it
surprised no one when he later climbed the coaching ladder through
Lawrence, Kansas, and South Bend, Indiana, before landing the top job

in Chapel Hill in 2000. Jordan had promoted Doherty, making calls, pushing for him. He was nothing if not loyal, and once Doherty's tenure went from early promise to player revolt, I had little doubt what Jordan's reaction would be. Then again, it now seemed to be our generation's transition time, middle age supplanting youth: Jordan was coming to the end of his playing career in Washington, a forty-year-old with creaky knees and sputtering fire. He had given up his role as the team's general manager to play these last two seasons, but no one doubted he still ran the show and no one knew, really, what he was getting out of it. It was fashionable to call this chapter a cynical play by Jordan the businessman, using Jordan the player to juice the box office. Ever since he returned to the court, Wizards home games had sold out.

I had been out to see the Wizards often enough, but never approached him. Jordan had boycotted *Sports Illustrated* ever since the magazine mocked his stint playing minor-league baseball in 1994, and that had been the last time we had spoken at length, in a dank Birmingham, Alabama, clubhouse where he stood too tall. Jordan's celebrity and wealth had only mushroomed since, and there were few casual moments with the press now; he came into the locker room in the most beautiful suits, a CEO wending his way through boysland, and there was no reason for me to stop him. We weren't close. Just two guys who knew each other once.

As it happened, the day after Doherty quit, I went to the Wizards game against the Sacramento Kings, the team I had cut my teeth on nearly twenty years before. It had been a decade since Monica Seles had been stabbed on a Hamburg tennis court, I was reporting a piece on sports security in the terror age, and I needed some NBA players and coaches. I didn't expect to see Jordan. His days of talking before games had ended long ago, and usually he secluded himself where no reporter or fan could reach. But when I walked into the near-empty locker room at 6:00 P.M., Jordan was sitting in a corner talking to Wizards assistant coach Patrick Ewing. "Scotty?" Jordan bellowed. "What are you doing here? Still slumming for *Sports Illustrated*?"

I walked over, and Ewing stopped talking and ducked his head to sort through a stack of mail. I told Jordan I'd been thinking about him, what with Doherty's departure, and he shook his head, mouth twisting. We ran down the list of people we had in common, and I mentioned one friend, Mark Vancil, who had just had his first baby boy after a string of daughters.

"I told Vanny," Jordan said. "If you want a boy, you've got to do it from behind. That's the only way."

I mumbled something, waiting for a grin to reveal the joke. But Jordan's face had taken on this serious cast, like someone playing a doctor on TV. Just as I was thinking about my newborn son, and mulling whether to discuss his conception, Ewing's head jerked up. "What?" he said. "Is that true?"

"I'm serious," Jordan said. "You've got to do it . . . from . . . behind."

Ewing chuckled. Jordan wasn't budging. I had, then, this odd moment of telescoping time: Twenty-one years before, Jordan's Tar Heels had met up with Ewing's Georgetown Hoyas in the 1982 national title game, a classic showdown. Ewing had been a freshman, too, that night in New Orleans, but until game time he was the bigger name. He blocked Carolina's every shot early on, got called for goaltending five times, set the tone. But Jordan's cool jumper with 17 seconds left wrapped up Dean Smith's first national title, made Michael an instant legend, and became the always-cited first sign of his supremacy. Ewing went on to have a fine career, even won an NCAA title himself two years later, but his professional life followed the pattern of that game. Always, he came up short against Jordan, his Knicks teams losing one clutch game after another to Jordan's Bulls. He never seemed to understand what he needed to do to win. Now he sat in Jordan's locker room, working for Jordan, letting the boss spout off, and I couldn't help but wonder how much of hiring Ewing had been friendly kindness and how much a subtle way of rubbing Ewing's face in it. Jordan could be kind, but no one more enjoyed making life as competitive as basketball.

"Come on," Ewing said, proferring some of his personal exceptions, but Jordan wouldn't have it. He listed some half-baked evidence, nodded emphatically, and I realized both of them had forgotten I was standing there. Standing at his locker, rookie Juan Dixon leaned in and said, "What? What's that you're talking about?" and Jordan told him and Dixon said, "No! Really?"

"Don't worry, rookie!" Jordan laughed. "You're so young you can do it any old way."

Ewing stood up shaking his head and walked off. I asked Jordan whether he knew what happened with Doherty.

"New-Jack players," Jordan said. "I mean, Matt yelled at 'em, but everybody gets yelled at. I wanted to quit my freshman year, too, but that's what happens. You don't go after the coach."

For fifteen minutes, then, Jordan kept on, talking about how the Carolina chancellor had violated Dean Smith's Tar Heel code by ripping Doherty publicly; how the fact that Doherty had failed to hire Carolina legend Phil Ford as an assistant killed him from the get-go; how he could never coach these players of today, too spoiled, too *sensitive*; how some former Carolina players in the NBA that he wouldn't name had, by phone, rallied the current Carolina team to revolt against Doherty. Jordan's disgust was so palpable, his distress so genuine, that I couldn't help but feel amazement. His critics found him too controlling, too slick, hypocritical even, but when it came to North Carolina, Jordan remained a freshman. He still cared too much.

I had turned down the Chicago job by then, but still hadn't decided when we'd take up the magazine's offer on Europe. The Bush administration had invaded Iraq in March, and Americans were unloved. Fran had had our third, Charlie, in January, and lack of sleep made a move seem foolish. But in mid-April, she came back from a trip to Miami and announced that Washington's grip was too flimsy to hold us. In early May, Jordan went into the office of Wizards owner Abe Pollin expecting to discuss plans for the following season. Pollin fired him.

Transition time, indeed: It suddenly seemed like lunacy to wait. How many chances like this, really, were we likely to get?

■ ■ ■

Of course it's a time of wonder. Of course it's a time of feeling life more intensely, because struggle with language and custom and driving rules knocks off the crust, opens you up, makes you needy and grateful. Aren't we in the South of France? It's good to be at the mercy of strangers for a while. Your antennae pick up every vibration, you blunder about uncalloused—a rare state of being, transcendent even, though incompatible with daily living. The most routine errand induces sensory overload; a broken cell phone, a stop for vegetables, provides keen miniatures of the culture, no matter that you just want to fix the phone or buy a carrot. We always knew our stay was temporary—twelve months and change—and the idea of an ever-ticking clock has inspired a sometimes desperate need to slow the days. Some afternoons I would find myself pedaling up our lane, *Chemin des Grillons*, feeling that it's all too much, new schools, new house, new faces, new work, too much living at once, the mundane and precious slipping by in a rush: words spoken, vistas seen, fleeting and replaced by the next small crisis, the next small glimpse of the new. Writing it here is the only way to grab hold. Only then can I believe the clock has stopped for a while.

Grab hold: There's four-year-old Addie wandering on a soft Saturday and picking flowers in the pitted backyard, correcting my French in a rage. There's one-year-old Charlie taking his first steps on a winter Sunday, screaming, when the hot months came, at the maroon-and-gold planes buzzing overhead in search of fire. There's the day we race against sundown up to the firetower, Jack loping ahead, Charlie on my shoulders, reaching the top for the first and last time and pointing down, down to the little speck that is the house we occupy and will soon leave. There are the nights for Fran and me alone in Aix, jabbering along the damp, chill streets, then taking that first bite, dripping in local oil and fresh basil and thick cheese, of the best pizza ever made.

I've held Aix at a distance during our time here. I know what it feels like when you fall for a small town, invest it with emotional weight, and come back years later. In the spring of 1999, I returned to Davis, my Northern California home, wandered again the streets I had wandered as a young man, the places where I had been perfectly buzzed and said one funny thing after another. I went through the motions of running the track and passing the parking lot that echoed with the laughter of careless women, the garage where I bought that '60 Plymouth. All my friends had moved on. All my life, I had loved going places where nobody knew my name. But here was the cost: Wait long enough, and eventually nobody there will know you again. Leave a place fondly, and someday it will hurt.

On our last visit into Aix, the annual Christmas fair is under way: carnival rides, food, trinkets for sale up and down the Cours Mirabeau. Addie wants desperately to get tickets for a minicar ride, all popping lights and music and garish vehicles sent spinning around a small track for three minutes or so. I move her to what seems to be the line, and we stand to wait our turn. The ride stops, kids scramble out, kids scramble in. Three minutes pass, and the same scramble occurs, but we don't move an inch. Addie is hopping with anticipation. After four such sequences, I realize: There is no line. The next time the ride stops, I grab her hand and race to a car, but am beaten by a woman shoving her boy behind the wheel. Addie starts to cry. I grab her hand, skulk back to our place, and feel myself getting angry. No line? Just chaos? I look around at the French faces. No one seems the least bit bothered. I make a decision.

"Get ready," I say.

As soon as the ride stops, I yank Addie out toward the nearest car and pick her up. A small, pointy-faced Frenchman has reached the other side at the same time, with the same idea; he's got his son in his arms. Simultaneously, we thrust our kids into the seat, cramming them kicking and howling against each other, trying to get purchase. The man refuses to catch my eye, but we are dueling just the same, viciously, and our children are the weapons of choice. Still, I was just a millisecond faster. I've wedged Addie's leg under the steering wheel, and the bell is now ringing, and the man sags. He pulls his son back. In the States, by now, we would be pummelling each other. But without a word, without a glance, he shuffles away.

Addie pats the steering wheel and says, "Whee!" I watch her spin round and round. I'm not sure I want to come back to Aix anytime soon.

The French are kind after Bush wins. No one subject to my cock-sure prediction shoves the result in my face. They pretend the election hasn't happened, but then, they have their own problems. A government report calls the rising wave of anti-Semitic attacks in France "not marginal subjects, even less so are they communal matters—they are at the heart of the evolution of our society." Two French journalists kidnapped in Iraq in late summer remain hostages into December; the hostage-takers, originally at least, declare they won't be released until France rescinds its ban on Muslim headscarves in public schools. French Muslims denounce the kidnapping, thousands rally in the streets and sing *La Marseillaise*, but as days and months pile up it's the words of Iraq prime minister Allad Allawi that sum up the tortured French position. The Americans may have blundered into and around Iraq, and the French can always congratulate themselves on an opposition that now appears wise and right. But their clumsy attempts to engage and control their own clash with Muslim culture seem no more palatable. "Neutrality doesn't exist," Allawi had said in August. "The French are deluding themselves if they think they can remain outside of this. Today, the extremists are targeting them, too."

So we call the movers, sell the furniture, throw out the scraps of a year outside. Jean-Philippe says he'll buy our appliances, and we use that pretext to stop over every few days to see Philippe's finishing touches on his son's apartment. I ask if the neighbor ever paid for the broken fence, but Philippe says no and we roll our eyes together: What a jerk. Jocelyne tells us she's starting a business shepherding tourists to the hidden world of Provence. They tell us how our French has improved, even mine. "You began here," Philippe says, his hand flat on the floor. He lifts it to his shin. "And now you're here."

The clock ticks nearer to zero and I drive the kids to school, down past the power plant towers, past the HyperChampion where we got our haircuts and food, past the Parc Roi Rene and the graffiti begging, *Le Pen Vite!* Late one afternoon near the end of November, I sit typing upstairs when the atmosphere seems to shift; I hear cries, and then a sudden swirl descends. Thousands of swallows fill the air like tiny jets, whirling about the house, screeching into trees. I squint until the reason becomes obvious, one by one. Each bird flies past holding in its beak a plump, shiny olive.

I spend the following Saturday on a ladder, reaching past the gray-green leaves, grabbing fistfuls of black, purple, and green olives, skimming the branches, dropping the year's final harvest into a bin below. Jocelyne stands on the other side of the yard. We don't speak much. I shake the stems and watch the weakest lose hold and fall. The noon heat lasts a few hours, then flees into a sky gone hazy and pink. It's slipping away, the day, the olives, the light. Hills fade into outline, and the dogs of Greasque and St. Savournin begin to call each other, back and forth in a mindless taunt: *You were never here . . . You were never here.*

A week later, on the way to the mailbox, Jocelyne sees me and says that we doubled last year's haul, she and I. I point to the tree where I had spent most of that morning and say, "From now on, you must promise, this will be called *L'Arbre Americain.*" And she laughs and says, "But of course"—and that's it, my last breakthrough, my last pure moment. I know she'll forget in the walk up to her house, but it doesn't matter. In the last days, we kiss everyone good-bye on both cheeks, and I stare at the mountains from our terrace. Here is a small life, I think. Grab hold . . .

Then, like ghosts, like the birds, we're gone.

Acknowledgments

These are brutal days for American journalism. I write at a moment when jobs are scarce and the industry fears for its future. The era of the visionary editor, manning the wall against the newspaper's business side, defending his or her staff for the sake of a good story, a good idea, a good writer—or even a bad one—seems, at the very least, to have been placed on hiatus. We may well never see such a time again.

Here, then, it seems right to thank first and foremost the bosses who made this book possible. Terry McDonell, *Sports Illustrated*'s managing editor, more than anyone saw the mad potential behind a half-baked request to send a staffer to Europe, gave me the time and space to roam, and never once wavered in his support. Without him, my family would never have had the adventure of a lifetime. He is one of the magazine world's last buccaneers.

Thanks also go to those who came before, and whose support and encouragement, looking back, seems even more confounding. At the *Miami Herald*: Edwin Pope, Paul Anger, Tom Shroder and Bill Greer. At the *Sacramento Bee*: Joe Hamelin and Jim Dawson, who took the biggest chance; Nancy Cooney, who endured all with perfect humor and touch; the incomparable Gregory Favre; and the best sports editor in America, Dan McGrath. At the *Daily Tar Heel*: Linda Robertson, who remains the best there is.

As for the manuscript, it would not have happened without the eternal good nature of the dozens of interviewees, fellow reporters, and unsuspecting citizens who gave up both their time and insight to help dispel my ignorance. For background on Bernard Tapie and Jean-Marie Le Pen, I leaned on Jonathan Fenby's 1998 classic work, "On the Brink: The Trouble with France." Any mistakes in understanding or expression, of course, are mine alone. Even with all that, there still would be no book without the meticulous editing, boundless generosity and invaluable suggestions of Bruce Schoenfeld who, here and always, saw the possibilities first; as well as Don Van Natta, Jr., Lizette Alvarez, and Bruce Jenkins. Thanks also to my mother Marilyn Price who, it turns out, can now add "superb copy editor" to her long list of talents.

Cecile Soler and Philippe Bouin helped me see French and American mind-sets anew, and endured my clumsy attempts to return the favor.

Bob Martin, the perfect road comrade, made Pakistan and Belgrade a surreal joy. I thank him for gracing this book with his sublime photography. I'm also grateful to Simon Bruty, for both his work on the cover and his friendship.

Day to day at the magazine, the burden of talking me off the ledge fell into the ever-patient hands of SI's unsung editorial staff, most notably Chris Hunt, Kostya Kennedy, Richard Deitsch, Julie Luu, and Jim Clements. Without Ann Kelly's help, I would've been lost.

Thanks also to Andrew Blauner, agent provocateur, whose enthusiasm and guidance kept the thing alive, and to editor Tom McCarthy, who brought it home. Their belief, in the end, remains with me like a gift. No book, not even a memoir, can ever fully capture the lives that produced it. So part of this, too, is for those who've gone, whose impact never ends: Irving Barnett, Jeremy Richard, John Wolin. I hear their laughter still.

But the biggest debt, of course, is owed to the family, old and new. The story is mine but the home—past and present—is theirs, too. Without my parents, without Sue, Todd, Steve, and Eric, there would be no life to write about. Without Fran, Jack, Addie, and Charlie, there would be no hope of understanding it.

Index

About the Author

S. L. Price has been a senior writer at *Sports Illustrated* since 1994. Previously, he was an award-winning columnist and feature writer at the *Miami Herald* and the *Sacramento Bee*. His work has appeared three times in the annual anthology, *Best American Sports Writing*; he is also the author of *Pitching Around Fidel: A Journey Into the Heart of Cuban Sports*, which was a finalist for the Los Angeles Times Book Prize. He lives in Washington, D.C.